Splendid Fare

The Albert Stockli Cookbook

Splendid
Fare

drawings by Bill Goldsmith

Alfred A. Knopf New York

The Albert Stockli
Cookbook

Contents

Introduction

The idea of this book is to bring my world of food into your kitchen. It truly is a *world*, because my recipes are selected and adapted from cuisines from all parts of the world.

Some experts claim that there is no such thing as an international cuisine, only a collection of national or ethnic cuisines. But in that respect my recipes are unique, because I have combined concepts and practices of different cuisines to create literally international recipes.

It was inevitable that I should want to do this, because, to start with, I am of Swiss origin, and the French, Italian, and German cultures of Switzerland intermingle and influence each other, especially gastronomically. In addition, I have traveled widely, not only throughout Europe but in the Orient as well, working in kitchens and learning the distinctive foods, methods, and dishes of the different countries. When I finally got to the United States, what impressed me most was the fantastic bounty of nature—the unequaled blessings of quantity and quality and variety and availability of the good things of the earth, in and out of season. I made up my mind that to combine the food products of America with the culinary experience and know-how of Europe and the Orient would be the greatest service I could perform, not only in the restaurant kitchens I operated, but also in a cookbook for American housewives.

Sharing meals, especially on festive occasions, is to my mind a kind of sacrament, and one of the most beautiful and loving aspects of family life. There are few childhood pleasures more glowing and more lasting than the memories of family festive dinners: the remembered excitement and bustle of preparation and anticipation; the tantalizing, never-to-be-forgotten smells and delicious sounds coming from the kitchen; the laughter and happiness of a family gathering; and, finally, the sheer enjoyment of favorite, long-awaited foods.

The love of good food starts in the home, and parents can do much to enrich the lives of their children by helping them develop their sense of taste. Just as children's ears can be trained and an appreciation of music developed by exposing them early to good music, so can their palates be trained and enjoyment of good food taught.

Certainly children will start out preferring hamburgers and hot dogs, and tuna-fish salad sandwiches and peanut butter and jelly sandwiches, and there is nothing wrong with these foods if they are of good quality and properly prepared. Most children also prefer comic books at first. Yet, thoughtful parents will lead them to good children's books and childhood classics as a first step to the enjoyment of great literature. The same can be done with food. Parents can set the example for their children by their own interest in food, care in its preparation, appreciation of quality and variety, and, especially, a willingness to try new things. And this effort will be repaid by seeing their children enjoy the unending pleasure that the knowledge and appreciation of fine food can give.

This is no exaggeration. The art of cooking and dining can provide a lifetime of the highest esthetic enjoyment. Delicate nuances, infinite variety, unexpected blends and contrasts, exciting new harmonies—indeed, all the elements of the creative process and of artistic achievement are inherent in fine cooking. Often at night I have paced the floor thinking about a new creative combination—composition, if you will. For a great dish is composed much as is a symphony, the elements arranged and blended to achieve the desired, special effects. Nor can there be any doubt that the art of cooking and dining is an essential aspect of culture; the history of civilization will always include the chronicle of man's efforts to beautify and otherwise enhance the food he eats.

One final note to reassure my readers. This book was written for you, not for the professional chef. Of course, you do not have available the equipment and organization and all the ingredients that are taken for granted in a large hotel or restaurant kitchen. But you do not need them, for you are not preparing huge quantities.

There is only one thing which you and a great chef both need—and that is, to care. You need to be sufficiently concerned so as not to become careless. You must be willing to give the extra little effort and attention that will make the difference in achieving superlative cooking. And with this attitude, and with these recipes, I can assure you that your results will match those achieved by the finest professional chefs.

Professional Hints to Improve Results in Your Kitchen

Following Recipes and Procedural Instructions

First, when a chef meets a new recipe he reads it through carefully before doing anything else. Then he "sets up." The culinary term is *mise en place* ("arranged in its place"). Set up all the ingredients side by side in the order in which they will be used, and have them in READY-TO-USE form. It is the height of inefficiency, for example, to have to start chopping or grating one of the ingredients at the time when you should be combining them. So in order to encourage you to follow the example of a good chef, I have set up the recipes with *all* preliminary preparation indicated at the outset—that is, in the listing of the ingredients. The onion is chopped, the egg lightly beaten, the butter softened *before* you start the recipe.

Planning the Timing

Set up a time schedule for preparation of the various parts of the meal; you won't necessarily do them in the same order as they will be eaten. If, for example, you are having a frozen dessert, you might make it first, put it away, and forget it until dessert time.

Oven Preheating

While there is some difference in gas and electric ovens and between older and newer types of ovens, 10 minutes of preheating is a safe rule.

Serve Hot

The best way to be sure that a course you serve is properly hot is by serving it on a very warm plate. Many ovens have plate-warming cabinets. Use them. Dishes may also be warmed by placing them in a warm corner on top of the range. Use your ingenuity.

Wine or Beer or Brandy

Some of my recipes call for wine or beer or brandy. Do not hesitate to use them, because the alcohol is completely cooked out and all that remains is the flavoring element. When you include these ingredients in preparing a recipe, you are definitely not using alcoholic beverages as such, and you need not hesitate to serve such dishes even to children.

Cooking with Beer

It is interesting that while so many cookbooks and recipes give suggestions for cooking with wine, relatively little attention, at least in the United States, is given to cooking with beer.

Yet some of my most successful dishes owe their unusual and delightful flavor to beer, for beer already contains many essences and flavors that blend with other recipe ingredients to add new and exciting tastes. In the cooking of certain food combinations, beer adds an element that no other liquid can duplicate.

You will find the use of beer in many of my recipes, such as beef or chicken in beer. But there are two essential recipes—beer batter for frying and *pâte à choux* made with beer—which are called for again and again in many of my dishes. Consequently, these two basic recipes using beer appear at the back of the book for easy reference.

Roux

One term you will run across constantly in professional recipes is *roux*. *Roux* is a blend of flour and melted butter (or other fat) and is essential in the making of a thickened sauce or gravy.

Forcemeat

Another term widely used in professional chef circles is *forcemeat*. It is primarily composed of finely chopped meat, fish, game, poultry, or mushrooms, with a binding or moistening agent and appropriate seasoning. Forcemeat is used as a stuffing and as an addition to other dishes.

The Glory of the Electric Blender

You will note that throughout in my recipes I recommend the use of the electric blender. This appliance is one of the greatest contributions to fine cooking. Speedily and beautifully, and with almost no labor, it makes possible the creation of smooth blends, purées, etc., which once was achieved only by pounding, pressing through sieves, and other hard work.

Reduce

Another term you will encounter not only in this book, but in many French recipes, is *reduce*. This means to cook a liquid over high heat so that some of the water evaporates, thus concentrating the flavor.

Sausages

While we consume great quantities of sausage in the United States, we eat them "as is," hot or cold. But in Europe, sausages are also used as an ingredient in salads and numerous main dishes, and I have included a number of such recipes. However, it is difficult to specify in my recipes types that are available everywhere in the United States.

Sausage makers usually distinguish four basic types: fresh, dried, smoked, or cooked. Of course, added variety is often obtained by combining methods of preparation: for example, smoking *and* drying.

The fresh sausages need to be cooked. In this category are "breakfast" sausages, such as Jones, Parks, and others. Included also are country sausages and the Polish type, *kielbasa*.

Most sausages, however, are either already cooked, cured, smoked, or dried, and need only to be warmed through if used in a hot dish. All forms of salami are in this category, and even frankfurters.

When you see sausages called for in one of my recipes, do not hesitate to substitute what is readily available in your local delicatessen or supermarket. When in doubt, you can always use a good quality frankfurter.

The Problem of Gravies

Frequently in my recipes I include among the necessary ingredients a ¼ cup or ½ cup of gravy—veal or beef or chicken. I realize, of course, that you cannot be expected to stop and cook a roast so that you can make some gravy. But there are some very practical things you can do.

One is that every time you make gravy, make an extra quantity. Put into small freezer containers. It will keep indefinitely in your freezer and even for a long time in your refrigerator. Then you will always have some available when a small amount is called for.

Also, in almost all cases, you can use chicken or veal or beef gravy interchangeably, or, for that matter, a blend of them would be even better. The purpose of gravy as an ingredient in a recipe is to enhance and enrich the flavor, not to overpower it.

The one thing I hope you will avoid is the use of canned gravies, which would impair the standard and quality of the rest of the recipe. Instead, in emergencies, I would suggest using your ingenuity. Essentially, gravy is a combination of fat, flour, and a liquid of meat juices. The usual proportions are 2 Tablespoons fat, 2 Tablespoons flour, and 1 cup of liquid. The flour is no problem and the fat can be butter or chicken or goose fat, etc. Brown the flour and fat together. Then, for the liquid, use canned chicken broth or beef broth or consommé with added Bovril or bouillon cubes, a little fresh onion juice, and Kitchen Bouquet, Maggi, or other concentrated seasonings. You'll be surprised how acceptable a gravy you can create.

Herbs, Spices, and Their Uses

Herbs and spices are vitally important ingredients in the art of cooking and, in fact, provide the soul of flavor in the kitchen. But they must be used with delicacy and restraint, in order to enhance and supplement flavors, not to suppress or overpower the flavor of the main ingredient.

At this point, I would like to plead with you: It is so important to the final result to have *fresh* herbs that you should make every effort to get them, instead of automatically resorting to the can or jar of dried products.

The fact is that it is so easy to grow at least a few of the essential herbs yourself, even in a window box in a city apartment, that it is more than worth the effort. Incidentally, be careful to note the recipe equivalents for fresh and dried herbs, because, contrary to some people's expectations, you usually need more fresh herbs than dried; the removal of the moisture content from the former makes the latter more concentrated.

Another plea I would make is that you be adventurous in the use of unusual spices and do not limit yourself to the same ones. My comments on individual herbs and spices and flavors may help.

Salt The oldest and most widely used of all spices.

Onion The most used and important single flavor in cooking, and delightful as a vegetable as well.

Leek A member of the onion family with a faint garlic overtone. Especially important in soups and stews.

Shallots Another member of the onion family but more delicate. Shallots are the secret of every fine sauce cook.

Garlic The most outstanding flavor of the onion family, yet surprisingly, despite its aroma, it has the most delicate of tastes.

Horseradish A sharp member of the radish family used only in grated form as an ingredient of cold and hot sauces.

Parsley The jewel of herbs, both in the pot and on the plate.

Chervil An aromatic herb related to parsley, but with a faint flavor reminiscent of anise. It is a blessing to cold sauces, fish, eggs, and chicken.

Watercress A pungent, peppery herb, a great delicacy in sauces, soups and salads, and as a garnish.

Fennel (Italian *finocchio*) Has a texture like celery and a flavor like licorice. Excellent as a vegetable, especially when braised. The leaves make a wonderful seasoning in fish cookery.

Anise Seed Slight licorice flavor. Excellent in baking and in making preserves.

Chives A slender, hollow, green-leaved herb which is related to the onion. A fresh flavor for cold soups and omelets.

Basil (Italian *basilico*) A member of the mint family, but the strong aroma combines a hint of licorice, pepper, and cloves.

Turmeric A yellow, bittersweet spice, related to the ginger family. The secret of curry powder and a golden touch to any dish.

Dill One of the most delightful and aromatic of all herbs. A "must" in game cookery, but ideal for vegetables and with sweet-and-sour soups and sauces.

Wild Marjoram (Italian *oregano*) Similar to regular marjoram, only much stronger. It is the secret of the sausage maker, but also universally valuable in soups, stews, and sauces, and for flavoring fish, game, or meat.

Sweet Marjoram Gives a more delicate, refined flavor.

Savory A delicate herb you can use in almost everything— in fact, anything except sweet food. Summer savory is milder than the "winter" variety.

Thyme One of the most widely used herbs, because it loves a great many foods, including other herbs. It is a standard for stuffings and is always present in a *bouquet garni*.

Sage A member of the mint family, it comes in many varieties. It is excellent with meat items, for stuffings and gravies.

Mint The refresher of all sauces—it should not be used only with lamb.

Rue A very bitter but not unpleasant herb, used as a flavoring for cold soups and sauces.

Cumin The dried seed of an herb related to the parsley family. Distinctive flavor, used especially in curries, chili and rye breads. Must be used carefully.

Caper The pickled flower bud of a European shrub (the best is Spanish). Is used as a garnish and adds piquancy to sauces, salads and fish.

Ginger The root of a tropical plant widely used in baking, but also valuable in cooking.

Pepper Covers a whole family of condiments—one of the most important of all seasonings. If you don't grind your own pepper in your kitchen, you can't know the true flavor of fresh pepper.

Black The most commonly known is the whole berry, ground.

White The ground inner seed. It has less flavor than black pepper and is used only where the black specks might make a white or cream sauce unsightly.

Cayenne A very strong, hot seasoning derived by grinding or crushing from capsicum or red peppers.

Paprika The mildest of the red pepper spices, coming from the sweet red pepper or pimento. But paprika is available in many different strengths. This is the spice that gives characteristic distinction to Hungarian cooking and can be used profitably in any cuisine.

Mustard The seed of the mustard plant—valuable not only as a condiment by itself, but should be used more often to pep up sauces, gravies, stews, etc., by adding it in dry powdered or prepared form.

Cloves Buds from a clove tree. Their affinity for ham should not limit you to that use. A pinch can add zest and flavor to many other foods, in addition to the natural affinity which cloves have for cinnamon in cakes and pastries.

Allspice A remarkable spice confusingly called pimento, which it is not. Rather, it is a seed with a restrained blend of the aromas of clove, nutmeg, and cinnamon.

Splendid Fare

The Albert Stockli Cookbook

Appetizers

Hot   Cold

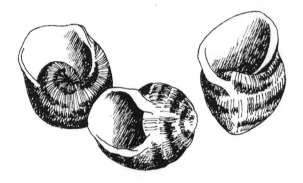

Appetizer is the English word for a delicate dainty or a small portion of appetizing dishes which are designed to whet the appetite before or at the start of a dinner. The German *Vorspeise*, the Italian *antipasti*, and the French *hors d'oeuvres* are in this category.

Every country in the world, in fact every region in any individual country, takes pride in its own special, distinctive appetizers—and a cuisine can be identified most readily by a glance at its appetizers. Appetizers are especially important in Scandinavia and the Northern "snow" countries, because traveling conditions make the arrival time of guests uncertain, and the "appetizer" part of the meal makes it possible to keep earlier guests occupied and entertained until all guests have arrived for dinner.

Appetizers are classified as *hot* or *cold*. Whichever they are, appetizers should be spicy and tasty to perform their function; you should never serve too many and they shouldn't be too heavy. For it is definitely not the purpose of appetizers to fill up the guests or spoil their appetites.

Most appetizers can be prepared in advance. They give the creative cook a good opportunity to make use of leftovers and to use imagination in devising new combinations and presenting them artistically.

When a single appetizer is served as the first course of a meal, it should be selected according to what will follow. A rich, creamy first course should be served only if the main course is a simple broiled fish or lamb chop. If the main course is elaborate and rich, a plain and simple first course should be selected.

A number of the appetizers I have suggested, both hot and cold, can be served as luncheon entrées.

Hot

Cold

Appetizers—Hot

Onion Tart à la Suisse

Serves 4 to 6

6 *medium onions, thinly sliced*
  (In the fall of the year when
  onions tend to be sweet,
  soak the slices in 1 teaspoon
  vinegar.)
2 *Tablespoons butter*
1 *teaspoon thyme*
1 *teaspoon salt (for onion*
  mixture)
½ *teaspoon brown sugar*
½ *teaspoon pepper*
4 *slices lean bacon, diced*
1 *pre-baked 10 × 2 inch pie shell*
  (see page 346)
1 *Tablespoon flour*
3 *eggs, beaten*
½ *cup milk*
1 *teaspoon salt (for flour*
  mixture)

Preheat oven to 400 degrees.

Slice the onions as thin as possible and sauté them in butter in a large skillet. Add thyme, salt, brown sugar, pepper, and diced bacon. Continue cooking until the onions are light brown. Drain off the excess fat. Pour the mixture into the pie shell.

    Sift the flour into a mixing bowl; add the beaten eggs, milk, and salt. Pour the mixture over the onions in the pie shell. Bake (400 degrees) for 25 to 30 minutes until golden brown. Serve warm.

Quiche with White Wine and Shallots

Serves 5 as main course, 8 as first course

My recipe for *quiche*, rich with eggs, cream, and Gruyère cheese, piquant with wine and shallots, is an elegant beginning to a meal, but the remaining courses should be light and simple. This *quiche* may also be served as a main course at luncheon with other dishes that are light.

This particular *quiche* remains popular and has become a stand-by on my menu. It is exciting to bring to the table: The crust is dry and flaky; the filling is puffed up and golden brown. The *quiche* should be served hot and reasonably soon after it is taken from the oven, but it will not fall like a soufflé.

The special refined flavor of imported Gruyère cheese is particularly delicious in this *quiche*. But I refer to the genuine "loaf" Gruyère, not to the small, packaged, "processed," so-called Gruyère. You will note that I do not use the chopped bacon or ham traditionally used in *quiche Lorraine*. The *quiche* rises higher if you avoid fat, but it is important to have the oven preheated at 400 degrees.

Try my *quiche* and I am certain you will make it your own specialty as it has so long been one of mine.

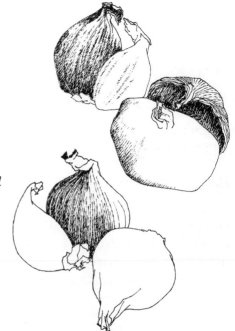

½ *cup shallots (or onions),*
    minced
½ *cup dry white wine*
 6 *eggs*
 3 *cups heavy cream*
 1 *teaspoon salt*
¼ *teaspoon white pepper*
    Dash nutmeg, freshly grated
12 *ounces Gruyère cheese, grated*
 1 *pre-baked 10 × 2 inch pie shell*

Preheat oven to 400 degrees.

Place the minced shallots and wine in a saucepan and bring to a boil. Lower heat and simmer for 2 minutes. Remove from the heat to cool.

Beat the eggs and cream together; add salt, pepper, nutmeg, and the wine-shallot mixture. Sprinkle the grated cheese evenly over the pie shell, then pour in the custard mixture. Bake (400 degrees) for 25 to 30 minutes or until golden brown.

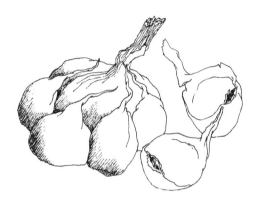

Shucked Oysters in Beer Batter, *Sauce Rémoulade*

Serves 4 to 6

24 *oysters*
   Juice of 1 lemon
 1 *teaspoon salt*

Flour, about 1 cup
Beer batter (see page 373)
Oil for deep frying

GARNISH
  Sauce rémoulade *(see page 89)*

Heat oil to 375 degrees.

Drain and dry the fresh oysters and sprinkle with the lemon juice and salt. Dust the oysters generously with flour, then dip into a small bowl of beer batter and fry 6 at a time (or more if your fryer is big enough) in deep oil (375 degrees) until golden brown.

Serve hot with *sauce rémoulade.*

Crisp Fried Shrimp in Beer Batter   *Serves 4 to 6*

Of the many uses for beer batter, perhaps deep-fried shrimp best illustrates the magic of this simple combination of beer and flour. The cooked shrimp will be tender and moist and free of fat. Medium or large fried shrimp are ideal as a first course of a full dinner or as a main course at luncheon, or a late supper.

16 *raw medium shrimp*   *Flour, about* 1 *cup*
  Juice of 2 *lemons*   *Beer batter (see page 373)*
  Oil for deep frying

GARNISH
  Parsley or watercress, lemon
  wedges
  Pungent fruit sauce
  (see page 94)

Have the shrimp at room temperature. Carefully peel off the shells, leaving the tail intact. Make an incision from the base of the tail down the center. Wash each shrimp under running water and remove the dark vein. Dry them and sprinkle with lemon juice.

Heat several cups of oil or fat in a fryer.

Dredge the shrimp in flour, coating them entirely, then grasp by the tail and dip into the beer batter, coating well. When the temperature of the oil or fat has reached 375 degrees, drop the shrimp in one by one and cook until they are golden brown and crisp. Drain on paper toweling.

PRESENTATION
If you are serving the shrimp at the table, garnish each plate with a lemon wedge and parsley or watercress and serve with fruit sauce. For cocktail parties, cover a large serving tray with doilies or a napkin, place a bowl of fruit sauce in the center, and surround with bouquets of parsley or watercress. Pile the golden shrimp all around the tray with lemon wedges placed among them.

Tiny Crabmeat Dumplings in Beer Batter

Serves 4 to 6

Dumplings of flaked fresh crabmeat are another of my favorite ways of using beer batter. The dumplings are light, crisp, and versatile enough to be served not only as hot canapés with cocktails but also as a first-course appetizer. The entire mixture may be made hours ahead, but do not deep fry them until the last minute so that you serve them hot and crisp.

½ pound cooked crabmeat,
  or Alaska King Crab
½ cup béchamel *sauce*
  (see page 81)
  Juice of 1 *lemon*
  Pâte à choux, *about* ¾ *cup*
  (see page 373)
½ *teaspoon horseradish*

½ *teaspoon dry English mustard*
½ *teaspoon salt*
¼ *teaspoon pepper*
 3 *drops Tabasco sauce*
  Oil for deep frying
  Flour, about 1 *cup*
  Beer batter (see page 373)

GARNISH

Pungent fruit sauce (see page 94)   *Parsley or watercress*
or sauce Lamaze *(see page 90)*

Flake the crabmeat and pick over to remove any bits of bone or shell. Combine in a mixing bowl the cold *béchamel* sauce, lemon juice, *pâte à choux*, horseradish, mustard, salt, pepper, and Tabasco sauce, and mix thoroughly. This dough should rest at least an hour and may be made some hours ahead.

Preheat oil to 375 degrees.

Roll a teaspoonful of the mixture between the palms of your hands, dredge in flour, then dip in beer batter. Fry 6 at a time until golden brown and crisp. Drain on absorbent paper and keep warm.

PRESENTATION

For cocktails, cover a tray or platter with a napkin or paper doily. In the center of the tray place a bowl of sauce surrounded by a garnish of parsley or watercress, and pile the hot dumplings around. A splendid accompaniment for these crabmeat dumplings is pungent fruit sauce, or you may use *sauce Lamaze.*

Calf's Brains in Beer Batter, *Sauce Rémoulade*

Serves 4 to 6

3 *calf's brains*
1 *teaspoon salt*
¼ *cup dry white wine*
   or cider vinegar

Oil for deep frying
Flour, about 1 cup
Beer batter (see page 373)

GARNISH
   Sauce rémoulade *(see page 89)*

Wash the brains. Remove the skin and delicate membrane; then cut each brain in half. To a quart of water in a saucepan add salt and wine or vinegar and bring to a boil. Reduce to a simmer and cook the brains over low heat for 20 minutes. Remove the brains, drain, and cool slightly.

Heat the oil to 375 degrees, using enough oil to submerge the brains.

Dredge the brains lightly in flour, then coat completely in beer batter, and drop into the hot oil for 5 minutes or until golden brown and crisp. Serve immediately with *sauce rémoulade.*

Coquille Jacqueline

Serves 4

12 *ounces bay scallops*
 4 *Tablespoons dry white wine*
 4 *Tablespoons clam juice*
 1 *teaspoon lemon juice*
    Pinch salt
 4 *scallop shells*

 1 *heaping teaspoon cornstarch,*
    dissolved in 2 Tablespoons
    water
¼ *cup heavy cream*
 2 *Tablespoons butter*
½ *avocado, diced*

Preheat oven to 450 degrees.

Wash the scallops under running water to remove any sand. In a saucepan combine the wine, clam juice, lemon juice, and salt and bring to a boil. Add the scallops, reduce the heat, and simmer for 5 minutes. With a slotted spoon remove the scallops and divide into the four shells.

To the wine mixture, now add the dissolved cornstarch, remove from the heat, and fold in the cream.

Melt the 2 Tablespoons of butter in a small frying pan and sauté half of the diced avocado until soft, setting aside the remaining half. Combine the wine mixture and the sautéed avocado to make the sauce.

Divide the raw diced avocado equally among the shells, mixing with the scallops. Pour the sauce over the scallop mixture and transfer the shells to a baking sheet. Bake (450 degrees) for about 8 minutes or until the top is lightly browned.

Artichokes with Baked Oysters *Serves 4 to 6*

1 *Tablespoon salt*   4 *artichokes*
   Juice of 2 *lemons*

THE STUFFING
3 *ounces dry white wine*   *Pinch of pepper*
40 *oysters, shucked*   *Juice of* ½ *lemon*
½ *teaspoon cornstarch dissolved*   ½ *teaspoon salt*
   in 1 *Tablespoon water*
½ *cup hollandaise sauce*
   (see page 86)

To a 4 quart saucepan of salted boiling water, add the juice of 2 lemons, then drop in artichokes and boil for 25 minutes, or until done. Test by pushing the leaves outward; if they stay out and make a cavity, the artichoke is done. Drain the artichokes, then remove the feather choke.

Preheat oven to 450 degrees.

Pour the white wine into a saucepan and bring to a light boil. Then reduce the heat, add half (20) of the oysters, and simmer for 5 minutes. Put the remaining oysters in the blender and blend until smooth. Add the puréed oysters to the oyster and wine mixture and bring again to a light boil. Add the dissolved cornstarch and mix well. Cool slightly.

Add the hollandaise sauce, pepper, the juice of ½ lemon, and ½ teaspoon salt. Spoon the mixture into each artichoke and place them in an ovenproof dish. Bake (450 degrees) for 10 minutes.

Snails in Garlic Butter   *Serves 4 to 6*

It has been my experience in this country that most people don't eat snails in garlic butter—at least at home. However, they are on my menu throughout the year and are one of the most called-for appetizers.

There is no reason why you can't enjoy them at home. The recipe I am giving you here is exactly as I prepare them in my kitchen. This quantity is enough to fill 36 small shells, although I prefer to use the small French ceramic pots, which are more durable, easier to clean, and don't topple over. The pots or shells may be prepared well in advance of serving and need only be popped into a hot oven on ovenproof serving dishes 10 minutes before they are eaten.

1 *bunch parsley,* 1 *bunch watercress (about* 2 *Tablespoons each when trimmed and chopped)*	1 *teaspoon salt*
	1 *teaspoon pepper*
¼ *cup shallots (or onions), peeled and chopped*	½ *ounce Pernod (an anise-flavored liqueur)*
6 *anchovy filets*	5 *drops Tabasco sauce*
¼ *cup almonds, blanched*	*Juice of* 1 *lemon*
8 *cloves garlic, peeled*	36 *snail shells or pots*
½ *pound butter*	36 *snails (imported French snails in cans are excellent)*

Preheat oven to 450 degrees.

GARLIC BUTTER

Wash and remove the stems from the parsley and watercress. Drain well and blot dry with paper towels. Put the parsley, watercress, shallots, anchovies, almonds, and garlic through the fine blade of the meat grinder. Cream the butter (which is more easily done on a chopping board with a pallet knife), add the ground mixture and season with salt and pepper. Then add the Pernod, Tabasco sauce, and the lemon juice. Work the mixture well until it is thoroughly blended.

Using a round-ended table knife, place a bit of the garlic butter in each shell or pot. Add one snail and fill to the top with more garlic butter. The filled snail shells or pots may then be refrigerated or left at room temperature until ready to use.

Bake (450 degrees) for 10 minutes and serve hot.

Avocado Filled with Cauliflower Mousse   *Serves 4*

One of America's most popular foods is the avocado and I can think of no reason why it should always be served cold. Heated through and served hot, the avocado is delicious, and this particular combination of lightly cooked cauliflower and avocado is a useful vegetable course, particularly as an accompaniment to roast beef or lamb. Or it is good as an appetizer, a main course for a light luncheon, or a late supper.

1 *head of cauliflower (1 pound)*	½ *teaspoon salt*
½ *cup* béchamel *sauce*	¼ *teaspoon pepper*
(see page 81)	2 *large ripe avocados*
¼ *cup hollandaise sauce*	1 *Tablespoon melted butter*
(see page 86)	4 *strips of pimiento*

Preheat oven to 400 degrees.

Trim the green leaves off the cauliflower; break or cut off the buds. Cook the buds in boiling water to cover for 15 minutes, leaving them slightly undercooked. Drain and put through the fine blade of the meat grinder. Stir in the *béchamel* sauce, the hollandaise sauce, and season with the salt and pepper. Keep warm.

Cut the avocados in half and remove the pit but leave the skin intact. Place them in a shallow baking dish and brush the inside of each with melted butter. Bake (400 degrees) for about 8 minutes, or until they are heated through.

Remove from the oven and fill each avocado with the cauliflower mousse—piling it as high as possible. Return to the oven for 10 minutes.

Serve the hot, stuffed avocados garnished with a strip of pimiento across the top of each.

Mushroom Caps Filled with Chopped Olives

Serves 4 to 6

Those of you who like garlic will enjoy this combination of barely cooked mushrooms, tart green olives, and anchovies bathed in beef marrow. I recall making up this dish at one Sunday lunch in my lakeside house when I had available only the ingredients listed below.

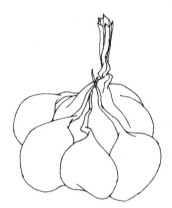

12 *large button mushrooms*
   Juice of 2 lemons
25 *large green olives, pitted and*
   finely chopped
 3 *or 4 cloves garlic, peeled and*
   finely chopped
 2 *anchovy filets, finely chopped*
 4 *ounces beef marrow, finely*
   diced
 1 *teaspoon salt*
¼ *teaspoon pepper*

Preheat oven to 450 degrees.

Wash mushrooms or wipe with damp cloth and carefully cut away the stems, leaving only the caps. Drop the mushrooms in enough boiling water to cover, add the lemon juice, and cook for 4 minutes, no longer. Drain them well, cover with a damp cloth and keep warm.

Prepare the filling by combining the finely chopped olives, garlic, and anchovies, the diced beef marrow, salt, and pepper. Fill each mushroom cap heaping full, place in a shallow ovenproof dish and bake (450 degrees) until heated through—about 10 minutes.

PRESENTATION

Your own imagination will best determine how and when to serve these delicious mushroom caps. Avoid any accompanying dish with garlic— the mushrooms are loaded. I enjoy them with a grilled steak, or you may serve them at a buffet on a *croustade* of bread so that you can pick the whole thing up and eat with your fingers.

Country Gentleman Stuffed Cabbage

Serves 4 as an entrée, 8 as an appetizer

8 *large outside cabbage leaves*
½ *pound bacon, coarsely chopped*
1 *medium onion, finely chopped*
¾ *pound lean ground beef*
1 *Tablespoon chili powder*
1 *Tablespoon chili sauce*

2 *cups fresh corn kernels,*
   cooked (or canned)
2 *eggs, beaten*
1 *teaspoon salt*
1 *teaspoon brown sugar*
2 *cups tomato juice*

Preheat oven to 400 degrees.

Remove from the cabbage 8 outside whole leaves of equal size and blanch them for 2 to 3 minutes in boiling water. Blot them dry and spread out on a flat surface.

Sauté the bacon until soft. Pour off the fat. Add the chopped onion, ground beef, chili powder, chili sauce, corn kernels, 2 beaten eggs, and salt, and continue to cook for 5 minutes.

Divide the mixture equally among the cabbage leaves, filling the center of each. Roll the front flap of the cabbage over the filling; fold the right side over, then the left, then roll. Place the stuffed leaves in a shallow, buttered baking dish.

Add the brown sugar to the tomato juice and pour over the stuffed cabbage leaves. Bake (400 degrees) for 25 minutes. Brush the top of the leaves several times with the pan juices during the baking time. Serve hot.

Dilled Cabbage and Ham

Serves 4

1½–2 *pounds cabbage,*
   thinly grated
 4 *ham steaks, 6 ounces each*
 1 *cup dry white wine*
 2 *cups water*
 1 *Tablespoon prepared*
   mustard

 1 *Tablespoon peanut or corn oil*
 1 *Tablespoon red or white*
   wine vinegar
 ½ *Tablespoon brown sugar*
 ½ *teaspoon salt*
 ¼ *cup fresh dill, finely*
   chopped

Grate the cabbage as fine as possible (as for sauerkraut), and blanch for 5 minutes in boiling salted water. Drain the cabbage and cool.

Simmer the ham steaks in 2 cups of water and 1 cup of white wine for 25 minutes. Remove the steaks (and keep warm) while you reduce the water/wine broth to half by boiling rapidly. Remove from the heat. Add the mustard, oil, vinegar, sugar, salt, and chopped dill. Toss the cabbage in this dressing, and serve at room temperature alongside the warm ham steaks.

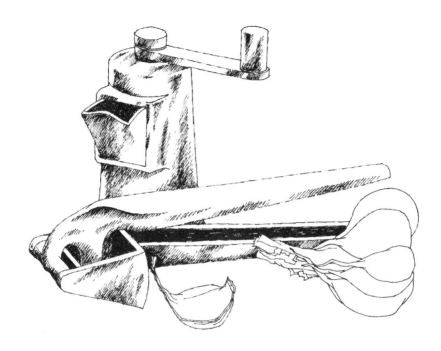

Chicken Livers *Béarnaise*   *Serves 4*

1 *pound chicken livers*
3 *Tablespoons butter*
1 *medium onion, finely chopped*
1 *ounce dry sherry*
1 *teaspoon paprika*

4 *slices of bread, trimmed of*
   crust
1 *cup* Béarnaise *sauce (see*
   page 81)

Preheat oven to 400 degrees.

Wash the chicken livers, cutting away any gall (greenish spots), and drain well. In a frying pan melt the butter, add the chopped onion, and sauté until light brown. Add the chicken livers, sherry, paprika, and sauté for only 2 minutes, leaving the livers rosy-colored inside, or 4 minutes for well done, if you prefer.

Toast the 4 slices of bread and place them on a small baking sheet. Divide the liver mixture equally on the pieces of toast, cover each piece with *Béarnaise* sauce and brown (400 degrees) for about 2 minutes.

Veal Meat Balls in White Wine and Cream

Serves 4 to 6

These delicately flavored meat balls simmered slowly in white wine and cream may be served in several ways. Originally, I created this recipe for a buffet supper, to balance the cold meats and salads. It is a beautiful dish served in a gleaming copper chafing dish, the meat balls swimming in a buttery white sauce sprinkled with bright green bits of chives.

This recipe will make about 128 small meat balls, or, if you want to serve them as a main course, make them about the size of a small egg. Even if you buy the veal ground, follow the directions in the recipe by putting it through the fine blade twice. The meat balls may be prepared some hours in advance and kept at room temperature, but the sauce should be made at the last minute.

1½ *pounds shoulder of veal*
  6 *Tablespoons softened butter*
    (¾ stick)
  1 *teaspoon marjoram*
  ½ *teaspoon rosemary*
1½ *teaspoons salt*
  ¼ *teaspoon pepper*
  3 *eggs, beaten*
  ¼ *cup heavy cream,*
    for meat balls

  ½ *cup dry white wine*
  ½ *cup heavy cream, for sauce*
  1 *teaspoon cornstarch,*
    dissolved in 2 Tablespoons
    water
  1 *Tablespoon shallots (or*
    onions), minced
2 *or 3 Tablespoons chives,*
    finely chopped

Preheat oven to 400 degrees.

Grind the veal very fine. In a large mixing bowl, mix together the ground veal, the softened butter, marjoram, rosemary, salt, pepper, and beaten eggs. Put the mixture once more through the fine blade of the meat grinder, then blend in ¼ cup of cream and shape into meat balls the size of small olives.

Butter a shallow ovenproof serving dish. Arrange the meat balls in the dish so that they do not touch, and bake (400 degrees) for 25 minutes.

Remove from the oven. Transfer the meat balls to another dish and keep warm. Add the white wine to the pan juices in the baking dish and stir, adding the ½ cup cream, the dissolved cornstarch, and the minced shallots.

Transfer the meat balls back into the baking dish with the sauce, and heat in the oven (400 degrees) for another 15 minutes. Sprinkle generously with chives and serve hot.

Chopped Chicken Liver with Apples   *Serves 4*

Cooked chicken livers tend to have a monotonous texture however one flavors them. When they are mixed with onion, hard-boiled eggs, and tart green apples, however, something new emerges. Watch the cooking times carefully. Overcooking will make a mush out of what is intended to create a variety of textures.

1 *pound chicken livers*	*coarsely chopped, and*
½ *cup corn oil*	*sprinkled with juice of* ½
1 *medium onion, finely chopped*	*lemon*
2 *Tablespoons dry sherry*	½ *teaspoon curry powder*
4 *hard-boiled eggs, chopped*	½ *teaspoon salt*
2 *tart green apples, peeled, cored,*	¼ *teaspoon pepper*

Wash the chicken livers and remove any greenish bits. Set aside to drain.

Heat the oil in a large frying pan, add the finely chopped onion and sauté until light gold. Cut the chicken livers into small pieces and add to onion, together with the sherry, chopped eggs, and chopped apples. Season with curry powder and salt and pepper. Sauté the mixture over medium heat for no longer than 3 minutes.

PRESENTATION

I generally serve this combination hot on buttered toast or tiny pastry shells, but it may also be served cold if that seems more appropriate to your meal.

Smoked Sausage with Mustard Dressing   *Serves 4*

1½ *pounds smoked small pork*
    link sausages (Or you may
    substitute cervelat or cooked
    frankfurters.)
  1 *Tablespoon vegetable oil*
  1 *Tablespoon prepared*
    mustard

  ½ *teaspoon mustard seed*
  1 *Tablespoon red or white*
    wine vinegar
  ½ *teaspoon salt*
  ½ *teaspoon pepper*

Place the pork sausages in water and bring to a boil. Cook just suffi-ciently to heat through.

In the meantime, mix together the rest of the ingredients to make the mustard dressing.

Remove the outer skin (if any) from the sausages, cut them into thin slices, cover with mustard dressing, and serve while still warm.

Spiced Pork Sausage in Wine and Raisins

Serves 4 to 6

  1 *cup white wine*
  1 *Tablespoon prepared mustard*
  ½ *cup brown stock (see page*
    45) (or use rich canned beef
    broth)
  ½ *teaspoon thyme*

  1 *pound smoked pork sausage*
    (Use Polish smoked Kielbasa,
    or you may substitute beef
    salami.)
  1 *cup white seedless raisins or*
    fresh green seedless grapes

Preheat oven to 400 degrees.

Pour the wine into a mixing bowl and add the mustard, brown stock, and thyme, and mix thoroughly.

Remove the outer skin of the sausage and cut into thick slices. Place the sausage slices in a shallow baking dish and pour the wine mixture over them. Add raisins or grapes, and place in oven (400 degrees) until heated through—about 10 minutes.

Smoked Sausages and Red Wine and Mustard Dressing

Serves 4 to 6

Select your favorite, well-seasoned smoked dry sausage to accompany this unusual wine dressing. Balance the hearty mustard flavor with more bland accompaniments. Whether you use it at a buffet, as a luncheon entrée or appetizer, you'll enjoy this Swiss farmhouse stand-by—prepared in minutes. I would suggest serving beer and perhaps small boiled new potatoes with it.

½ *cup red wine*
¼ *cup prepared mustard*
  Pinch thyme
¼ *teaspoon pepper*
½ *teaspoon salt*

½ *Tablespoon shallots*
  (or scallions), finely chopped
1 *pound smoked dried sausage*
  (Kielbasa or cervelat)

Pour the wine into a saucepan, add the mustard, thyme, pepper, salt, and chopped shallots. Bring to a boil, reduce heat and simmer for 5 minutes, stirring frequently.

Remove the outer skin from the sausages, slice thick, and simmer in the wine sauce until heated through.

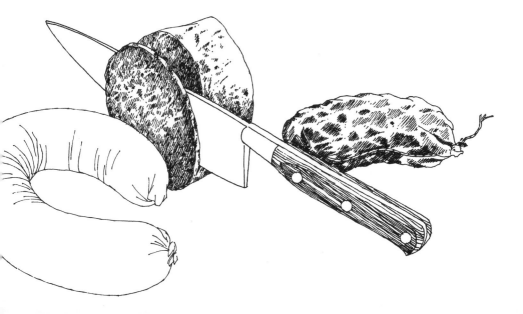

Appetizers—Cold

Country *Terrine*

Yield 3 pounds

For holiday meals and during seasons of frequent entertaining, it is a great convenience to have at least one course ready for the table, and this chunky country *terrine* of pork, veal, calves' brains, and livers marinated in brandy, sherry, and spices is a good choice. A *terrine* is an earthenware pot (from the French *terre* meaning earth)—and this container has given its name to the pâté which it contains. *Terrine* usually means a product coarser and chunkier than the usual pâté, especially with the "country" reference.

The *terrine* may be refrigerated and kept up to ten days. With my recipe, which is simple to make, this *terrine* needs no lining of fat and makes its own gelatine, which keeps it moist.

1 *pound lean pork neck*	2 *Tablespoons brandy*
½ *pound veal*	2 *Tablespoons dry sherry*
½ *pound salt pork, trimmed*	¼ *teaspoon each of thyme,*
of thick outer skin	*savory, mace, and marjoram*
½ *pound calf's brains,*	½ *teaspoon ground coriander*
trimmed of outer skin	1 *teaspoon salt*
¼ *pound chicken livers,*	½ *teaspoon pepper*
trimmed of any greenish spots,	4 *eggs, beaten with ¼ cup*
washed and drained	*water*
⅓ *cup (2 ounces) whole,*	
peeled pistachios	

GARNISH

Cumberland sauce (see page   *Lettuce*
94)

Put the pork, veal, salt pork, brains, livers, and pistachios through the coarse blade of the grinder (or have your butcher do it). Place in a large mixing bowl and stir in the brandy and sherry, the seasonings, and the beaten eggs.

Let the mixture marinate uncovered overnight in the refrigerator or for at least several hours at room temperature. Pack the *terrine* mixture into a greased 2½ quart, thin, metal loaf-baking pan and cover with cooking foil. (If you use a crockery *terrine* dish with its own cover, proceed the same way.)

Preheat oven to 450 degrees.

Place the pan into a larger pan filled with enough boiling water to come three quarters of the way up to the top of the smaller pan. Bake for 1½ hours (450 degrees). This will leave the center of the *terrine* pink, which is the way it should be.

Allow to cool and then refrigerate for several hours, before serving or cutting into pieces for storage.

PRESENTATION

I prefer to serve this country *terrine* with a Cumberland sauce, tart and dark red, about 1 teaspoon over two slices of *terrine* on a lettuce leaf.

Baked Eggplant with Seafood Orientale

Serves 6 to 8 as an appetizer, 4 to 6 as a main course

1 cup peanut or corn oil
1 eggplant (about 1 pound),
  peeled and diced
2 cloves garlic, finely minced
2 Tablespoons onion, finely
  chopped
1 Tablespoon curry powder
8 ounces tuna, flaked
  (or whitefish, flaked)
1 cup mussels, cooked 2 minutes
  in boiling, salted water (or 1
  6-ounce can, drained)

6 anchovy filets, coarsely
  chopped
1 cup piñon nuts (pine nuts),
  toasted
1 Tablespoon tomato purée
2 green apples, peeled, cored,
  and chopped (or 1 cup fresh
  chopped pineapple)
  Juice of 1 lemon
1 teaspoon salt
½ Tablespoon vinegar

GARNISH
  Tomato wedges

  Watercress or parsley

Preheat oven to 400 degrees.

Combine the oil and diced eggplant in an ovenproof dish and bake (400 degrees) until soft—about 25 minutes. In a large salad bowl combine the eggplant with all of the other ingredients. Toss lightly and chill well before serving.

PRESENTATION
This cold salad is substantial enough for a main luncheon course if you serve it on individual plates, garnished with wedges of tomato and tiny bouquets of watercress or sprigs of parsley. I sometimes use this chilled salad on a buffet as a colorful accompaniment to meats.

Mussels and Cucumber *Polonaise*   *Serves 4 to 6*

1 *pound cucumbers, peeled and sliced very thin*
1 *teaspoon salt*
Juice *of 1 lemon*
1/3 *cup heavy cream*
1 *cup sour cream*
4 *Tablespoons corn oil*
2 *Tablespoons cider vinegar*
2 *Tablespoons fresh dill, finely chopped (or 1 Tablespoon dried)*

1 *teaspoon salt*
1/2 *teaspoon pepper*
1/2 *cup mayonnaise*
3 *cups mussels (canned), drained of liquid*
1 *egg, hard-boiled, finely chopped or rubbed through a sieve*

Place the sliced (you may use the coarse side of a hand grater) cucumbers in a bowl and sprinkle with salt. Allow them to "sweat" for at least 1 hour. Squeeze all moisture out of the cucumbers and pour the lemon juice and the heavy cream over them.

In another bowl mix together the sour cream, oil, vinegar, chopped dill, salt, pepper, and mayonnaise. Pour this mixture over the cucumber slices and add the well-drained mussels.

Chill well and just before serving sprinkle the top with chopped egg.

Stonehenge Curried Mussels with Celery Root (Celeriac)

Serves 6

4 *cups fresh cooked and drained*
  mussels, or 4 six-ounce cans,
  drained
1 *teaspoon salt*
1 *teaspoon peanut oil*
  Juice of ½ lemon (for cooking
  mussels)

4 *medium celery roots (celeriac)*
2 *cups mayonnaise*
½ *cup heavy cream*
1 *Tablespoon curry powder*
  Juice of 2 lemons (for sauce)
1 *teaspoon salt*
½ *teaspoon pepper*

If fresh, 40 to 55 mussels will serve 4 people. Wash fresh mussels free of sand, put in a saucepan with a cup of water, a teaspoon of salt, a teaspoon of peanut oil, and juice of ½ lemon. Cover, bring to a boil, cook from 3 to 5 minutes or until the mussels open up. Remove from shells and drain.

Peel and wash the celery roots; grate finely into a mixing bowl. Add the mayonnaise, cream, curry powder, juice of 2 lemons, salt, pepper. Mix thoroughly and add the drained mussels. Serve chilled.

Salmon Mousse with Horseradish *Mousseline* Sauce

Serves 4 to 6

1 *pound salmon (If you use the*
  1-pound can, include the liquid.
  Remove skin and bones.
  With poached fresh salmon,
  add 3 ounces dry white wine.)
1 *Tablespoon shallots or*
  scallions, finely chopped

½ *cup heavy cream*
¼ *teaspoon each of pepper,*
  salt, and savory
3 *eggs*
1 *teaspoon parsley, finely*
  chopped

GARNISH
  Horseradish mousseline *sauce*
  (see page 87)

Lettuce

Preheat oven to 400 degrees.

Put the fish and its liquid (or wine) into the blender with all of the other ingredients and purée until smooth. Pour the mousse into a lightly oiled mold that holds 4 cups, or into 4 separate cups. Place the mold or cups into a baking pan and pour in boiling water to reach three-quarters of the way up the mold. Bake (400 degrees) for about 40 minutes, or until the mousse is firm to the touch.

Remove mold or cups from the water to cool. Unmold the mousse and serve chilled, either whole or cut into thick slices, on lettuce leaves, with horseradish *mousseline* sauce.

Shrimp and Crabmeat Salad with *Sauce Lamaze*

Serves 4 to 6

15 *medium-sized shrimp,
    cooked and peeled*
½ *can lump crabmeat (7
    ounces)*
1 *hard-boiled egg, coarsely
    chopped*
1 *cup celery, finely chopped*
1 *medium white radish or 4 red
    radishes, finely grated*

1 *medium carrot, finely grated
    Juice of 2 lemons*
1½ *cups sauce Lamaze
    (see page 90)*
½ *teaspoon salt
    Dash each of mace and
    savory*

GARNISH

    Lettuce leaves
8–12 *whole red radishes*

1 *tomato cut into 4 or 6
    wedges*

Place the cooked and peeled shrimp in a mixing bowl. Pick over the crabmeat to make sure all bones are removed and add to the shrimp along with the chopped egg and celery, the grated radishes and carrot, and lemon juice. Add the *sauce Lamaze* and mix thoroughly. Then season with salt, mace, and savory, and serve on plates garnished with lettuce leaves, wedges of tomato, and red radishes.

Lump Crabmeat *Ravigote*   *Serves 4 to 6*

1 *can lump crabmeat (14 ounces), or Alaskan King Crab*
1 *teaspoon dry English mustard*
½ *green pepper, finely chopped with ribs and seeds removed*
½ *red pepper or pimiento, finely chopped*

½ *small onion, finely chopped*
Juice of 3 lemons
½ *teaspoon salt*
1 *cup mayonnaise (for binding mixture)*

GARNISH
Lettuce leaves
½ *cup mayonnaise, mixed with*
1 *Tablespoon water*

Capers
1 *egg, hard-boiled and quartered*
Tomato wedges

Pick over the crabmeat to remove bones and place in a mixing bowl. Sprinkle with mustard and stir well. Add the chopped green pepper, red pepper, onion, lemon juice, and salt. Mix in 1 cup mayonnaise. Arrange on individual plates on lettuce leaves. Cover the crabmeat mixture with mayonnaise mixed with 1 Tablespoon warm water and sprinkle with capers. Garnish the plates with quartered egg and wedges of tomato.

Artichoke Hearts with Tuna, Sauce Vinaigrette
Serves 4 to 6

2 *No. 2 cans artichoke hearts, or 1 pound frozen artichokes*
1 *eight-ounce can tuna fish, flaked*
1 *whole pimiento, coarsely chopped*
1 *clove garlic, finely chopped*
2 *hard-boiled eggs, coarsely chopped*

½ *cup piñon nuts (pine nuts), toasted for 3–5 minutes in 450 degree oven*
1½ *cups sauce vinaigrette (see page 90)*

Drain the artichoke hearts (if frozen, cook according to packaged directions and drain), and put them into a mixing bowl. Add the tuna, pimiento, garlic, eggs, piñon nuts, and sauce vinaigrette. Mix thoroughly and chill before serving.

Artichokes Filled with Eggplant Salad   *Serves 4*

4 *large fresh artichokes*   ½ *teaspoon salt*
  Juice of 2 lemons

FILLING
¼ *cup corn oil for sautéing*   6 *anchovy filets, finely chopped*
  vegetables   ¼ *cup blanched almonds, sliced*
1 *eggplant, peeled and finely*   *and toasted in the oven for*
  diced (about 12 ounces)   *about 3–5 minutes*
1 *clove garlic, minced*   1 *Tablespoon capers*
½ *onion, chopped*   ¼ *cup white wine vinegar*
2 *tomatoes, peeled, seeded,*   ½ *cup olive oil*
  and diced   ¼ *teaspoon paprika*
20 *pitted, green olives,*   1 *teaspoon salt*
  coarsely chopped

Trim the artichokes of dry leaves, remove the stems, and cut 1 inch off the top with a sharp knife. Place the artichokes in a saucepan and cover with boiling water, add lemon juice and salt, and cook until tender, about 25 minutes. Test by seeing if one of the center leaves pulls away easily. Drain the artichokes well and spread the leaves; then, using a pointed spoon, remove the weedy choke from the inside, leaving only the large leaves and bottom (heart). While preparing the filling, chill the trimmed artichokes.

Pour ¼ cup oil into a frying pan and add the diced eggplant, the minced garlic, chopped onion, and diced tomatoes. Sauté the vegetables for about 15 minutes or until tender. Pour the mixture into a mixing bowl. When cool, add the chopped olives and anchovies, the toasted almonds, the capers, vinegar, olive oil, and seasonings. Mix well. Fill each of the artichokes, heaping the filling high. Chill before serving.

Raw Mushrooms and Country Sausage   *Serves 4 to 6*

½ *pound raw mushrooms, rinsed*
   and sliced fine
   Juice of 1 *lemon*
¼ *cup onion, finely chopped*
¼ *cup celery, finely chopped*
 1 *teaspoon salt*

¼ *teaspoon pepper*
¼ *cup corn oil*
 1 *well-seasoned smoked sausage*
   (Kielbasa or cervelat), about
   5 ounces, sliced
4–6 *lettuce leaves*

Rinse the mushrooms and wipe dry. Trim the stems. Slice the mushrooms as thin as possible (very sharp knife or grater) into a salad bowl and moisten them immediately with the lemon juice. Add the chopped onion and celery, salt, pepper, and oil. Skin the sausage and slice very thin into the mushroom salad. Mix and serve well chilled on a lettuce leaf.

Chicken Liver Pâté   *Serves 4 to 6*

This simple pâté is quickly prepared and has a great many possibilities for serving. I squeeze it from a pastry bag into puff balls on top of very thin bread to make tiny cocktail sandwiches. Or, for an appetizer, I serve it on a lettuce leaf garnished with finely chopped egg yolk, green onions, perhaps some capers, and accompanied by melba toast or that crispy Norwegian flatbread.

1 *pound chicken livers*
6 *ounces butter, softened*
  but not melted
½ *teaspoon thyme*
  Pinch cinnamon
2 *Tablespoons dry sherry*

1 *small onion, finely chopped*
1 *teaspoon salt*
¼ *teaspoon pepper*
1 *hard-boiled egg, finely chopped*

Wash the chicken livers and remove any greenish spots. Blanch them in enough boiling water to cover, no longer than 3 minutes, leaving them slightly undercooked. Drain the livers and put them in the blender with the butter, and purée until smooth. Add the thyme, cinnamon, sherry, chopped onion, salt, and pepper, and blend until smooth. Chill well before serving. Garnish with chopped egg.

Fresh Peach Stuffed with Curried Ham or Chicken

Serves 4

⅓ *pound cooked ham or cooked chicken*
½ *teaspoon curry powder*
3 *Tablespoons softened butter*
1 *teaspoon chutney syrup from jar (leaving solid pieces)*

½ *ounce dry sherry*
  Pinch salt
  Pinch pepper
4 *large fresh peaches*
  Lettuce leaves

Put the ham or chicken through the fine blade of the grinder. Blend with the curry powder, butter, chutney syrup, sherry, salt, and pepper, to make a smooth paste. Chill while preparing the peaches.

Dip the peaches into boiling water for a few seconds and remove the skin. Cut the top off of each peach and with a sharp-pointed spoon remove the pit. Slice ⅛ inch off the bottom of peaches so they will stand firmly. Fill each peach with the mousse, piling it high above the top. Serve the peaches well chilled on a bed of lettuce leaves.

Pineapple Stuffed with Curried Seafood   *Serves 4*

¼ *pound shrimp*
4 *ounces canned tuna fish*
4 *ounces canned boneless*
   sardines, drained and
   coarsely chopped

1 *Tablespoon curry powder*
  Pinch salt
2 *ripe pineapples*
½ *cup* sauce Lamaze
  (see page 90)

GARNISH
Watercress

Lemon wedges

Peel the shrimp and cook according to their size: about 10 minutes for large shrimp, about 6 minutes for small ones.

Place the cooked shrimp in a mixing bowl. Flake the tuna and add, along with the chopped sardines, to the shrimp. Sprinkle the mixture with the curry powder and salt.

Cut off the top of each pineapple and split in half from top to bottom. With a small sharp knife cut along both sides of the core at an angle, pull out the core and discard. Now carefully cut out the ripe pineapple flesh and cut into thin strips. Add the pineapple strips to the seafood mixture, pour the *sauce Lamaze* over it and mix thoroughly. Fill each pineapple shell with mixture and chill before serving. Garnish with watercress and a wedge of lemon.

Swiss Mountain Ham with Melon or Fresh Pear

This unusual ham is brought to perfect flavor in the dry mountain air of the Alps of Switzerland. It reaches us in this country boneless and with the faintest suggestion of salt. It is similar to Italian prosciutto, but I think the Swiss ham has more flavor. If your delicatessen counter does not have Swiss ham, prosciutto or Westphalian type ham may be substituted. It must be sliced paper thin on a slicing machine, so get it at a delicatessen.

2 or 3 slices ham per serving   *Parsley sprigs*
2 slices melon or pear per serving

Cover each portion of melon or pear with ham and serve well chilled and garnished with a sprig of parsley.

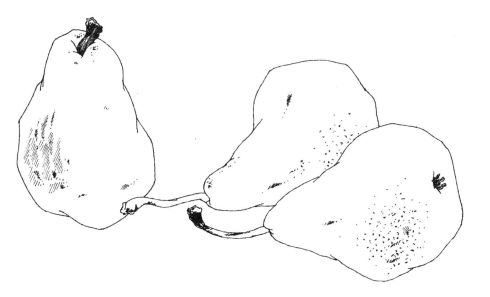

Marrow Beans and Country Sausage   *Serves 4 to 6*

1 *pound marrow beans or navy*
beans
Ham bone or a piece of bacon
rind (about 3 ounces)
½ *cup corn oil*
¼ *cup white wine vinegar*
1 *medium onion, finely chopped*
½ *teaspoon salt*

¼ *teaspoon pepper*
1 *pound smoked dried pork*
sausage, thinly sliced. (You can
substitute salami, bologna, or
cooked frankfurters.)
1 *teaspoon fresh horseradish,*
finely grated

Cook the beans for 1 hour, 45 minutes in 2 quarts of salted boiling water, with the ham bone or bacon rind to give flavor. Keep beans covered with water at all times.

In a serving bowl mix together the oil, vinegar, chopped onion, salt, and pepper. Add the cooked, drained beans and thinly sliced pork sausage. Sprinkle the salad mixture with horseradish and chill before serving.

Tomato Filled with Country Sausage   *Serves 4*

4 *large ripe tomatoes*
2 *smoked dried sausages, about*
4 ounces, or use cervelat, salami,
bologna, or cooked frankfurters
2 *Tablespoons onion, finely*
chopped
2 *teaspoons prepared*
domestic mustard

5 *Tablespoons corn oil*
2 *teaspoons white wine vinegar*
¼ *cup finely grated cheese*
(about 1½ ounces), imported
Gruyère or other hard white
cheese
½ *teaspoon salt*
¼ *teaspoon pepper*

GARNISH
Lettuce

Watercress or parsley

Select ripe but firm tomatoes. Slice off the tops of the tomatoes and scoop out the pulp and seeds. Turn upside down to drain thoroughly before filling.

Remove the skin from the sausages, slice lengthwise into four pieces and then slice vertically as thinly as possible. Place sausage pieces in a mixing bowl, and add the finely chopped onion, mustard, oil, vinegar, and grated cheese. Season with the salt and pepper. Mix thoroughly and use to fill the tomatoes. Chill.

PRESENTATION

These filled tomatoes are ideal for a buffet supper, an appetizer, or main-course luncheon dish served on crisp lettuce and garnished with watercress or parsley.

Soups

Stocks   Hot   Hot or Cold   Cold

There is an old European saying which illustrates my feeling about soup: "Taste the soup and you know what to expect from the rest of the meal."

Soups can be delightful hot or cold and can be made of every imaginable ingredient. In fact there is no edible material that cannot or has not been used in making soup. Moist porridges were considered soup, as were various liquids flavored with beer and wine. Many soups are enjoyed today with sherry or madeira wine added.

Fruit soups are popular in Europe, especially in Scandinavia, and soups made from flower petals are enjoyed in India and the Near East.

Soup is a wonderfully practical dish for the housewife because it can be prepared well in advance. In fact it is often enhanced by long simmering. You can capitalize on locally available ingredients and can make use of all sorts of leftovers; your soup can be kept for days in the refrigerator or even frozen.

Above all, here is a chance to show some creativity and ingenuity. The main danger is heavy-handedness in seasoning, for a prolonged cooking which evaporates the liquid might result in an over-salty or over-seasoned flavor.

The glory of soup lies in the blend of flavors it provides—and exciting new tastes can be developed by skillfully mixing together leftover soups. The limitless variety can be extended even further by the addition of various garnishes, dumplings, etc.

Usually, soups are classified as clear or thick soups—but there are many gradations in between. Soups are closely related to stews, and, therefore, an appropriate soup can be a main dish in itself. At the same time, soups are also closely related to sauces and leftover sauces can make a great contribution to soup.

The average housewife does not have available the basic soup stocks which a large restaurant kitchen can command, but she has more than she thinks. Canned consommé or broth can be used, the liquid from canned mushrooms or canned vegetables can be saved and used, as well as the liquid from the vegetables she has cooked. Of course for superlative flavor it is worth the extra effort of making soup stock, for which I have included simplified recipes.

Stocks

Hot

Hot or Cold

Cold

Stocks

Clear Chicken Stock

Yield 1 quart

The flavor of freshly made chicken stock is always preferable to that of canned or the kind produced from bouillon cubes and is well worth the extra trouble. You can reduce the stock by boiling it an extra 25 or 30 minutes and then freezing it in cube form to be reconstituted when needed by adding ½ cup water per medium cube.

To make the best stock you need *raw* bones or chicken pieces, not leftover cooked chicken. You should be able to get raw chicken wings, necks, gizzards, etc., at a supermarket.

1 *carrot, unpeeled, rinsed, and coarsely chopped*
1 *medium onion, unpeeled, rinsed, and coarsely chopped*
1 *whole leek (or additional onion), unpeeled, rinsed, and coarsely chopped*
2 *stalks celery, rinsed, and finely chopped*

1 *Tablespoon butter*
1 *pound raw chicken carcass, or fresh chicken pieces*
1 *calf's foot, or several veal marrow bones*
½ *teaspoon salt*
¼ *teaspoon pepper*
1½ *quarts water*

BOUQUET GARNI
6 *sprigs parsley, 2 sprigs fresh thyme (or ½ teaspoon dried), 1 bayleaf, tied together in cheesecloth.*

In a large saucepan sauté the rinsed and chopped vegetables in butter over high heat for 5 minutes. Add the chicken bones or pieces, calf's foot or veal bones, salt, pepper, water, and bouquet garni. Simmer uncovered over medium heat for 45 minutes.

Strain the soup and allow to cool before refrigerating. When the stock is thoroughly chilled, skim off the fat. It is now ready for use or may be further reduced and frozen as noted above.

Basic Beef Stock

Yield 1½ quarts

You may, of course, use canned beef broth or other substitutes (bouillon cubes, etc.) for your own beef stock in recipes calling for this ingredient. But if you cook regularly for your family or entertain frequently, you will find that your own strong beef stock will improve immeasurably the dishes in which you use it. It is easy to make and inexpensive—much less in fact than the alternative bouillon cubes or canned broth. And it will keep indefinitely if frozen.

NOTE: In my beef and chicken stock recipes I have specified that the vegetables be rinsed but remain unpeeled, as the peel when left on and cooked gives the resulting stock a much stronger, richer color.

3 *stalks celery, rinsed, and cut in chunks*

2 *carrots, unpeeled, rinsed, and cut in chunks*

1 *onion, unpeeled, rinsed, and cut in chunks*

1 or 2 *leeks (or 3 or 4 scallions), rinsed and cut in chunks*

1 *turnip, unpeeled, rinsed, and cut in chunks*

2 *quarts water*

3 *pounds beef shank (the meat and bones)*

BOUQUET GARNI

6 or 8 *sprigs of parsley, sprig of fresh thyme (or ¼ teaspoon dried), and 1 bayleaf, tied together in cheesecloth.*

In a large saucepan combine the rinsed, coarsely chopped vegetables with 2 quarts of cold water and the soup meat and bones. Add the bouquet garni and simmer uncovered for at least 2½ hours. Season the stock only lightly with salt and pepper, as subsequent use of stock will include seasoning.

Strain the stock into a container and de-grease thoroughly. It is easier to do this when the stock is cold.

It is now ready for use or may be frozen for future use.

Basic Brown Stock

While the ingredients for brown stock and basic beef stock are similar, in this case the initial browning produces a rich, dark brown, thick base which is used frequently in sauces and for flavoring a number of dishes in this volume.

3 *pounds beef shank (the meat and the bones)*

2 *carrots, unpeeled, rinsed, and cut in chunks*

1 *large onion, unpeeled, rinsed, and cut in chunks*

2 *quarts water*

2 *stalks celery, unpeeled, rinsed, and cut in chunks*

1 *turnip, unpeeled, rinsed, and cut in chunks*

1 *teaspoon salt*

½ *teaspoon pepper*

B O U Q U E T   G A R N I
6 *or 8 sprigs parsley, sprig of fresh thyme (or ¼ teaspoon dried), 1 bayleaf, tied together in cheesecloth.*

Preheat oven to 500 degrees.

Place the meat and bones in a baking pan and roast (500 degrees) for twenty minutes, turning them once or twice.

Reduce heat to 450 degrees. Add the coarsely chopped carrots and onion, and roast (450 degrees) for about 30 minutes more or until the meat and vegetables have taken on a good color. Turn the pieces several times to insure even browning.

Transfer the contents to a large saucepan, pour off the fat, and add enough water to the baking pan to loosen the juices. Then pour the juices from the baking pan, and the remaining water, into the saucepan over the bones. Add the celery, turnip, salt, pepper, and bouquet garni. Simmer uncovered for at least 2 hours, removing with a slotted spoon any scum that appears on the surface.

Strain into another saucepan and boil until the quantity of stock is reduced to half.

This rich essence of beef and vegetables is now ready for immediate use or to be further reduced and frozen until required.

White Fish *Fumet* (Fish Stock)

Yield 2 cups

2 *pounds raw fish bones (any white fish)*
1 *quart water*
1 *onion, peeled, stuck with two cloves*

1 *leek, white part only (or 2 scallions, white part only)*
1 *pinch thyme*
1 *stalk celery*

Simmer fish bones, water, onion, leek, thyme, and celery for 15 minutes, uncovered, skimming foam off the top while cooking. Then simmer for 15 minutes more. Strain through a fine sieve.

Use to poach fish, or as a basic fish stock in making white fish sauces.

White Veal Stock

Yield 1 quart

1 *carrot, peeled and coarsely chopped*
1 *medium onion, peeled and coarsely chopped*
1 *leek, white part only (or additional onion), peeled and coarsely chopped*
2 *stalks celery, finely chopped*

1 *Tablespoon butter*
2 *pounds raw veal bones*
1 *calf's foot (or calf's knuckle)*
½ *teaspoon salt*
¼ *teaspoon pepper*
1½ *quarts water*

BOUQUET GARNI
6 *sprigs parsley, 2 sprigs thyme (or ½ teaspoon dried), 1 bayleaf, tied together in cheesecloth.*

In a large saucepan, sauté the chopped vegetables in butter for 5 minutes. Add the veal bones, calf's foot, bouquet garni, salt, pepper, and water. Simmer, uncovered, over medium heat for 1½ hours, skimming foam off the top while cooking.

Strain the stock and allow to cool before refrigerating. When the stock is thoroughly chilled, skim off the fat. It is now ready for use, or may be frozen for future use.

Hot Soups

Bisque of Butternut Squash with Apple   *Serves 4 to 6*

1 *small butternut squash (about 1 pound), unpeeled, cut in half, and seeded*

2 *tart green apples, peeled, cored, and coarsely chopped*

1 *medium onion, coarsely chopped*

Pinch rosemary

Pinch marjoram

1 *quart chicken stock (see page 43) (or use rich canned chicken broth)*

2 *slices white bread, trimmed and cubed*

1½ *teaspoons salt*

¼ *teaspoon pepper*

2 *egg yolks*

¼ *cup heavy cream*

Combine the squash halves, the chopped apples and onion, herbs, stock, bread cubes, salt, and pepper in a large heavy saucepan. Bring to a boil and simmer uncovered for about 45 minutes, or until the vegetables are soft.

Scoop the flesh of the squash out, discard the skins, and return the pulp to soup. Purée the soup, to which you have returned the squash, in the blender until smooth. (You will probably have two blender loads.) Return the puréed soup to the saucepan.

In a small bowl, beat the egg yolks and cream together. Beat in a little of the hot soup, then stir back into the saucepan. Heat, but do not boil, and serve immediately.

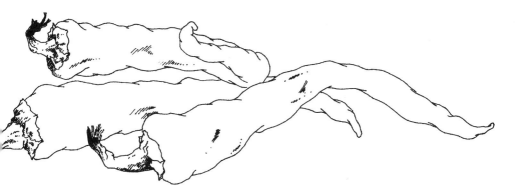

Bisque of Summer Squash

American squash, in such great variety and so many flavors, has always seemed to me a much neglected basic food. I long ago began to experiment with this plentiful and delicious vegetable, and through the years guests have been enthusiastic over the various soups and bisques made from squash. I am giving you several of my favorites and I think you'll agree that this simple and inexpensive soup makes a nourishing and delicious first course.

1 *pound summer squash,*
  unpeeled and coarsely chopped
1 *onion, coarsely chopped*
1 *stalk of celery, coarsely*
  chopped
5 *sprigs of fresh parsley*
1 *leek, white part only (or 2*
  scallions, white part only),
  coarsely chopped

3 *cups chicken stock (see page*
  43) (or use rich canned
  chicken broth)
  Salt and pepper to taste
2 *egg yolks*
¼ *cup light cream*

Scrub the squash, cut into small pieces, and place in a large saucepan. Add the onion, celery, parsley, leek, chicken stock, salt, and pepper. Bring to a boil and simmer uncovered over medium heat for 40 minutes.

Pour the soup mixture into the blender and purée until smooth. Return to the saucepan. Beat the egg yolks and cream together, add a bit of the hot soup mixture, then pour back and stir into the saucepan. Heat but do not boil.

Bisque of Smelts and Avocado

One of the real joys in creating new recipes is to consider what might be done with a particular food which is in abundant supply, high in nutrients, and inexpensive. If you are near the coast, smelts fall into this category. And, when combined with mushrooms, onions, and avocado, they make a smooth and delicate soup—a rather elegant beginning to a dinner.

½ *pound whole, cleaned smelts*
⅓ *cup dry white wine*
3 *cups water*
1 *teaspoon salt*
¼ *teaspoon pepper*
1 *Tablespoon mushroom, diced*
1 *Tablespoon onion, finely*
  chopped
1 *Tablespoon cooked rice or*
  uncooked quick-cooking rice
1 *medium avocado, peeled*
  and chopped
  Pinch each of oregano, basil,
  thyme
2 *cups light cream or milk*
  Garnish of croutons or finely
  chopped parsley

Gut the smelts, leaving on head and tail, and wash them under running water. Place them in a large saucepan, add the white wine, water, salt, pepper, diced mushroom, chopped onion, and rice. Cook, covered, for 15 minutes over medium heat.

Remove from the fire. Lift out the smelts and remove backbone, head, and tail, and discard.

Put the fish into the blender and add the contents of the saucepan plus the chopped avocado, the oregano, basil, and thyme. Purée until smooth (you may have to do it in two loads).

Pour the puréed soup back into the saucepan, stir in the cream or milk, and reheat but do not boil. Serve garnished with croutons or finely chopped parsley.

Oxtail Soup

Like so many dishes that have become American, oxtail soup has European origins. It was created by beleaguered chefs during the deprivations of the French Revolution, and it became a mainstay of the American kitchen during less affluent times.

1 *oxtail (about 1½ pounds) cut into* 6 *or* 8 *pieces*
2 *stalks celery, washed and coarsely chopped*
1 *whole leek (or ½ onion), washed and coarsely chopped*
1 *carrot, peeled and coarsely chopped*
½ *medium onion, coarsely chopped*
  Pinch each of rosemary, thyme, mace, marjoram

1 *small bayleaf*
1 *Tablespoon tomato purée*
1 *clove garlic, minced*
1 *teaspoon salt*
¼ *teaspoon pepper*
¼ *cup red wine*
½ *cup dry sherry*
6 *cups clear brown stock (see page 45) (or use a rich canned beef broth)*

GARNISH
1 *stalk celery, coarsely chopped*
1 *carrot, peeled, coarsely chopped*

1 *small turnip, peeled, coarsely chopped*

Preheat oven to 500 *degrees.*

In a roasting pan roast (500 degrees) the oxtail pieces for 25 minutes. Add coarsely chopped celery, leek, carrot, onion, herbs, tomato purée, minced garlic, salt, and pepper, and return to the oven for another 10 minutes.

Remove from oven and transfer the contents to a large saucepan. Add the red wine, sherry, and brown stock, and simmer uncovered for 3 hours.

While the soup is simmering, prepare the garnish: Chop the celery, carrot, and turnip, and cook them until tender in lightly salted water. Drain and set them aside.

After the soup has simmered, let it cool, then chill it, skim off the fat and strain.

Remove the meat from the oxtail bones and add the meat and the garnish to the strained soup.

Reheat just before serving.

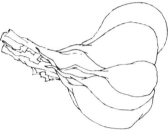

Cream of Pheasant with Giblets   *Serves 6*

P H E A S A N T   B R O T H   (makes 4 cups)

Use one pheasant, cut up, and including the giblets. Simmer the pheasant and giblets in 1½ quarts of water, lightly salted, uncovered, for about 1 hour. Strain the broth, cut the meat from the bones, chop it into medium pieces, and reserve with the giblets. Reduce the liquid over high heat to 4 cups.

2 *Tablespoons butter*	2 *Tablespoons flour*
½ *medium onion, coarsely*	1 *teaspoon salt*
chopped	¼ *teaspoon pepper*
1 *small whole leek (or 1 whole*	4 *cups pheasant broth (from*
scallion), washed, coarsely	*above)*
chopped	1 *cup heavy cream*
1 *stalk celery, coarsely chopped*	

Melt the butter in a large saucepan. Sauté the chopped onion, leek, and celery for 5 minutes. Sprinkle the flour, salt, and pepper over the mixture, add the 4 cups broth gradually, stir, and simmer uncovered for 35 minutes.

Pour the soup into the blender and purée until smooth. Return the soup to the saucepan over low heat. Add the chopped pheasant meat and giblets. Stir in the cream and reheat, but do not boil.

Game Soup

3 *pounds raw neck bones of*
  venison, OR
3 *pounds rabbit, cut in pieces,* OR

3 *pounds pheasant, partridge, or*
  duck, cut in pieces (can be a
  combination of these)

MARINADE

2 *cups dry red wine*
2 *cups water*
1 *onion, coarsely chopped*

1 *carrot, coarsely chopped*
1 *bayleaf*

Cover the bones and meat with the wine and water. Add the coarsely chopped onion and carrot and the bayleaf. Allow to marinate, uncovered, for several hours at room temperature, or overnight in the refrigerator.

1 *pound beef marrow bones*
¼ *pound salt pork, coarsely*
  chopped
  Onions and carrots from
  marinade
1 *clove garlic, peeled and*
  chopped
1 *teaspoon salt*

¼ *teaspoon pepper*
6 *cups cold water with* 1 *cup*
  marinade
2 *Tablespoons butter*
1 *Tablespoon flour*
2 *Tablespoons rolled oats*
2 *egg yolks*
2 *ounces dry sherry*

Place the marinated bones and meat in a large saucepan, discard the bayleaf from the marinade, but reserve the vegetables and the liquid. Add the beef marrow bones, chopped salt pork, the onion and carrot from the marinade, the chopped garlic, salt and pepper to the saucepan. Add cold water and 1 cup marinade, and simmer, uncovered, for 2 hours. Skim the foam off the top during cooking time.

Strain the soup and skim off the fat. Cut the meat off the marrow bones, dice it and set it aside. Discard bones. (If you make this soup well in advance of serving, the easiest way to remove the fat is to cool the soup and then skim the risen fat off the surface.)

In another large saucepan, melt the butter, stir in the flour and rolled oats, and cook for two minutes. Add a little of the hot strained soup, and stir until smooth. Add the remainder of the hot soup, stirring constantly, then add the diced meat.

Just before serving, beat the egg yolks and sherry into a small bowl, add a little of the hot soup, then stir back into the remaining soup. Reheat, but do not let boil.

European Cream of Barley Soup   *Serves 4 to 6*

This rich country soup has long been a favorite of mine, and the aroma of barley and freshly made chicken stock takes me back to my childhood.

1 *Tablespoon butter*	½ *cup pearl barley*
1 *carrot*	*Salt and pepper to taste*
1 *medium onion* ⎫ *all finely*	3 *egg yolks*
1 *whole leek* ⎬ *chopped*	½ *cup heavy or light cream*
2 *stalks celery* ⎭	2 *Tablespoons chives, finely*
5 *cups chicken stock (see page*	*chopped*
43) (or use rich canned	
chicken broth)	

Melt the butter in a large saucepan and sauté the chopped carrot, onion, leek, and celery for 5 minutes. Add the chicken stock, barley, salt and pepper, and simmer uncovered over medium heat for 1 hour. Remove from heat.

Beat together the egg yolks and cream. Add about ½ cup of the hot soup, and stir quickly to prevent the egg from curdling. Stir back into the soup and reheat, but do not boil.

PRESENTATION
I prefer to serve this soup from a tureen at the table into deep bowls or soup plates, and sprinkled generously with finely chopped chives.

Cream of Leek, Country Style

Serves 4 to 6

3 *slices bacon, coarsely chopped (or ¼ cup chopped ham ends)*
½ *medium onion, coarsely chopped*
2 *stalks celery, coarsely chopped*
3 *small whole leeks (about ½ pound), washed and coarsely chopped, or 6 scallions*
3 *cups chicken stock (see page 43) (or use rich canned chicken broth)*
½ *teaspoon salt*
¼ *teaspoon pepper*
Pinch nutmeg
1 *smoked farmer sausage, or use either bauernwurst, cervelat, Kielbasa, pig's*

knuckles, or small pork link sausages (about 5 ounces)
1 *cup light cream*
1 *Tablespoon chives, finely chopped*

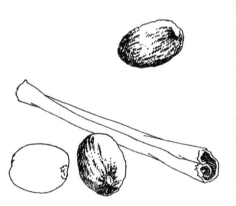

Sauté the chopped bacon in a large saucepan for 3 minutes. Add the chopped onion, celery, leeks, and sauté for 5 minutes. Pour in the stock, season with salt, pepper, and nutmeg.

Add the sausage. (If the sausage is fatty, first simmer *separately* in boiling water for 5 minutes to remove excess fat.) Simmer over medium heat, uncovered, for 45 minutes or until the leeks are soft and well cooked.

Remove the sausage and keep warm. Pour the soup into the blender (you may have to do it in two loads) and purée until smooth, or strain through a fine sieve.

Return the soup to the saucepan and stir in light cream. Heat, but do not boil.

Remove the skin from the sausage, slice it very thin and add to the soup.

Serve sprinkled with finely chopped chives.

Cream of Broccoli Soup

Serves 4 to 6

1 *Tablespoon butter*
½ *medium onion, coarsely chopped*
1 *small leek (or 1 scallion), coarsely chopped*
1 *stalk celery, coarsely chopped*
1 *Tablespoon flour*
4 *cups stock: chicken or beef (see pages 43 and 44) (or use rich canned chicken or beef broth)*

1 *bunch fresh broccoli, trimmed as indicated (about 1 pound)*
½ *teaspoon salt*
¼ *teaspoon pepper*
Dash nutmeg
1 *cup light cream*
1 *Tablespoon parsley or chives, finely chopped*

Melt the butter in a large saucepan and sauté the chopped onion, leek, and celery for 5 minutes. Sprinkle the flour over the vegetables and mix. Add the stock, bring to a boil, lower heat, and simmer uncovered for 15 minutes.

Trim the head of the broccoli from the coarse stalk just where the buds begin. Break or cut the head into buds and add to the soup, cover and simmer for another 15 minutes. Pour the mixture into the blender and purée until smooth. (You will probably have two blender loads.) Strain through a fine sieve into a clean saucepan. Season with salt, pepper, and nutmeg, and stir in the cream. Reheat but do not boil. Garnish with chopped parsley or chives.

Variation: Cream of Cauliflower with Savory

Serves 4 to 6

Use the same recipe as for cream of broccoli, substituting for the broccoli 1 pound or a good-sized head of cauliflower, trimmed by cutting out the stem or core. Also, substitute ½ teaspoon of savory for the dash of nutmeg.

Cream of Celeriac

Serves 4 to 6

For reasons I've never understood, celeriac (celery root) is often difficult to find in the markets, and if it is not available in your area you may have to grow it yourself. This gnarled root has a wide variety of uses in my own kitchens; for instance, you will find a recipe for braised celeriac under Accompaniments.

1½ *pounds celeriac, peeled and
      diced
      Juice of ½ lemon*
  2 *Tablespoons butter*
  2 *Tablespoons flour*
  2 *Tablespoons rolled oats*

  1 *bunch leeks, white part only,
      about 4 ounces net, or 12 or
      14 scallions (1 or 2 bunches),
      using white part only, finely
      chopped*
  1 *medium onion, finely
      chopped*
  3 *cups chicken stock (see page
      43) (or use rich canned
      chicken broth)*
  ½ *teaspoon salt*
  ¼ *teaspoon pepper*
  1 *cup light cream or milk*

Peel and dice the celeriac, reserving one good slice—about ½ inch thick—for garnish. Grate this piece and sprinkle with lemon juice.

Melt the butter in a large saucepan, add the flour and oats, and stir into a *roux;* before it takes on color, add the diced celeriac and chopped leeks and onion, chicken stock, salt, and pepper. Bring to a boil, reduce heat and simmer uncovered for 30 minutes.

Lift out the vegetables into the blender, add enough liquid to cover, and purée until smooth. Strain the puréed vegetables and remaining liquid into a saucepan. Add the light cream or milk and reheat, but do not boil.

Sprinkle the grated celeriac into the soup as a garnish.

Alpine Cheese Soup

Serves 4 to 6

I can remember, as a boy, seeing herdsmen in the Alps, surrounded by their cattle, using a stick to stir a large iron pot of steaming soup. Undoubtedly they were making an Alpine cheese soup, a health soup born of necessity and often varied according to the vegetables available. My own version here has been developed to include year-around vegetables and while you most probably will not make it in an iron pot or stir it with a stout stick, I'm sure you will enjoy this family soup—hearty enough as a main course with hot crisp breads.

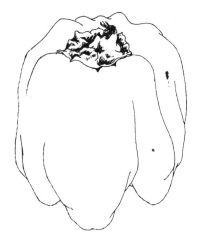

  4 *slices lean raw bacon,*
    coarsely chopped
½ *medium onion, coarsely chopped*
  1 *stalk celery, coarsely chopped*
  1 *leek (or 3 scallions),*
    coarsely chopped
½ *cup rolled oats*
  1 *teaspoon salt*
½ *teaspoon pepper*
  5 *cups chicken stock*
    (see page 43) (or use rich
    canned chicken broth)
½ *cup Gruyère cheese, grated*
¼ *cup heavy or light cream*
  1 *Tablespoon parsley, finely*
    chopped

Sauté the chopped bacon in a large saucepan for 3 minutes. Add the chopped onion, celery, and leek, and sauté for another 5 minutes. Add the rolled oats, salt, pepper, and chicken stock, and simmer uncovered over medium heat for 40 minutes.

    Pour the soup into the blender and purée until smooth. Return the soup to the saucepan over medium heat, add the grated cheese a little at a time and stir until melted. Stir in the cream. Do not boil. Serve sprinkled with chopped parsley.

New England Cheese Soup

Serves 6

5 cups chicken stock (see page 43) (or use rich canned chicken broth)
1 whole leek (or 3 whole scallions), unpeeled, rinsed and coarsely chopped
½ medium onion, coarsely chopped
1 stalk celery, rinsed and coarsely chopped
½ teaspoon salt
¼ teaspoon pepper
⅛ teaspoon grated nutmeg
1 cup (5 ounces) mild Vermont cheddar cheese, grated
1 Tablespoon cornstarch dissolved in 3 Tablespoons cold water
1 egg yolk
½ cup light cream
2 Tablespoons dry white wine

Pour the stock into a large saucepan, add the chopped leek, onion, and celery, salt, pepper, and nutmeg, and simmer uncovered over medium heat for 30 minutes.

Pour the soup into the blender and purée until smooth. (You may have to do it in two loads.) Return to the saucepan. Over medium heat, add the grated cheese a little at a time, and stir until cheese is melted. Stir in the dissolved cornstarch.

In a small bowl beat together the egg yolk and cream and beat in ½ cup of the hot soup. Beat this back into the soup. Add the white wine, and reheat, but do not let the soup boil.

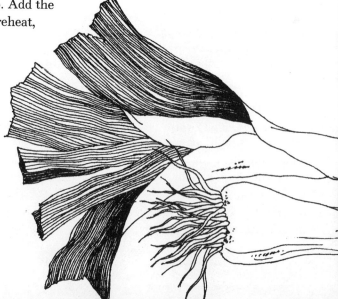

Swiss Potato Soup with Gruyère

Serves 3 to 5

6 *slices lean bacon, coarsely chopped*
½ *medium onion, coarsely chopped*
1 *leek (or 2 scallions), coarsely chopped*
½ *pound white cabbage (about ¼ head), coarsely chopped*
1 *pound raw potatoes (2 medium), peeled, coarsely chopped*

3 *cups chicken stock (see page 43) (or use rich canned chicken broth)*
Salt to taste
¼ *teaspoon pepper*
1 *cup Gruyère cheese, grated*
½ *cup light cream*
1 *Tablespoon fresh dill, finely chopped, or 1½ teaspoons dried dill*

Sauté the chopped bacon in a large saucepan over medium heat for 3 minutes. Add the chopped onion, leek, and cabbage, and continue to sauté for another 5 minutes. Add the chopped potatoes, pour in the chicken stock, and season with salt and pepper. Bring to a boil, lower the heat and simmer uncovered for 40 minutes.

Pour the soup into blender and purée until smooth. Strain the soup through a fine sieve back into the saucepan, and over medium heat add the cheese a little at a time and stir until melted. Do not boil. Just before serving, salt to taste, stir in the cream, and sprinkle with chopped dill.

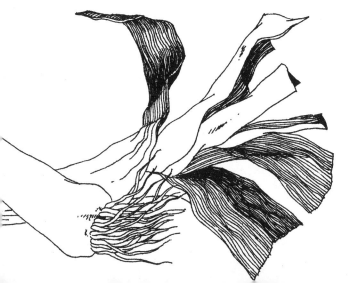

Potato Soup with Dill

Serves 4 to 6

3 *slices bacon, coarsely chopped*
½ *cup lean cooked ham*
   or ham ends, coarsely chopped
1 *medium onion, coarsely*
   chopped
2 *stalks celery, coarsely chopped*
1 *large leek (or 3 scallions),*
   coarsely chopped
4 *cups beef or chicken stock*

(see pages 43 and 44) (or
use rich canned broth)
Pinch pepper and nutmeg
¾ *pound raw potatoes, peeled*
   and coarsely chopped
Salt to taste
1 *teaspoon finely chopped fresh*
   dill, or ½ teaspoon dried
   dill

Sauté the chopped bacon, ham, and onion in a large saucepan for 5 minutes over high heat. Add the chopped celery and leek and cook 5 minutes longer. Pour in the stock and add the pepper, nutmeg, chopped potatoes, and salt to taste. Simmer over medium heat for 40 minutes.

Pour the soup mixture into the blender (you may have to do it in two loads) and purée until smooth. Return to the saucepan and warm over low heat. Do not boil. Sprinkle with chopped dill before serving.

Onion Soup Gratinée with Calvados

Serves 4

Onions as a food are as old as civilization. Alexander the Great found the onion in Egypt and brought it to Greece, where he used this humble vegetable to condition his troops for battle. Later it was considered an aphrodisiac and a panacea for all ills, especially colds. Whatever its virtues, the onion is very much a part of our lives today. I like to blend the strong flavor of onion with the Calvados of Normandy.

2 *medium onions, thinly sliced*
2 *Tablespoons butter*
½ *teaspoon thyme*
4 *cups chicken stock (see page*
   43) (or use rich canned
   chicken broth)

Salt and pepper to taste
1 *liquid ounce Calvados*
   (or applejack)
8 *triangles thinly sliced bread*
½ *cup Gruyère cheese, grated*

Sauté the sliced onions in butter in a large saucepan until they are lightly colored. Add the thyme and chicken stock. Season with salt and pepper and simmer covered over medium heat for 20 minutes.

Preheat oven to 450 degrees.

Add the Calvados and pour into four individual heatproof bowls. Top each with two triangles of bread, sprinkle with grated cheese, and bake (450 degrees) for 5 to 7 minutes or until golden brown. Serve at once.

Variation: Onion Soup with Cheese Dumplings

Serves 4

Prepare the onion soup, eliminating the Calvados, bread, and Gruyère cheese.

CHEESE DUMPLINGS

¼ cup water
1½ Tablespoons butter
    Pinch each: salt, pepper, nutmeg

¼ cup sifted flour
2 eggs
3 Tablespoons Gruyère cheese, grated

Pour the water into a 1 quart saucepan, add the butter, salt, pepper, and nutmeg, and bring to a boil. Remove from heat, add the sifted flour all at once and stir vigorously. Return to low heat and stir the dough until it leaves the sides of the pan and forms a solid mass. Add one egg at a time and mix each thoroughly into the dough. Add the grated cheese and stir until the cheese is melted and thoroughly mixed.

In a large saucepan, bring 2 quarts of lightly salted water to simmer. Use two teaspoons to make the tiny cheese dumplings. Fill one spoon with dough and use the other to scoop it off into the water. Dip the spoons into the simmering water each time. Cook no more than 6 or 8 at a time. The dumplings will rise to the surface when cooked. Remove them and keep warm in cooking foil. These tiny dumplings may be made about an hour before you place them in the hot soup.

Preheat oven to 375 degrees.

Top each bowl of hot soup with dumplings and bake (375 degrees) 3 to 4 minutes. Serve immediately.

European Beer Soup

Serves 4 to 6

Does this suggestion appear odd to you? Strangely enough, though I call it "European," this same soup was popular in America during the early 1900's. Families of European origin made it frequently and served it as a main course, but with the advent of prohibition it vanished from American tables. However you serve it, I know you will be glad to be part of its revival. Forget about the minute amount of alcohol—as I pointed out in my introduction, the end result contains none at all, as alcohol used in cooking is rapidly burned up whether it is beer or wine.

2 cups bread cubes, tightly packed (use only hard-crust bread or rolls)	3 cups beef or chicken stock (see pages 43 and 44) (or use rich canned beef or chicken broth)
3 Tablespoons corn oil	1 teaspoon salt
1 clove garlic, peeled and finely chopped	½ teaspoon pepper
1½ medium onions, finely chopped	2 Tablespoons parsley, finely chopped
1 cup dry bread crumbs	1 cup Gruyère cheese, grated
1 can light domestic beer (12 ounces)	1 teaspoon paprika

Preheat oven to 400 degrees.

Place the bread cubes on a baking sheet in a 400 degree oven until well toasted.

Combine the oil, chopped garlic, and onions in a large saucepan, and sauté over medium heat until the onions are golden.

Stir in the bread crumbs and the bread cubes, add the beer and stock and bring to a boil. Add the salt, pepper, and chopped parsley, and pour the soup into a 2 quart heatproof casserole or individual heatproof bowls. Sprinkle the grated cheese evenly over the top of the soup and dust with paprika. Place under the broiler until the cheese is melted and golden brown.

Tomato Soup with Wild Thyme

Serves 4

This soup is seasonal, according to the availability of fresh wild thyme. The aroma and flavor of fresh wild thyme is so important to the final result of this delicious soup that I don't recommend using dried thyme. If you don't have a garden or a vegetable market nearby which carries fresh herbs, thyme is easy to grow in a pot or window box.

1 *slice ham, coarsely chopped,*
  (about 1–1½ ounces) or
1 *calf's foot, or several*
  beef or veal marrow bones
½ *medium onion, coarsely*
  chopped
1 *small leek, unpeeled, rinsed*
  and coarsely chopped
1 *stalk celery, rinsed and*
  coarsely chopped
1 *Tablespoon fresh wild thyme,*
  coarsely chopped
1½ *pounds tomatoes, unpeeled,*
  cored and cut in quarters
2 *cups of beef or chicken stock*
  (see pages 43 and 44)
  (or use rich canned beef or
  chicken broth)

Salt and pepper to taste
A pinch of sugar
1 *teaspoon lemon juice*

In a large saucepan, combine the chopped ham, the chopped onion, leek, and celery, the thyme, and quartered tomatoes, and pour the stock over them. Season with salt, pepper, and a pinch of sugar, bring to a boil, then lower heat and simmer uncovered for 30 minutes.

Remove the bones, pour the mixture into the blender, and purée until smooth. (You may have to do this in two loads.) Strain through a fine sieve into the saucepan, add the lemon juice, and reheat just before serving.

Soups—Hot or Cold

Cream of Artichoke with Sherry

Serves 4 to 6

½ medium onion, coarsely
  chopped
1 small leek (or two scallions),
  coarsely chopped
1 stalk celery, coarsely chopped
4½ cups chicken stock
  (see page 43) (or use rich
  canned chicken broth)
2 medium size fresh artichokes,
  cut in quarters (Cut off
  green part 1½ inch from top.
  Remove outside leaves.)
  Or 9 ounces net of frozen or
  canned artichoke hearts
  Salt and pepper to taste
1 Tablespoon cornstarch
  dissolved in 3 Tablespoons
  stock
¼ cup dry sherry
½ cup light cream

Combine the chopped onion, leek, and celery, the chicken stock, artichokes, salt, and pepper in a large saucepan. Bring to a boil and simmer uncovered over medium heat for 30 minutes. Pour the vegetables and stock into the blender and purée until smooth. Strain through a fine sieve. Return to saucepan. Over medium heat stir in the dissolved cornstarch. Do not boil. Just before serving, stir in the sherry and cream.

PRESENTATION
This soup may also be served cold, sprinkled with finely chopped chives. Chill, but do not add sherry and cream until just before serving.

Bisque of Clams *Serves 4 to 6*

24 *clams in shells*
½ *cup dry white wine*
1 *cup milk*
    Handful of fresh parsley
6 *Tablespoons butter*
1 *cup white bread, trimmed of crust and diced*

2 *cloves garlic, minced*
2 *Tablespoons onion, finely chopped*
¼ *teaspoon marjoram*
¼ *teaspoon pepper*
½ *cup clam juice (canned or bottled)*

Wash and scrub the clam shells and place them in a heavy saucepan with a lid. Pour in the wine and milk and cover with fresh parsley. Cook over medium heat, covered, for about 25 minutes or until the shells have opened.

While the clams are cooking, melt the butter in a large heavy saucepan, add the diced bread, minced garlic, chopped onions, marjoram, and pepper (but no salt, as the canned clam juice is salty). Sauté over medium heat until the bread cubes are golden, stirring constantly.

Remove the clams from the saucepan and set aside. Then strain the broth into the sautéed bread cubes. Remove the clams from the shells and add to the bread and broth. Add the canned clam juice and simmer for 15 minutes. Pour the mixture into the blender and purée until smooth. Return to saucepan and reheat, but do not boil. If the soup is too thick, add a little hot milk.

PRESENTATION
If bisque is to be served cold, add a bit more clam juice and cold milk.

Cream of Tomato Soup with Avocado   *Serves 4 to 5*

3 *slices bacon, blanched for*
  1 minute in boiling water,
  and drained, and then
  coarsely chopped
1 *leek (or 2 scallions),*
  coarsely chopped
1 *stalk celery, coarsely*
  chopped
½ *medium onion, coarsely*
  chopped
2 *cups beef or chicken stock*
  (see pages 43 and 44)
  (or use rich canned beef or
  chicken broth)

½ *teaspoon salt*
¼ *teaspoon pepper*
1½ *pounds fresh tomatoes*
  (5 medium, unpeeled), cut
  in quarters
1 *ripe avocado*
  Juice of ½ lemon
½ *cup light cream*
1 *Tablespoon chives, finely*
  chopped

Sauté the chopped bacon in a large saucepan over medium heat for 3 minutes. Add the chopped leek, celery, and onion and sauté for another 5 minutes. Add the stock, salt, pepper, and tomatoes, and simmer uncovered for 30 minutes. Pour the mixture into blender and purée until smooth. Strain through a fine sieve into the saucepan. Peel the avocado and sprinkle with lemon juice. Then place in the blender, pour in the cream and purée until smooth. Add the strained soup to the avocado purée and blend for 1 minute; then pour back into the saucepan and reheat, but do not boil. Serve sprinkled with chives.

This soup may also be served chilled.

Soups—Cold

Vichyssoise (and Its Variations)

Serves 4 to 6

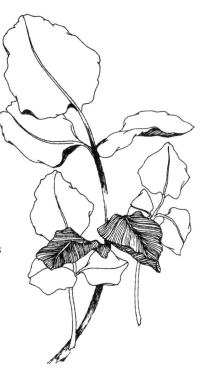

From this basic soup you can quickly and easily prepare a number of colorful and delicious variations. Freshly made vichyssoise, delicately flavored with slightly sour green apples, fresh carrots, or watercress, for example, is a gentle and subtle beginning to a dinner where more substantial courses are to follow.

BASIC VICHYSSOISE RECIPE

2 *small leeks, white part only (or 4 scallions, white part only), coarsely chopped*
½ *medium onion, coarsely chopped*
1 *pound (about 3 medium) potatoes, peeled and chopped*
2 *cups chicken or veal stock (see pages 43 and 46) (or use rich canned beef or chicken broth)*

1 *teaspoon salt*
¼ *teaspoon white pepper*
4 *cups cold milk*
1 *Tablespoon chopped chives*

Combine the chopped leeks, onion, potatoes, stock, and seasoning in a saucepan, and bring to a boil. Reduce heat and simmer uncovered until the vegetables are tender—about 30 minutes.

Pour the contents into the blender and when smooth transfer to a large mixing bowl. Add the cold milk and allow to cool to room temperature before chilling well. Garnish with chopped chives.

Variation: Fresh Watercress Vichyssoise   *Serves 4 to 6*

Prepare the basic vichyssoise and pour into the blender. Wash and pick over one bunch of watercress, removing any brown leaves. Drain well, chop coarsely and add to the liquid in the blender. Continue as in the basic recipe and serve well chilled and generously sprinkled with finely chopped watercress.

Variations: Fresh Apple or Pear Vichyssoise

Serves 4 to 6

Proceed as in the basic recipe, using only ½ pound of potatoes. When the vegetables have been cooked and are in the blender (you may have to do it in 2 loads) add ½ pound of tart green apples—unpeeled, but cored. After blending I suggest pressing through a sieve or food mill before adding the milk.

For pear vichyssoise, peel the pears, then chop and add them, instead of the apples, to cooked vegetables in the blender.

Serve well chilled.

Variation: Fresh Carrot Vichyssoise   *Serves 4 to 6*

Prepare the basic vichyssoise, substituting for the pound of potatoes ½ pound potatoes and ½ pound (4 or 5) scrubbed young carrots. I don't peel the carrots for this soup as much of the flavor is retained in the skin. Add ¼ teaspoon of sugar and cook the vegetables until tender. Continue as in the basic recipe. Be certain to sprinkle generously with finely chopped chives before serving.

Serve well chilled.

Variation: Celeriac Vichyssoise

Serves 4 to 6

(Celeriac is a root vegetable also known as celery root.)

Prepare the basic recipe using only ½ pound potatoes and adding one large celeriac root, peeled and coarsely chopped, to the vegetables to be cooked.

Serve well chilled.

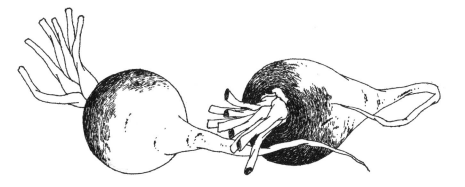

Variation: Turnip Vichyssoise

Serves 4 to 6

Prepare the basic recipe using only ½ pound potatoes and adding ½ pound white turnips, peeled and coarsely chopped, to the vegetables to be cooked.

Serve well chilled.

Vichyssoise with Dill

Serves 4 to 6

Prepare potato soup with dill (see page 60). Pour the soup mixture into the blender and blend until smooth, then strain into a bowl. Add 1 cup heavy cream and chill in refrigerator. Serve garnished with finely chopped chives.

This soup may also be served hot.

Madrilène of Beet and Onion *Serves 4 to 6*

Whatever the season, a sparkling, chilled madrilène of fresh beets and onion can add a touch of elegance to your menu. Of course you can make it with canned broth and beets but it will be a long way from the flavor you get by combining your own chicken stock and fresh beets free of preservatives. This madrilène is simple to make, inexpensive, and may be prepared well in advance of serving.

1 *medium onion, cut in half and sliced paper thin*
4 *small beets, peeled (about ½ pound)*
1 *teaspoon salt*
¼ *teaspoon sugar*
1½ *teaspoons vinegar*

1 *quart chicken stock, skimmed of all fat (see page 43) (or use rich canned chicken broth)*
1 *level Tablespoon (1 envelope) unflavored gelatin*

GARNISH
Lemon wedges
Sprigs of parsley

In a large saucepan cook the sliced onion in enough water to cover, for about 10 minutes or until soft. Grate the raw beets into the onion, add the salt, sugar, and vinegar, and pour in the strained chicken stock. Bring to a boil, lower heat and simmer uncovered for 15 minutes. Remove from the heat and strain.

Dissolve the gelatin in ¼ cup cold water to make a smooth paste, and add some of the hot soup to make it thoroughly liquid. Stir the gelatin into the strained soup. Set aside to cool and then refrigerate for at least 2 hours until it is firm. It should not be too solid or rubbery.

PRESENTATION
Use a knife to break up the madrilène into small pieces. Serve it in a glass bowl set in a larger bowl of cracked ice and garnish with lemon wedges and parsley.

Chilled Gazpacho

Serves 4 to 6

A Tingling Blend of Fresh Vegetables and Spices

Is there any more appetizing way that you can give your family a great dollop of vitamins with a minimum of effort than by serving gazpacho? I have worked out a balance of flavors in this particular recipe to avoid any one predominating taste. The two raw eggs are essential to bind the soup, so do not leave them out. The garlic? Well, omit it if you must, but I recommend that you include this dash of flavor and say nothing about it.

3 *very ripe, medium tomatoes, seeded (reserve ¼ tomato for garnish)*

1 *medium green pepper, cleaned and seeded (reserve ¼ pepper for garnish)*

1 *medium cucumber, seeded (reserve a 2-inch slice for garnish)*

2 *stalks celery*

1 *medium onion*

12-*ounce can tomato juice*

2 *cloves garlic, peeled and finely chopped*

4 *Tablespoons tomato purée*

¼ *teaspoon each of savory, thyme, pepper, and salt*

2 *Tablespoons vinegar*

1 *Tablespoon corn oil*

2 *raw eggs*

¼ *teaspoon Tabasco sauce*

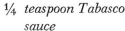

Wash and dry the vegetables, chop them, unpeeled but seeded, and place them in blender with enough tomato juice to partially cover. Add garlic, tomato purée, savory, thyme, pepper, salt, vinegar, oil, eggs, and Tabasco, and purée until smooth. Pour the mixture into a bowl and stir in the remainder of the tomato juice. Chill at least 1 hour.

PRESENTATION

Serve the gazpacho in individual bowls or soup plates. Chop the remaining bits of tomato, green pepper, and cucumber separately and sprinkle them separately on top of the soup. Be certain the gazpacho is well chilled.

Chilled Chicken Senegalese

Serves 4 to 6

1 *quart chicken stock, skimmed
of fat (see page 43) (or
use rich canned chicken
broth)*
1½ *cups milk*
2½ *teaspoons curry powder*
2 *Tablespoons cornstarch*
½ *cup flour*
Juice of ½ lemon

1 *large green apple, peeled,
cored, and finely grated (or
an equal amount of mango,
finely chopped)*
1½ *teaspoons salt*
¼ *teaspoon sugar*
¼ *cup heavy or light cream*
¼ *cup grated coconut, lightly
toasted in the oven*

Bring the chicken stock to a simmer in a large saucepan.

Pour the milk into a mixing bowl and stir in the curry powder, cornstarch and flour, then stir into the chicken stock. Add the lemon juice and grated apple and simmer uncovered for 20 minutes.

Remove from heat and cool. Add the salt and sugar, and stir in the cream. Chill well before serving. Serve in individual bowls sprinkled with the toasted grated coconut.

Chilled Soup of Apple and Walnut

Serves 4 to 6

The autumn in America is a glorious season to me—especially now that I live in the hills of Connecticut where the leaves are red and gold and baskets of colorful ripe apples seem to be everywhere. My kitchen reflects this bounty of the surrounding farms and I use apples in many ways on my early winter menu.

My chilled soup of apple and walnut is popular here, particularly with guests who choose to follow the game of the season—partridge, quail, venison, or elk. Whatever meat course you choose, apple soup makes a pleasant start and can be prepared well in advance of serving.

3 *green or tart apples, unpeeled,*
  cored and diced
1 *small white turnip, trimmed*
  but unpeeled
4 *ounces hard cider (or 2*
  ounces sweet cider mixed with
  2 ounces applejack)
3 *cups water (or 2 cups of water*
  and 1 cup of apple juice)

Pinch each of ground
  cinnamon and cloves
1 *teaspoon salt*
¼ *teaspoon pepper*
½ *teaspoon sugar*
  Juice of ½ lemon
2 *slices bacon, diced*
4 *Tablespoons walnut meats,*
  finely ground

Combine all of the ingredients except the walnuts in a saucepan and simmer uncovered until the mixture is a pulp—about 30 minutes.

Pour the mixture into the blender and purée until smooth. (You may have to do it in two loads.) Strain into the saucepan, add one half ground walnuts and bring to a boil.

Remove from the fire and allow to cool before chilling in the refrigerator. If the soup is too thick, add additional apple juice. To serve, sprinkle the remaining ground walnuts on top.

Fruits of the Season in a Chilled Soup   *Serves 4*

Ripe peaches, bursting plums, the berries of midsummer, grapes, well-ripened apricots, pieces of melon—the bounty of fresh fruits in America is almost endless in variety. With these plentiful fruits I make a delicious chilled soup, an exciting and colorful beginning to a meal. Try this soup and vary it from time to time with the ripest of fruits available on your trees or in the markets, or use some of the fruits that are frozen successfully.

3 *cups of fresh, ripe fruit (juicy),*
   pitted and coarsely chopped,
   unpeeled (You may combine
   cherries, peaches, apricots,
   grapes, mangoes, plums—
   selecting both tart and mildly
   sweet fruits.)
   Juice of 1 *lemon*
¼ *cup dry sherry*

¼ *cup dry white wine*
1 *cup cake crumbs, or diced*
   leftover pound cake or similar
   cake
   Pinch ground cloves
½ *teaspoon ground ginger*
½ *teaspoon cinnamon*
1 *cup light cream*

Place the chopped fruit and lemon juice in a saucepan, pour in the sherry and white wine and bring to a boil. Lower the heat and simmer until the fruit is soft.

Set aside to cool, and then pour the cooked fruit and liquid into the blender. (You may have to do it in two loads.) Add the cake crumbs, cloves, ginger, and cinnamon, and purée at low speed until smooth. Transfer to a bowl, stir in the cream and chill well.

Variation: Chilled Cherry Soup   *Serves 4 to 6*

This tart cherry soup is a variation of the chilled fruit soup (above). Select dark, ripe cherries, remove the pits, cut in half enough to fill 3 cups. Or, you may use the dark pitted cherries in cans; I have found the best quality to be those imported from Switzerland. Follow the recipe

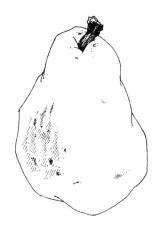

for chilled fruit soup, using 3 cups of cherries instead of 3 cups of fresh assorted fruit.

Serve well chilled.

Fall Fruit Soup

The combination of fruits I have listed is only a suggestion, but the dark plums of autumn do give a special flavor. Cold weather need not require that only hot soup be served. This particular soup, easy to prepare, is a refreshing beginning to a meal where you plan to serve a substantial meat course such as venison or roasts. Fall fruit soup may be prepared well in advance of serving, adding the cream just before it goes to the table.

2 *winter pears, unpeeled, cored and diced*	⅔ *cup dry red wine*
5 *Italian plums of the season, pitted (about 10 ounces), unpeeled*	¼ *cup dry sherry*
	1 *cup water*
	½ *cup cake crumbs (leftover white cake or sponge)*
1 *apple, unpeeled, cored and diced*	1 *cup light cream*
1 *cup grapes, cut in half, seeded*	

Combine all of the above ingredients except the cream in a saucepan. Bring to a boil and simmer uncovered for about 20 minutes or until the fruit is soft.

Pour the mixture into the blender (you may have to do it in two loads) and purée until smooth. Strain through a fine sieve into a bowl; allow to cool and then chill in the refrigerator for several hours.

When ready to serve, stir in the cream. If it is too thick add some milk.

Sauces

To me sauces are the essence and soul of cookery. The word *sauce* comes from the Latin and is related in origin to the words *salt, salad,* and *sausage;* it may roughly be defined as any kind of liquid or semi-liquid seasoning used on food. Thus sauces can range from the juice of roast meat, which becomes gravy when flour and seasoning are added, to the most elaborate prepared sauces. Clearly salad dressings are sauces, as are many bottled condiments. And I have already pointed out how closely related sauces are to soups, in view of their common foundation in basic stocks.

We use sauces to enhance, vary, and harmonize flavors, to improve the appearance of food, to overcome the dryness of certain meats or fish, and sometimes to "bind" together the elements of a dish. The one thing we don't use them for is what some critics unfairly claim is the purpose of sauces in French cuisine—to cover up the taste or lack of taste of inferior foods. While French cuisine has advanced the art of sauce-making to the highest and most sophisticated levels, every cuisine has excellent sauces.

Although imagination may be used in flavoring and seasoning sauces, they must be made with great care; this is one area of culinary art where the chemistry of cooking must control the imagination of the chef. Wines should be added with finesse, and care should be taken to enhance the flavor of the basic stock, not to destroy its distinctive characteristics.

There are probably more than 600 sauces but only about half a dozen basic or "mother" sauces from which they derive. For this section I have selected these basic sauces as well as some which are unusual and seem to be particularly well liked.

One final note. Generally one cup or 8 ounces of sauce will provide for 4 ample servings.

Basic Brown Sauce (*Also called* Sauce Espagnole)   *Yield 2 quarts*

This, like the other basic or mother sauces, is used as a base to make other more complicated or sophisticated sauces.

4 *pounds raw cut veal bones*
2 *pounds raw pork bones*
2 *pounds raw chicken bones*
2 *Tablespoons butter*
2 *Tablespoons flour*
1 *carrot, coarsely chopped*
2 *Tablespoons onion, coarsely chopped*
1 *stalk celery, coarsely chopped*

2 *quarts beef stock (see page 44)* (*or use rich canned beef broth*)
2 *cups water*
1 *Tablespoon tomato purée (or 3 ripe tomatoes, coarsely chopped)*
½ *teaspoon salt*
¼ *teaspoon pepper*

Preheat oven to 500 degrees.

In a large open roasting pan, spread the veal, pork, and chicken bones and brown them in the oven for 20 minutes, turning them once or twice.

Meanwhile, heat 2 Tablespoons butter in a saucepan and stir in 2 Tablespoons flour. Add chopped vegetables (carrot, onion, and celery) and sauté until they have taken on a deep brown color.

In a heavy-bottomed pot, place the browned bones, browned vegetables, beef stock, water, tomato purée, salt, and pepper, and simmer uncovered for 2 hours. Remove the bones and strain the sauce through a fine sieve.

Demi-Glace   *Yield 4 cups*

This more concentrated form of the basic brown sauce (see above) is used in making stronger sauces for meat and game.

Reduce 2 quarts of basic brown sauce to 1 quart by simmering, uncovered, about 30 to 40 minutes.

Onion and Mustard Sauce

Yield 1½ cups

This is a good sauce to use with fish, lamb, beef, ham, and pork dishes.

1 *Tablespoon butter*
1 *Tablespoon corn oil*
2 *medium onions, finely sliced*
¼ *cup dry white wine*
½ *cup basic brown sauce*
   (see page 79)

⅛ *teaspoon pepper*
¼ *teaspoon salt*
2 *teaspoons vinegar*
4 *teaspoons prepared mustard*
½ *teaspoon sugar*

Place the butter and oil in a skillet and sauté the onions until golden. Add the wine, brown sauce, pepper, salt, vinegar, mustard, and sugar. Simmer over medium heat until the sauce is reduced by one quarter.

This sauce can be stored for some days in the refrigerator and easily reheated. It can also be frozen for future use.

Basic White Sauce

Yield 2 cups

Basic white sauce is prepared with strong chicken or veal stock. The stock must be clear and white.

2 *Tablespoons butter, melted*
1 *Tablespoon flour*
2 *cups veal or chicken stock*
   (see pages 43 or 46) (or use
   rich canned chicken broth)
1 *whole onion, peeled, stuck*
   with 2 cloves

1 *leek, white part only (or*
   2 scallions, white parts only)
5 *peppercorns*
1 *Tablespoon salt*
½ *cup mushroom stems*

Melt the butter slowly in a heavy 1–1½ quart saucepan; blend in flour to make a *roux*. (A *roux* is a smooth, creamed blend.) Add the veal or chicken stock and stir until thickened. Add the remainder of ingredients and simmer uncovered for 40 minutes, skimming foam from the top with a skimmer or slotted spoon while cooking. Strain through a fine sieve.

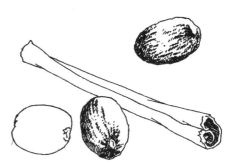

Béchamel or White Milk Sauce

Yield 2 cups

Béchamel sauce is particularly good with fish, chicken, egg, and mushroom dishes and also blends with other sauces.

2 *Tablespoons butter*
1 *small onion, sliced*
3 *Tablespoons flour*
   Pinch thyme

   Pinch nutmeg
2 *cups milk*
¼ *teaspoon salt*

Melt butter in a saucepan. Add onion and sauté until transparent. Stir in flour and cook over medium heat until a *roux* (a smooth blend) is formed. Mix in thyme and nutmeg.

    In another saucepan, bring milk and salt to a boil. Pour hot milk quickly into *roux,* and stir until thickened. Simmer slowly for 15 minutes, stirring constantly. Strain the sauce through a fine sieve.

White Wine Sauce

Yield ¾ cup

This sauce is used primarily on fish, chicken, or egg dishes.

⅓ *cup dry white wine*
¾ *cup basic white sauce (see page 80)*

Boil wine until reduced by one half. Add basic white sauce and stir until blended.

Sauce Piquant

Yield 1 cup

This is particularly good with pork dishes and can be used on cooked meats.

¼ cup dry white wine
¼ cup vinegar
 2 Tablespoons shallots
   (or scallions), finely chopped
 1 cup basic brown sauce
   (see page 79)
   Pinch cayenne pepper
 4 Tablespoons (½ stick)
   softened butter

2 sour gherkins, finely diced
1 Tablespoon parsley, finely
  chopped
½ Tablespoon each of fresh
  tarragon, chervil, chives, finely
  chopped (if dried, use ½ the
  amount)

In a heavy saucepan simmer wine, vinegar, and shallots until the liquid is reduced by half. Add basic brown sauce and pepper. Add butter and stir until the sauce is smooth and thick. Add gherkins, parsley, tarragon, chervil, and chives, and simmer 2 to 3 minutes more.

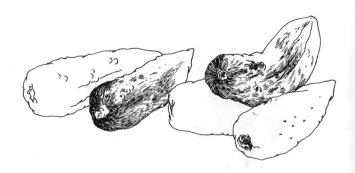

Sauce Velouté

Yield 2 cups

2 Tablespoons butter
3 Tablespoons flour
2 cups white fish fumet, or clear

chicken stock, or white veal
  stock (see pages 43 and 46)
¼ teaspoon salt

Melt butter in a saucepan. Stir in flour and cook over medium heat until a *roux* (a smooth, creamed blend) is formed and bubbles slightly. In another saucepan, bring stock and salt to a boil. Pour hot stock quickly into *roux* and stir until thickened. Simmer slowly for 15 minutes, stirring constantly. Strain the sauce through a fine sieve.

If made with white fish *fumet*, serve with fish or shellfish.

If made with clear chicken or white veal stock, serve with chicken, eggs, or calf's brains.

Mornay Sauce

Yield 2 cups

Mornay is one of the most useful of the cheese sauces, giving flavor to a wide range of appetizers and main dishes, such as fish, chicken, egg, and vegetable dishes. This sauce is always served hot, and a few minutes under the broiler turns it a golden color. *Mornay* may be prepared well in advance of serving and may be refrigerated for a limited time.

2 *cups* béchamel *sauce*
  (*see page 81*)
6 *egg yolks*
4 *Tablespoons butter, softened*
3 *Tablespoons finely grated*
  Parmesan cheese

2 *Tablespoons Gruyère cheese,*
  grated
¼ *cup heavy cream*

Heat the *béchamel* sauce in a heavy-bottomed saucepan over medium heat. Remove from heat. In a bowl, beat the yolks until lemon-colored and then stir them into the warm *béchamel*. Add the butter and cheeses, stirring until smooth. Reheat, but do not boil.

Just before serving, whip the cream and fold into the sauce.

White Cream Sauce

Yield 2 cups

Use white fish *fumet* for a white cream sauce to be used on fish or seafood.

Use clear chicken stock for a white cream sauce to be used on eggs and poultry.

Use white veal stock for a white cream sauce to be used on veal, calf's brains, sweetbreads, etc.

2 *Tablespoons butter*	*veal stock (see pages 43*
3 *Tablespoons flour*	*and 46)*
2 *cups white fish* fumet,	¼ *teaspoon salt*
clear chicken stock, or white	½ *cup heavy cream*

Melt butter in a saucepan. Stir in flour and cook over medium heat until a *roux* (a smooth, creamed blend) is formed and bubbles slightly. In another saucepan, bring stock and salt to a boil. Pour hot stock quickly into *roux* and stir until thickened. Simmer slowly for 15 minutes, stirring constantly. Add heavy cream to sauce and simmer for 5 minutes more. Strain the sauce through a fine sieve.

Sauce Polonaise

Yield 1½ cups

8 *Tablespoons butter*	½ *teaspoon dried fennel*
½ *cup sifted flour*	1 *Tablespoon shallots (or small*
1 *cup white veal stock*	*onion), finely chopped*
(see page 46)	½ *Tablespoon chives, finely*
1 *cup sour cream*	*chopped*
Juice of 3 lemons	3 *hard-boiled eggs, finely*
1 *Tablespoon prepared*	*chopped*
horseradish	*Pinch cayenne pepper*

In a heavy saucepan, melt the butter until it is foamy. Stir in flour gradually. Add white veal stock and simmer over low heat until thick and smooth. Stir in sour cream and lemon juice. Add horseradish, fennel, shallots, chives, eggs, and pepper.

I find this sauce particularly good with cauliflower and other vegetables. It can also be served with fish, veal, and pork dishes.

Béarnaise Sauce

Yield 1 cup

This is a perfect *Béarnaise* sauce, but if you do not have the basic brown sauce on hand you may omit it and still have a fine *Béarnaise*.

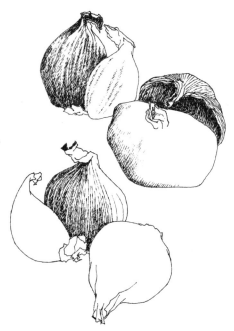

- 1 *Tablespoon shallots (or onion), finely chopped*
- ½ *cup tarragon vinegar*
- 1 *teaspoon parsley, finely chopped*
- 1 *Tablespoon fresh tarragon, finely chopped (or ½ Tablespoon dried)*
- ¼ *teaspoon freshly cracked pepper*
   Pinch salt
- ¾ *cup hollandaise sauce (see page 86)*
- 1½ *Tablespoons basic brown sauce (see page 79)*

Combine the shallots, vinegar, parsley, half of the tarragon, the cracked pepper, and the salt in a small saucepan. Bring to a boil, then simmer until the liquid is reduced to about 2 Tablespoons. Add the hollandaise and brown sauce. Stir in the remaining tarragon.

Serve on steaks or other broiled meat, or on baked or broiled fish.

Hollandaise Sauce

3 *egg yolks*
2 *teaspoons water*
1 *teaspoon white vinegar*
½ *teaspoon salt*

Pinch white pepper
¾ *cup melted butter*
Juice of ½ lemon

Use a stainless steel, glass, or copper bowl. Do not use aluminum, because the aluminum will discolor the sauce. Beat egg yolks, water, vinegar, salt, and pepper in a bowl which has been set over a pot of slowly simmering water (or on the edge of a low flame on the range) until a slightly stiff and foamy texture has been obtained.

Remove from fire and beat for about 1 minute to cool slightly. Beat in the melted butter slowly. Add the lemon juice. Keep warm, not hot, on the edge of the stove or on the top of the range (away from the fire), maintaining the sauce at room temperature. Stir occasionally to prevent skin from forming on top.

NOTES ON HOLLANDAISE

Fresh, homemade hollandaise sauce should never be refrigerated—in fact it should not be allowed to go below 65 degrees.

If it is not convenient to make fresh hollandaise or if only small quantities are required to blend with other sauces, as is true in some of my recipes, I have two alternative suggestions to offer:

One is to get the commercial variety in a jar which is available in the refrigerator cases of some food specialty shops.

The second is to make the following simplified substitute which will produce, if not the classic hollandaise, an acceptable substitute.

½ *cup white cream sauce (see page 84)*
¼ *cup mayonnaise (Use only the commercial homogenized type.)*

1 *egg yolk*
A few drops of lemon juice

Mix together in a bowl which has been set over a pot of simmering water.

(By adding 2 Tablespoons of grated Parmesan cheese this will make an acceptable version of *Mornay* sauce.)

Mousseline Sauce

Yield 2½ cups

This is a delicate but rich and fluffy sauce that is especially delightful with fish or chicken dishes.

4 *egg yolks, beaten lightly*
  (or 2 Tablespoons hollandaise)
½ *cup heavy cream, beaten*

1 *cup warm* béchamel *sauce*
  (see page 81)

Fold the egg yolks and heavy cream into the warm *béchamel* sauce. Keep warm and serve as soon as possible.

Horseradish *Mousseline* Sauce

Yield 1 cup

½ *cup hollandaise sauce (see*
  page 86)
½ *cup whipped cream*

1 *teaspoon freshly grated*
  horseradish or 1½ teaspoons
  prepared horseradish

Combine the above ingredients and serve at room temperature.

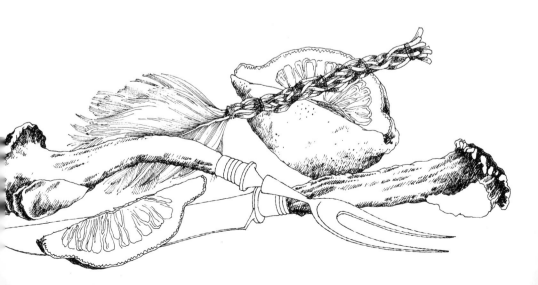

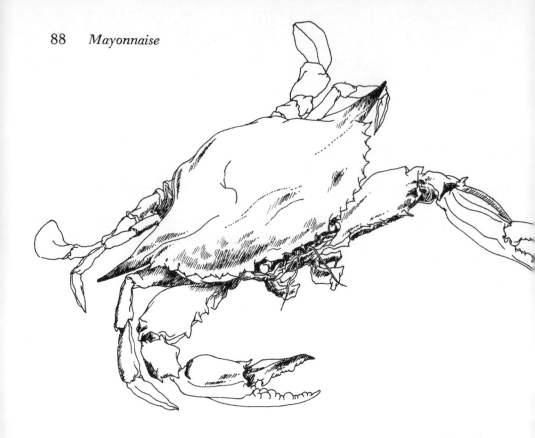

Mayonnaise

The uses of mayonnaise are too well known to need any suggestions. In fact, Americans use it too often instead of some of the more interesting variations.

2 *egg yolks*
1 *teaspoon warm water*
½ *teaspoon prepared mustard*
  Juice of ½ lemon
½ *teaspoon salt*

Pinch pepper
½ *teaspoon vinegar*
¾ *cup corn oil, at room*
  temperature

Using a wire whisk, beat all ingredients except oil until creamy. Add oil slowly, a few drops at first, then in a very thin stream, beating constantly until the mixture thickens.

Mayonnaise will "break" or curdle if oil is too cold or poured in too fast. Curdling can be remedied by whipping up a portion of the mayonnaise with an egg yolk and beating this back into the remainder of the mayonnaise.

Rémoulade Sauce

Yield 2½ cups

This variation of mayonnaise is ideal with cold seafood cocktails.

2 *cups mayonnaise*
  (see page 88)
2 *Tablespoons capers, drained*
  and finely chopped
2 *Tablespoons dill pickle or sour*
  gherkins, finely chopped
1 *Tablespoon onion, grated*

1 *Tablespoon prepared mustard*
¼ *teaspoon anchovy paste*
2 *teaspoons each of fresh parsley,*
  tarragon, chives, chervil, finely
  chopped (if dried, 1 teaspoon
  each)

Mix all the ingredients with the mayonnaise in a mixing bowl, and
stir to blend thoroughly.

Stonehenge Country Dressing

Yield 3 cups

This may be used for any cold salad but is especially good on crabmeat,
lobster, or shrimp.

1½ *cups mayonnaise (see page*
   88)
 ⅔ *cup heavy cream*
 1 *Tablespoon prepared mustard*
 ¼ *teaspoon each of thyme,*
   savory, and pepper
 2 *Tablespoons sago cheese,*
   finely grated

2 *Tablespoons onion, finely*
  grated
1 *Tablespoon salt*
2 *Tablespoons white vinegar*
1 *cup Gruyère cheese, grated*
½ *clove garlic, peeled and*
  minced

Place all the ingredients in a mixing bowl and blend thoroughly by hand
or with an electric mixer. Chill several hours before use.

Cold *Sauce Lamaze*

Lamaze sauce is excellent on seafood, eggs, or poultry, and may also be used as a salad dressing on any cold salad.

In a mixing bowl blend thoroughly:

1½ *cups mayonnaise*
   (see page 88)
  1 *Tablespoon prepared mustard*

1 *Tablespoon tomato ketchup*
½ *Tablespoon chili sauce*
½ *teaspoon A-1 sauce*

Then add the following:

1 *Tablespoon pimientos,*
  finely chopped
1 *Tablespoon celery,*
  finely chopped
½ *Tablespoon chives,*
  finely chopped
½ *Tablespoon green pepper,*
  seeded and finely chopped

½ *Tablespoon parsley,*
  finely chopped
1 *hard-boiled egg,*
  finely chopped
½ *Tablespoon horseradish,*
  grated (or use the prepared)

Blend all ingredients and mix vigorously.

Sauce Vinaigrette

This splendid, colorful sauce will remain fresh for some days in the refrigerator. It can be used on lightly cooked fresh asparagus or cauliflower, or with avocado and green salads. Try it also with baked or cold fish, with cold calf's brains, tuna fish, or eggs.

In a bowl mix together:

¼ *cup vinegar*
½ *cup oil*

1 *teaspoon salt*
⅛ *teaspoon pepper*

Add the following ingredients, all finely chopped (or they may be put through the small blade in meat grinder):

1 *Tablespoon parsley*
¼ *Tablespoon chervil or watercress*
¼ *Tablespoon chives*
¼ *Tablespoon tarragon*
1 *Tablespoon onion*
½ *Tablespoon capers*
1 *Tablespoon dill pickle*
½ *Tablespoon pimiento*
½ *Tablespoon green pepper*
1 *hard-boiled egg*

(If dried herbs are used, use half the amount.)

Vinaigrette sauce is usually served cold or at room temperature. It may also be served hot on such salads as spinach or green bean salad, but for this purpose omit the egg from the recipe.

White Fish Sauce

Yield 2 cups

2 *pounds raw fish bones (any white fish)*
1 *quart water*
1 *onion stuck with 2 cloves*
1 *leek, white part only (or 2 scallions, white parts only)*

1 *stalk celery*
1 *teaspoon salt*
   Pinch thyme
2 *Tablespoons butter*
1 *Tablespoon flour*

Boil fish bones, water, onion stuck with cloves, leek, celery, salt, and thyme for 15 minutes, uncovered, skimming foam off the top while cooking. Meanwhile make a *roux* (a smooth blend) of butter and flour; add to the liquid and simmer for 15 minutes more. Strain through a fine sieve.

Or if you have 2 cups of leftover fish *fumet* (see page 46), make a similar sauce by blending in *roux* of 2 Tablespoons butter blended with 1 Tablespoon flour. Simmer for 15 minutes and strain through a fine sieve.

Cold *Sauce Gribiche* for Fish

Yield 2 cups—Serves 6 to 8

Sauce Gribiche is equally good with hot or cold fish. Use with striped bass, carp, shad, or trout.

3 *yolks of hard-boiled eggs*
3 *whites of hard-boiled eggs,*
   cut into thin strips
¼ *teaspoon each of thyme*
   and savory
¼ *cup cider vinegar*
½ *Tablespoon prepared mustard*
½ *Tablespoon lemon juice*
1 *teaspoon salt*

½ *teaspoon pepper*
½ *cup corn oil*
1 *Tablespoon parsley, finely*
   chopped
1 *Tablespoon fresh tarragon,*
   finely chopped (If dried, use
   half the amount.)
1 *Tablespoon capers*
1 *Tablespoon boiling water*

Press the hard egg yolks through a fine sieve into a mixing bowl. Add the remainder of the ingredients and mix well. (The 1 Tablespoon of boiling water will ensure a smooth blending with the oil.)

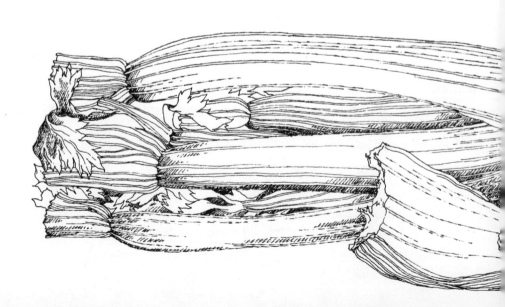

Tomato Sauce

Yield 4 cups

A tomato sauce like this one may be used with spaghetti dishes, fish, or cooked meats.

4 *slices raw bacon, diced*
1 *onion, finely chopped*
1 *pound tomatoes, unpeeled,*
  rinsed, and coarsely chopped
3 *Tablespoons tomato purée*
2 *stalks celery, rinsed and*
  coarsely chopped
2 *cups tomato juice*

2 *cups water*
  Pinch each of oregano, thyme,
  and savory
1 *clove garlic, peeled*
  and chopped
1 *teaspoon salt*
½ *teaspoon pepper*
  Pinch sugar

Combine the above ingredients in a saucepan and cook over medium heat for 30 minutes. Pour the sauce into the blender and purée until smooth. Strain the sauce through a fine sieve into the saucepan. The tomato sauce may be refrigerated for no more than 4 to 6 days or frozen for future use.

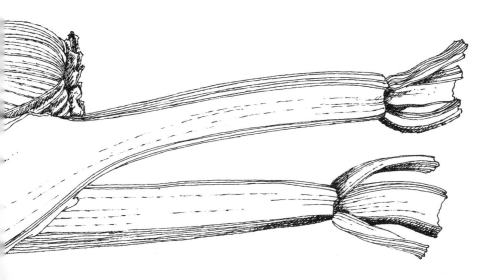

Pungent Fruit Sauce

Yield 1 cup

A lively sauce for cold seafood, cold game, or cold meats.

¾ cup orange marmalade
4 Tablespoons lemon juice
2 Tablespoons orange juice
2 teaspoons horseradish, grated
   (or use the prepared)

½ teaspoon powdered ginger
½ teaspoon salt
½ teaspoon dry English mustard
   (optional)

Combine the orange marmalade, lemon juice, and orange juice in the blender and purée until smooth. Pour into a bowl and add the horseradish, powdered ginger, and salt. If desired, add dry English mustard.

Cumberland Sauce

Yield 2 cups

Here is a sauce to be served with cold *terrine*, venison, or game.

5 shallots (or ¼ medium-sized
   onion), peeled and finely
   chopped
   Juice of 1 orange, reserve peel
   and cut into julienne strips
   Juice of ½ lemon, reserve peel
   and cut into julienne strips
1 cup port wine

¼ cup red currant jelly, melted
1 teaspoon prepared mustard
   (or 1 teaspoon dry English
   mustard dissolved in 1 Tablespoon water)
¼ teaspoon powdered ginger
   Pinch cayenne pepper

Simmer the shallots and the orange and lemon peel in their juices for 15 minutes or until tender. Add the wine and melted currant jelly. Stir in the mustard and season with ginger and cayenne. Let sauce cool before serving. Do not refrigerate.

Brown Butter Sauce

Yield 1 cup

This is a lovely sauce for brook trout, any poached fish, or sautéed calf's liver.

8 *Tablespoons sweet or salted*   1 *Tablespoon capers*
  butter (¼ pound)   1 *teaspoon parsley, chopped*
2 *teaspoons vinegar, or juice*
  of ½ lemon

Heat butter in a saucepan until it smokes and turns brown. Add vinegar. Stir in capers and parsley and remove from heat.

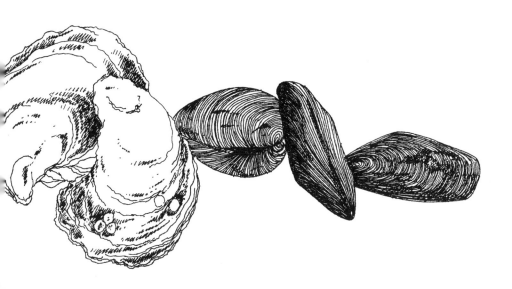

Curries

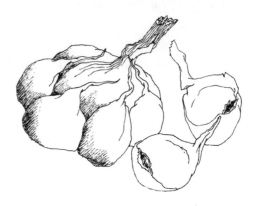

Curry is a basic flavoring in vast areas of our globe, but no two cooks ever agree on its preparation. I can give you basic recipes and some suggestions for using this colorful seasoning.

Disagreements arise mainly over the strength of the curry powder. So much depends upon where curry is served and to whom. You can be certain of pleasing any guest by controlling not only the ingredients that make up the basic powder but the amount you use in the sauce.

Fifteen to twenty herbs, spices, and seeds are generally used to make the bottled curry powder we buy in this country. It remains for you to find the blend and aroma most pleasing. If you are adventurous enough you can easily make your own curry powder in your blender—in small amounts, as it does lose its strength and aroma with age. The common ingredients for curry powder are pepper, nutmeg, cardamom, cinnamon, cloves, turmeric, coriander, caraway, fenugreek (an herb resembling clover), cayenne or red pepper, ginger, lime, and garlic. Remember that the chili pepper—the red, fiery kind—is what makes some curry powders offensive to Western palates.

Your curry sauce should be ardent and sultry rather than torrid or biting. Once you have found a pungent and delicately flavored curry powder a great new world of food is open to you. Add to it fruits such as apricots, or whatever is in season.

The amount of curry sauce needed per serving varies from 3 ounces to a full cup (8 ounces). When curry sauce is used with cut-up fruits or on cut-up pieces of chicken, more sauce will be needed. When poured over large pieces of meat, etc., much less will be needed.

Curries can be very valuable in your kitchen to relieve the bland monotony of egg, fish, chicken, or veal dishes, and especially of rice dishes. Curry dishes are a wonderful way of using cooked meats—chicken, turkey, veal, and lamb—and will always add pungency and variety to a menu in which the other elements are mild.

Above all, curry dishes are the answer to jaded appetites or hot weather lack of appetite, for contrary to popular impression, curries are as appropriate and appreciated on hot summer days as on cold winter nights. Remember that curries are most popular in the torrid countries of the Orient.

Basic Javanese Curry

Yield 4 cups

Some years ago I spent considerable time traveling among the islands of the East Indies, where curried meals are by far the most popular. I had long since tired of endless Indian curries, often full of fire and little else. I realized then that the answer is not only a bit less curry powder but additional ingredients to complement the main purpose of the curry —whether it is meat, poultry, or fish. The East Indians avoid a harsh fiery taste by lavish use of fresh fruit. My own version of Javanese curry, I think, reflects the American preference and is made with ingredients easily obtainable. This splendid curry sauce may be refrigerated for no more than a week or frozen, and the convenience of having it on hand is obvious.

1 *medium onion, finely chopped*
½ *cup cooked ham, finely chopped*
2 *slices raw bacon, finely chopped*
4 *Tablespoons curry powder*
1 *Tablespoon flour*
1 *unpeeled apple, cored and coarsely chopped*

¼ *cup preserved mango or kumquat*
1 *Tablespoon tomato paste*
3 *teaspoons salt*
Juice of 1 lemon
1 *Tablespoon honey*
2 *cups chicken stock (see page 43) (or use rich canned chicken broth)*

Sauté the chopped onion, ham, and bacon over medium heat until the onions are golden. Add the curry powder and sauté 1 minute. Add flour, apple, preserved fruit, tomato paste, salt, lemon juice, honey, and chicken stock. Simmer over medium heat for 25 minutes.

Set aside to cool, then put into blender and blend until smooth.

Green Olive Curry

Yield 2½ cups

This curry is used often during hot weather and mostly for non-meat items. It may be used either as a cold or hot sauce, and may be served as an appetizer, main course, or *hors d'oeuvre*.

1 *cup green olives, finely chopped*
1½ *Tablespoons vegetable oil*
2 *cloves garlic, crushed*
1 *cup watercress leaves, finely chopped*
1 *teaspoon turmeric*
¼ *cup onions, finely chopped*

2 *cups basic Javanese curry sauce (see page 99)*
¼ *cup pimientos, finely chopped*
Juice of ½ lemon
1½ *Tablespoons apricot jam, strained*
1 *teaspoon salt*
1 *teaspoon pepper*

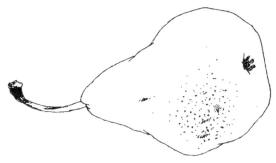

GARNISH

Toasted coconut   *Toasted pine nuts*

In a large sauté pan, combine green olives, vegetable oil, garlic, watercress, turmeric, and onions, and sauté very lightly for 2½ minutes. Add Javanese curry sauce, pimientos, lemon juice, apricot jam, salt, and pepper. Cover and simmer for 15 minutes.

SUGGESTIONS

Pour the hot curry sauce over chilled hard-boiled eggs, melon balls, peeled and cored pears, plums, pickled apricots, or other stewed, raw, or cooked fruit.

PRESENTATION

Sprinkle with toasted coconut and toasted pine nuts.

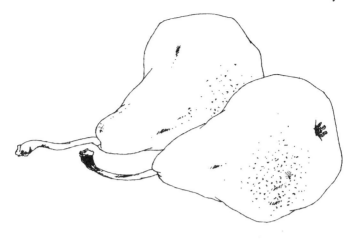

Beer Curry

Yield 2 cups

1 *medium onion, finely chopped*
1 *clove garlic, minced*
1 *Tablespoon butter*
3 *Tablespoons prepared mustard*
3 *Tablespoons bottled chili sauce*

3 *Tablespoons curry powder*
1 *cup light domestic beer*
  Juice of 2 lemons
1 *teaspoon salt*
1 *cup basic Javanese curry sauce (see page 99)*

Sauté the chopped onion and minced garlic in butter over medium heat until golden in color. Add the mustard, chili sauce, curry powder, beer, lemon juice, and salt, and simmer over low heat for 25 minutes. Put into a blender and blend until smooth. Combine this beer curry with the Javanese curry sauce.

SUGGESTIONS
Use this curry with frog's legs, chicken, lamb, beef, or veal.

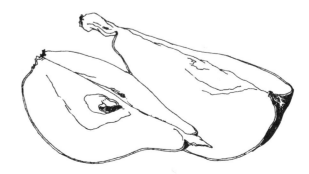

Vindaloo Fruit Curry

Yield 4 cups

1 *medium onion, minced*
2 *cloves garlic, minced*
3 *Tablespoons vegetable*
  or corn oil
1 *Tablespoon coriander*
2 *teaspoons turmeric*
1 *teaspoon cumin*
1 *teaspoon chili peppers,*
  dried and crushed
1 *teaspoon ginger*
1 *teaspoon dry English mustard*
½ *teaspoon dried fennel*
½ *teaspoon black pepper*
¼ *cup white vinegar*
1 *cup mango, sliced*

½ *cup pineapple chunks*
1 *medium size banana, sliced*
½ *cup tomato juice*
1 *Tablespoon honey*
1 *teaspoon salt*
  Juice of ½ lemon

Put all ingredients in large pot and simmer, covered, for 15 minutes.

SUGGESTIONS

Fruit curry may be used with meatless dishes. Select 2½ cups cauliflower buds, peas, carrots, broccoli, leeks, scallions, celery, spinach, or lettuce, and combine any of these vegetables or use only one if you prefer. Cook the vegetables and cut them into small, regular pieces, then cool to room temperature; or, if they are raw, slice them very thin. Or select melons, pears, apples, or peaches, sliced and chilled. Then serve the fruit or vegetables with the fruit curry poured over it.

ALSO WITH

2 *cups either cooked chicken,*
  lamb, beef, or seafood
6 *hard-boiled eggs*
1 *pound small shrimp, peeled and*
  deveined (Add to sauce during
  last 2 minutes of cooking.)

1 *cooked lobster, cut in serving*
  pieces
1 *8-ounce can Alaskan*
  king crab

SuSu Cream Curry

Yield 2 cups

This is a creamed curry usually made with coconut milk, but I prefer my recipe for its flavor and simplicity.

2 *cups basic Javanese curry sauce (see page 99)*
½ *cup heavy cream*
1 *Tablespoon horseradish, finely grated*

2 *Tablespoons coconut, finely chopped*
 Juice of ½ lemon
1 *teaspoon salt*
2 *dashes Tabasco*

Combine the basic Javanese curry sauce with the heavy cream, and simmer for 5 minutes. Remove from the fire and mix in the horseradish, coconut, lemon juice, salt, and Tabasco.

SUGGESTIONS
This sauce is excellent with cooked chicken, meat balls, beef, fish, or shrimp.

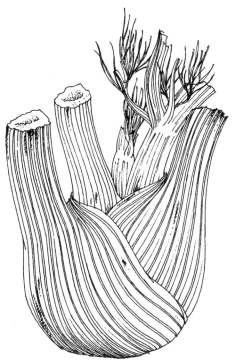

Crêpes
and Soufflés

Batters   Entrée Crêpes   Dessert Crêpes
Basic Beer Soufflé   Basic Soufflé

Crêpes are thin, delicate pancakes. Pancakes are one of the oldest forms of cooked food, probably the forerunner of bread, because before ovens were invented batter mixtures were heated on flat, hot stones.

The American and European concepts of pancakes are completely different. To Americans, pancakes are a hearty breakfast dish with a standard sauce—butter and syrup. But to Europeans, the pancake—or thin, flavorful *crêpe*—has an unlimited versatility. By adding beer or wine, herbs and other flavorings to the batter, by selecting from a multitude of tangy fillings to roll inside the *crêpe* and mouth-watering sauces to cover them, *crêpes* provide new, different, and exciting opportunities for any meal and as any course—appetizer, entrée, or dessert.

A great advantage of *crêpes* is that they can be prepared in advance, and frozen or stored in the refrigerator. They can thus be kept available for quick, easy, and utterly delicious dishes. Another advantage is that they provide a wonderful way to use cooked meat, fish, or vegetables.

One note which applies to all the *crêpe* recipes: The special, so-called "*crêpe* pan" is 6 inches in diameter. Two *crêpes* of this size make a normal portion as an appetizer or dessert, three or four for a main course. But if you prefer to use your 12 inch standard frying pan, one per person is sufficient as an appetizer or two as a main course. That is why recipes for four will specify 4 or 8 *crêpes*.

Another glamorous and delicious contribution to a meal is the soufflé. Like *crêpes*, a soufflé may be served as an appetizer or a main course for luncheon, or for dessert. And a soufflé may also be flavored with almost any edible materials, although they must always be grated, finely chopped, or puréed.

Amateur cooks are awed or frightened at the idea of attempting to prepare a soufflé because they have heard about the dangers of its not rising or of its falling after it has risen. There is some basis for this fear, but not too much. Many amateurs have successfully made soufflés on their first try. However, fear serves a good purpose if it makes you very careful to follow instructions and to have everything ready so that the soufflé can be served immediately.

Batters

Entrée Crêpes

Dessert Crêpes

Batters

Basic *Crêpes*

Serves 4 to 6

1 *cup all-purpose flour*	2 *eggs*
Pinch salt	2 *egg yolks*
½ *cup milk*	1 *Tablespoon melted butter*
½ *cup water*	

Sift the flour and salt into a mixing bowl, add the milk and water and stir until smooth. Beat the whole eggs and egg yolks together in a small bowl and pour into the flour and milk. Add the melted butter and whisk until smooth. (This batter may be used at once or prepared a few hours ahead.)

Wipe the surface of a 6 inch *crêpe* pan with oil. Place the pan over high heat and pour in enough batter to coat the surface thinly. Pour off any excess. When the *crêpe* forms slight bubbles, loosen the edges, and when lightly browned, turn over, using a spatula, and let the other side cook for a few moments.

If the first *crêpe* seems uneven, discard it. Repeat, making individual *crêpes* until the batter is used up. Wipe the pan with oil as necessary after each 2 or 3 *crêpes*. Stack the *crêpes* and keep warm.

Fines Herbes Crêpes

Serves 4 to 6

Prepare the basic *crêpe* batter (see page 109) and stir in:

1 *teaspoon fresh tarragon, finely*
  chopped (or 1½ teaspoons
  dried)
1 *teaspoon chives,*
  finely chopped

1 *teaspoon shallots (or onion),*
  finely chopped
1 *teaspoon parsley, finely*
  chopped

Make individual *crêpes* as in basic *crêpes*.

These may be served as appetizers or entrées, plain, or filled with chicken, caviar, or fish.

Onion *Crêpes*

Serves 4 to 6

1¼ *cups all-purpose flour*
  1 *teaspoon salt*
  ½ *medium onion, finely grated*
  ½ *cup milk*

½ *cup water*
2 *eggs*
2 *egg yolks*
1 *Tablespoon melted butter*

Sift the flour and salt into a bowl. Add the onion, milk, and water. Beat the eggs and egg yolks together and pour into the batter. Add the melted butter and whisk until smooth.

Make individual *crêpes* as in basic *crêpes* (page 109).

The onion batter is particularly good with chicken or mushroom fillings.

Buckwheat *Crêpes*   *Serves 4 to 6*

1 *cup buckwheat flour, sifted*   2 *eggs*
1 *teaspoon salt*   2 *egg yolks*
1 *cup milk*   1 *Tablespoon melted butter*

Sift the flour and salt into a bowl; pour in the milk. Beat the eggs and egg yolks together in a small bowl, and stir into the batter. Add the melted butter and whisk until smooth.

Make individual *crêpes* as in basic *crêpes* (page 109).

These *crêpes* go well with pork or ham dishes.

Beer *Crêpes*   *Serves 4 to 6*

1 *cup all-purpose flour*   2 *egg yolks*
1 *teaspoon salt*   1 *Tablespoon sour cream*
1 *cup light domestic beer*   1 *Tablespoon melted butter*
2 *eggs*

Sift the flour and salt into a mixing bowl. Stir in the beer until smooth. Beat the eggs and egg yolks in a small bowl, add to the batter, and whisk until smooth. Add the sour cream and melted butter.

Make individual *crêpes* as in basic *crêpes* (page 109).

Beer *crêpes* are particularly good with seafood filling.

Entrée *Crêpes*

Chicken Livers in Onion *Crêpes*

Serves 4 to 6

12 *onion* crêpes *(see page 110)*
1 *pound chicken livers*
4 *Tablespoons butter*
1 *Tablespoon onion, finely*
   chopped
Pinch each of savory and marjoram

2 *Tablespoons dry sherry*
   Juice of ½ lemon
1 *cup hollandaise sauce (see*
   page 86) or sauce Béarnaise
   (see page 85)

Prepare the *crêpes* according to onion *crêpes* directions.
   Preheat broiler.
   Clean the chicken livers of any greenish spots, drain, and cut into small pieces. Melt the butter in a frying pan, add the livers, onion, savory, marjoram, sherry, and lemon juice. Sauté about 5 minutes or until the livers are cooked through. Remove from heat.
   Spread the cooked *crêpes* out flat and fill the center of each with the liver mixture. Roll up each *crêpe* and place in a shallow, ovenproof, buttered baking dish. Pour hollandaise sauce over the 12 *crêpes* and place them under the preheated broiler until golden brown.

Summer Corn and Clam *Crêpes*

Serves 4 to 6

4 *or* 8 *basic* crêpes *(see*
   page 109)
½ *cup cooked corn, chopped*
½ *cup cooked clams, chopped*
¼ *teaspoon fresh dill, finely*
   chopped

½ *cup sour cream*
2 *hard-cooked eggs, finely*
   chopped
¼ *teaspoon prepared mustard*

Prepare the *crêpes* according to basic *crêpes* directions.
   Preheat oven to 375 degrees.

In a bowl, mix together the corn, clams, dill, 1 Tablespoon of the sour cream, the eggs, and mustard.

Spread the *crêpes* out flat and divide the mixture among them. Roll up each *crêpe* and place in a shallow buttered ovenproof dish. Cover *crêpes* with the remaining sour cream and bake (375 degrees) for 10 minutes.

A delightful variation of this recipe is achieved by substituting finely chopped herring for the clams. (Chopped herring may be bought in jars.)

Mousse of Ham in *Crêpes*   Serves 4 to 6

Fines herbes *or basic* crêpes
(8 if 6-inch, 4 if 12-inch)
(see pages 109 or 110)
½ *pound (or 1 cup) cooked ham,*
  finely chopped (ends and
  pieces may be used)
¼ *teaspoon salt*
 1 *Tablespoon softened butter*
 1 *teaspoon thyme*

5 *preserved kumquats, drained*
2 *small gherkins, finely chopped*
¼ *cup cold* béchamel *sauce (see*
  page 81)
1 *teaspoon prepared mustard*
1 *egg*
4 *Tablespoons butter*
1 *teaspoon brown sugar*

Prepare the *crêpes* according to *fines herbes* or basic *crêpes* directions. *Preheat oven to 375 degrees.*

Place the ham in the blender and add the salt, butter, thyme, kumquats, gherkins, and *béchamel* sauce, and blend until smooth.

Spread the cooked *crêpes* out and put only enough filling on each to allow for folding over. Place the folded *crêpes* side by side in a shallow ovenproof buttered baking dish.

In a small mixing bowl, place the mustard, egg, butter, and brown sugar. Beat to a smooth liquid and coat each *crêpe*. Bake (375 degrees) for 10 minutes and serve.

As a variation which imparts an unusual flavor, I suggest using 4 tablespoons orange marmalade instead of brown sugar.

This makes an excellent luncheon dish.

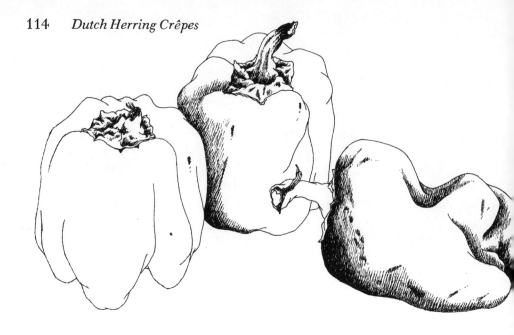

Dutch Herring *Crêpes* with Sour Cream   *Serves 4*

For this recipe I prefer to use uncooked schmaltz herring, as salted and cured herring is not really raw. However, some people, especially the British, prefer to sauté the herring.

4 *basic* crêpes *(see page 109)*
4 *Tablespoons onion, minced*
3 *ounces light domestic beer*
1 *teaspoon prepared mustard*
¼ *teaspoon curry powder*
¼ *teaspoon cornstarch, dissolved in 1 teaspoon water*

4 *filets of boneless herrings, salted and cured*
½ *cup sour cream*
1 *Tablespoon green pepper, finely chopped*

Prepare the *crêpes* according to basic *crêpes* directions.
   Preheat oven to 400 degrees.
   Cook the onion, beer, mustard, and curry powder in a frying pan for 3 minutes. Add the dissolved cornstarch and let thicken. Lay the herring filets on top to heat through.
   Spread the *crêpes* out flat, put a herring filet in the center of each, and divide the beer and onion sauce over them. Roll up each *crêpe* and place in a buttered ovenproof dish. Cover the *crêpes* with sour cream, sprinkle with chopped green pepper and bake (400 degrees) for 10 minutes.

Crêpes Finlandia with Herring

Serves 4

8 *basic, beer, or onion crêpes*
   (6-inch) (see pages 109, 110,
   or 111)
1 *Tablespoon red wine vinegar*
1 *Tablespoon tomato purée*
¼ *teaspoon pepper*
1 *Tablespoon bottled chili sauce*
¼ *teaspoon fresh dill, finely*
   chopped

½ *apple, peeled and grated*
4 *boneless herrings, sautéed*
2 *Tablespoons butter*
¼ *cup bread crumbs*
1 *Tablespoon parsley, finely*
   chopped

Prepare the *crêpes* according to basic, beer, or onion *crêpes* directions.
Preheat oven to 400 degrees.

In a saucepan over medium heat combine the vinegar, tomato purée, pepper, chili sauce, dill, and apple. Add the herrings, and simmer for 10 minutes.

After herrings have been sautéed and are cooked through, split them lengthwise. Lay the *crêpes* out flat and place half a herring in each *crêpe*. Divide the sauce mixture evenly among the *crêpes*, spooning it over the herring. Roll up the *crêpes* and place them in a buttered oven-proof serving dish.

Melt the butter in a small saucepan, toss in the bread crumbs and shake the pan until the butter is absorbed, add the parsley, and sprinkle the mixture over the *crêpes*. Bake (400 degrees) about 10 minutes or until light brown on top. Serve hot.

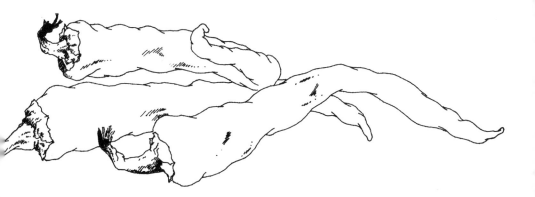

Spinach *Crêpes Orientale*   *Serves 4*

Basic crêpes *(4 if 12-inch,*
8 if 6-inch) (see page 109)
½ *onion, finely chopped*
1 *clove garlic, finely chopped*
3 *Tablespoons butter*
½ *teaspoon curry powder*
1 *cup spinach, cooked and*
chopped
½ *teaspoon salt*

12 *very small shrimp*
2 *hard-boiled eggs, finely chopped*
¼ *cup brown stock (see page 45)*
or beef gravy (to improvise
gravy see page xiii)
1 *Tablespoon pimiento, finely*
chopped
¼ *cup prepared mustard*
¼ *cup bottled chili sauce*

Prepare the *crêpes* according to basic *crêpes* directions.

Preheat oven to 350 degrees.

Sauté the chopped onion and garlic in the butter until lightly golden. Add the curry powder, spinach, salt, shrimp, eggs, stock, pimiento, and simmer over low heat for 5 minutes.

Spread out the *crêpes* and fill the center of each. Roll up the *crêpes* and place in a buttered ovenproof baking dish.

In a small bowl, mix the mustard and chili sauce and brush tops of *crêpes* generously. Bake (350 degrees) for 10 minutes. Serve hot.

Ideal as an appetizer or as a luncheon main course. If the latter, make extra *crêpes*.

Spiced Crabmeat *Crêpes*   *Serves 4 to 6*

8 *to 12 beer* crêpes *(see page 111)*
8 *to 10 ounces crabmeat (canned*
or cooked)
1 *teaspoon shallots (or onions),*
finely chopped
½ *teaspoon dry English mustard*
¼ *teaspoon prepared horseradish*
Pinch each of salt and pepper
Juice of 1 lemon
⅓ *cup* béchamel *sauce (see page 81)*

3 *Tablespoons mayonnaise*
½ *cup fine bread crumbs,*
freshly made in blender
1 *Tablespoon corn oil*
1 *clove garlic, peeled and*
minced
1 *teaspoon each parsley and*
chives, finely chopped
1 *Tablespoon Parmesan cheese,*
grated

Prepare the *crêpes* according to beer *crêpes* directions.

Preheat oven to 400 degrees.

Pick over the crabmeat and remove any bits of shell. In the top of double boiler over simmering water combine the crabmeat with the shallots, mustard, horseradish, salt, pepper, lemon juice, *béchamel* sauce, and mayonnaise. Cook for about 5 minutes until heated through.

Spread the *crêpes* out flat and fill the center of each *crêpe* with the crabmeat mixture. Roll the *crêpes* up and transfer them to a shallow, buttered ovenproof dish.

In a mixing bowl combine the bread crumbs, oil, garlic, parsley, chives, and cheese. Mix well and sprinkle over the filled *crêpes*.

Bake (400 degrees) for about 15 minutes, or until the tops are golden brown. Serve hot.

Crêpes of Fresh Sardines, Glazed Lemon   *Serves 4*

4 *large basic, beer, or onion* crêpes *(see pages 109, 110, or 111)*	1 *Tablespoon butter*
	2 *Tablespoons onion, finely grated*
4 *fresh sardines*	2 *Tablespoons tomato purée*
2 *Tablespoons prepared mustard*	*Juice of ½ lemon*
¼ *teaspoon pepper*	1 *lemon, sliced paper thin*

Prepare the *crêpes* according to basic, beer, or onion *crêpes* directions.

Preheat oven to 375 degrees.

Prepare the sardines by cutting off the heads and tails. Cover them with mustard and sprinkle with pepper.

Melt the butter in a skillet, add the onion, and sauté until transparent. Add the tomato purée, lemon juice, and the sardines, and cook over medium heat for 6 minutes. Lift out the sardines, split them, and carefully remove the backbones with a fork. They will come out easily.

Lay the *crêpes* out flat, place a sardine in each, and cover with the tomato and onion sauce. Roll the *crêpes* up and transfer to a buttered ovenproof dish. Cover the *crêpes* with the lemon slices and bake (375 degrees) for 10 minutes. Serve hot.

Mushroom Beer *Crêpes*   *Serves 4 to 6*

4 *large or* 8 *small beer* crêpes (*see page 111*)	3 *Tablespoons heavy cream*
3 *Tablespoons butter*	2 *ounces* (¼ *cup) cooked ham, cut in thin strips*
½ *medium onion, finely chopped*	6 *ounces* (1½ *cups) Gruyère cheese, grated*
1½ *cups mushrooms, finely sliced*	1 *teaspoon cornstarch dissolved in 2 Tablespoons water*
1 *Tablespoon lemon juice*	½ *teaspoon salt*
6 *ounces domestic light beer*	¼ *teaspoon pepper*

Prepare the *crêpes* according to beer *crêpes* directions.

Preheat broiler.

In a frying pan heat the butter, add the chopped onion and sauté until transparent. Add the sliced mushrooms, sprinkle with lemon juice and cook for 4 minutes. Add the beer and bring to a light boil. Remove from the heat and stir in the cream.

Return to the heat and simmer for 5 minutes or until the sauce is blended and slightly reduced. Add the ham and 1 cup of cheese a little at a time so that it does not lump, and stir vigorously until melted. Stir in the dissolved cornstarch and cook until the sauce thickens. Season with the salt and pepper.

Lay the *crêpes* out flat and divide the mushroom filling among them. Roll the *crêpes* up, place them in a buttered, shallow ovenproof dish, and sprinkle the remaining ½ cup of cheese on top. Place under the broiler until the cheese is melted and lightly browned.

Crabmeat *Crêpes Impériale*

Serves 4

4 *large (or 8 small) basic,*
  beer, or onion crêpes
  (see pages 109, 110, or 111)
2 *Tablespoons butter*
¼ *green pepper, finely chopped*
¼ *cup canned pimiento,*
  finely chopped
2 *Tablespoons onion, grated*
½ *teaspoon fresh ginger, finely*
  chopped (or ¼ teaspoon
  powdered ginger)
2 *Tablespoons dry sherry*
¼ *teaspoon dry English mustard*
1 *cup* béchamel *sauce*
  (see page 81)
2 *egg yolks*
2 *Tablespoons mayonnaise*
½ *teaspoon salt*
¼ *teaspoon pepper*
8 *ounces crabmeat, flaked*

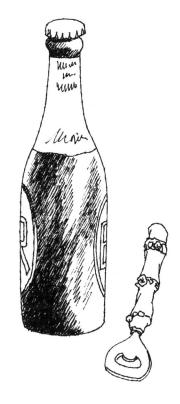

Prepare the *crêpes* according to basic, beer, or onion *crêpes* directions.

Preheat oven to 375 degrees.

Melt the butter in a frying pan, add the chopped green pepper, pimiento, onion, and ginger, and sauté over medium heat for 3 minutes. Add the sherry and dry mustard, cook for 1 minute longer and remove from fire.

Mix together the *béchamel,* egg yolks, mayonnaise, salt, and pepper in a mixing bowl. Add half the sauce to the sautéed vegetables and fold in the crabmeat.

Lay the *crêpes* out flat and divide the filling among them. Roll up each *crêpe* and transfer to a buttered ovenproof serving dish. Pour the remaining sauce over the *crêpes* and bake (375 degrees) for about 15 minutes, or until golden brown on top. Serve hot.

Creamed Mushroom *Crêpes, Mornay*   *Serves 4 to 6*

12 *onion* crêpes *(see page 110)*
 2 *Tablespoons butter*
½ *pound button mushrooms,*
   thinly sliced
 1 *Tablespoon onion, finely*
   chopped
   Pinch savory
   Juice of 1 *lemon*

½ *cup heavy cream*
 1 *teaspoon cornstarch*
 1 *Tablespoon dry white wine*
½ *cup Gruyère cheese, grated*
 1 *Tablespoon chives, finely*
   chopped
1½ *cups* Mornay *sauce (see page*
   83)

Prepare the *crêpes* according to onion *crêpes* directions.

Preheat oven to 400 degrees.

Melt butter in frying pan over medium heat, add the sliced mushrooms, chopped onion, savory, lemon juice, and sauté until the mushrooms are soft. Stir in the cream. Dissolve the cornstarch in the white wine and stir in. Add the cheese and chives.

Spread the *crêpes* out on a flat surface and divide the mixture equally among them, then roll up each *crêpe*. Place the *crêpes* in a shallow baking dish and cover with *Mornay* sauce. Bake (400 degrees) 5 minutes, or until they are lightly colored. Serve hot.

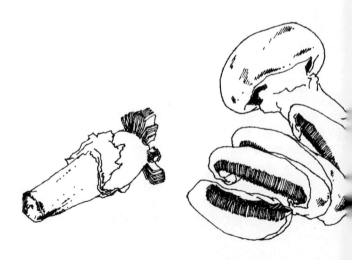

Green *Crêpes* with Prosciutto

Serves 4 to 6

8 *large basic* crêpes *(see page 109), made with addition of 3 Tablespoons cooked spinach, finely chopped*
2 *Tablespoons butter*
6 *paper-thin slices of Swiss mountain ham or prosciutto, cut in julienne strips*
½ *cup cooked spinach, finely chopped*

¼ *clove garlic, peeled and minced*
¼ *onion, finely chopped*
2 *Tablespoons tomato purée*
½ *teaspoon salt*
   Pinch pepper
1 *cup tomato sauce (see page 93)*
3 *Tablespoons Parmesan cheese, grated*

When making the basic *crêpes* add 3 tablespoons of spinach to the batter. Make 8 large *crêpes* and keep them warm while preparing the filling.

Preheat oven to 375 degrees.

Melt the butter in a frying pan, add the ham, the ½ cup of spinach, garlic, onion, tomato purée, salt, and pepper. Sauté for 5 minutes, stirring constantly.

Spread out the *crêpes* and divide the filling among them. Roll up the filled *crêpes* and place them in a heavily buttered, shallow ovenproof dish. Pour the tomato sauce over the *crêpes*, sprinkle with Parmesan cheese, and bake (375 degrees) for 10 minutes or until the cheese is melted and golden. Serve at once.

Dessert *Crêpes*

Crêpes Suzette

Serves 4 to 6

12 6-inch basic crêpes *(see*
   page 109)
 8 *Tablespoons (1 stick) butter,*
   melted
½ *cup granulated sugar*
   Grated rind of 1 *orange and* 1
   lemon

Juice of 1 *orange and* 1 *lemon*
3 *ounces brandy*
3 *ounces Cointreau or Grand*
   Marnier

Prepare the *crêpes* according to basic *crêpes* directions.

   Melt the butter in a chafing dish or copper frying pan. Stir in the sugar
and orange and lemon rind, and cook until caramelized. One by one
pass each *crêpe* through the syrup in the pan until each is completely
coated. Without removing from the pan fold each *crêpe* over twice,
making them into a triangular shape. Push the folded *crêpes* to the
edge of the pan until all are coated and folded. Add the orange and
lemon juice, brandy, and Cointreau or Grand Marnier. Mix thoroughly
and ignite, spooning the flaming liquid over each *crêpe*. Serve immediately.

Crêpes Hélène Flambées

Serves 4 to 6

12 *to* 16 *basic* crêpes *(see page 109)*
 1 *cup pure maple syrup*
 8 *Tablespoons (1 stick) butter*
 1 *teaspoon sugar*

Juice and grated rind of 2
   lemons
3 *ounces brandy*
3 *ounces rum*

Prepare the *crêpes* according to basic *crêpes* directions.

   Pour the cup of maple syrup into a large frying pan or chafing dish and bring to a boil. Stir in the butter, sugar, lemon juice, and grated rind.

Add the *crêpes* one at a time, and saturate with the mixture; fold into triangles and move to the edge of the pan until all the *crêpes* have been coated and folded.

Pour in the brandy and rum and ignite, spooning the flaming liquid over the *crêpes*. Serve the *crêpes* covered with the sauce.

Crêpes with Strawberry Cream *Flambées*   Serves 4 to 6

12 *basic* crêpes, 6-*inch*
    (*see page 109*)
½ *cup fresh strawberries*
2 *Tablespoons Cointreau*
2 *Tablespoons sugar*
1 *cup custard cream*
    (*see page 347*)

1 *teaspoon pistachio nuts, finely*
    chopped
2 *Tablespoons butter*
2 *Tablespoons sugar*
¼ *cup brandy*

Prepare the *crêpes* according to basic *crêpes* directions.

Combine the strawberries, Cointreau, and sugar, and crush to a coarse pulp. Add the custard cream and pistachio nuts and mix until smooth.

Lay the *crêpes* out flat and divide the strawberry cream among them. Roll them up carefully to retain the cream.

PRESENTATION
The filled *crêpes* are best served at table from a chafing dish or copper frying pan. Melt the butter in the chafing dish, stir in the sugar, and place the filled *crêpes* in the pan. Pour the brandy in, ignite, and spoon the flaming liquid over the *crêpes*. Serve warm.

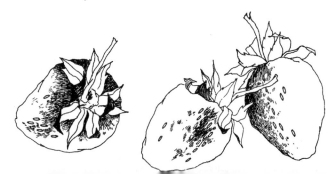

Souffléed *Crêpes* Grand Marnier

Serves 4 to 6

18 *to* 20 *6-inch basic* crêpes
(see page 109)

½ *the recipe for Grand Marnier
soufflé (see page 128)*

Preheat oven to 350 degrees.

Prepare the *crêpes* according to basic *crêpes* directions.

Prepare half the amount of the Grand Marnier soufflé.

Fold the *crêpes* into cones and fill each half full of the soufflé mixture. Place them in a large buttered baking dish and bake (350 degrees) for 15 minutes or until the filling has puffed and is golden. Serve at once.

Caramelized Strawberry *Crêpes*

Serves 4 to 6

16 *basic* crêpes, 6 *inches or
smaller (see page 109)*
8 *Tablespoons (1 stick) butter*
½ *cup sugar*

½ *pound whole, fresh strawberries, washed and drained*
¼ *cup brandy*

Prepare the *crêpes* according to basic *crêpes* directions.

In a chafing dish or copper frying pan melt the butter and sugar and cook until lightly caramelized. Add each *crêpe* and saturate thoroughly with the syrup, several at a time; then remove to a large platter.

Fill each *crêpe* with 2 or 3 strawberries, roll up, and return to the pan. Pour in the brandy, ignite, and spoon the flaming liquid over the *crêpes*. Serve at once.

Soufflés

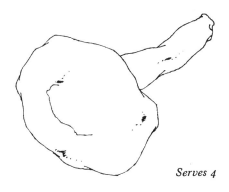

Basic Beer Soufflé

Serves 4

12 *ounces light domestic beer*
⅓ *cup scallion greens or chives,*
  finely chopped
 1 *teaspoon salt*
¼ *teaspoon sugar*

 6 *Tablespoons butter*
⅓ *cup onions, minced*
 6 *Tablespoons all-purpose flour*
  Dash cayenne pepper
 5 *eggs, separated*

Preheat oven to 450 degrees.

Butter bottom and sides of a 1½ quart soufflé dish and dust all over with flour. Set aside.

In a saucepan bring beer, scallion greens or chives, salt, and sugar to a boil. Then set aside to cool.

Meanwhile, in separate saucepan, melt butter until it foams; then add minced onions and sauté until transparent. Add the flour and cayenne pepper and stir briskly until mixture rolls away from sides of pan. Remove from the heat to cool slightly (about 5 minutes). Add egg yolks to dough mixture one at a time, stirring with a wire whisk until they are blended in. Pour in beer mixture and whip until smooth.

Beat egg whites to soft peaks and fold in. Don't overmix. Pour into prepared soufflé dish, filling to 1 inch from top. Place on bottom rack of oven and bake (450 degrees) for 30 minutes.

SUGGESTED FLAVORINGS
Use only half the amount of onions and add about ⅓ cup of any of the following:

Grated cheddar or Parmesan cheese
Chopped tomatoes
Chopped herring
Chopped eggplant
Diced cooked ham

Flaked tuna fish
2 *chopped anchovies*

Basic Soufflé

1 *cup milk*
5 *eggs (at room temperature)*
4 *Tablespoons flour*
3 *Tablespoons softened butter*
   Flavoring: as suggested on
   following pages

Preheat oven to 450 degrees.

Lightly butter a 1½ or 2 quart soufflé dish, dust it with flour, and set aside. Heat the milk in a medium-sized, heavy-bottomed saucepan. Separate the eggs—whites in one bowl and yolks in another. Beat the yolks until lemon-colored and sift the flour into the beaten egg yolks, stirring to a smooth paste. Add about half of the hot milk and all the softened butter and stir until smooth. Then scrape this mixture into the milk remaining in the saucepan and stir constantly over medium heat until the batter thickens. Remove from heat.

At this point, add one of the flavorings suggested, and stir until entirely melted or thoroughly mixed with the batter.

Beat the egg whites until they form soft peaks and add half of the egg whites to the batter, mixing thoroughly, then lightly fold in the remainder. Pour the soufflé batter into the buttered and floured soufflé dish, smoothing over the top with a knife.

Place in oven (450 degrees). After 15 minutes, reduce the temperature to 400 degrees. By this time, the soufflé will have risen over the top of the dish. Insert the tip of a pointed knife around the edge of the soufflé and downward toward the bottom, and cut entirely around. This will permit the soufflé to rise even higher and prevent it from spilling over the sides.

Bake (400 degrees) another 15 minutes or until the top is golden brown. Serve immediately.

Ideas for combinations and surprises include:

Bits of smoked salmon or bacon or anchovy in cheese soufflés or fish soufflés.

Bits of various seafoods in fish soufflés.

Bits of smoked sausage in a beer soufflé.

Bits of mustard fruits in a ham soufflé.

Curry powder or bits of curried chicken in a soufflé.

In dessert soufflés, try various kinds of fruit, liqueur, or concentrated fruit juice, jams, etc., singly and in combinations.

Suggestions for Entrée Soufflés

LOBSTER
½ cup cooked lobster, finely chopped

SHRIMP
6 medium cooked shrimp, finely chopped

RED CAVIAR
3 Tablespoons red caviar

CHEESE
4 ounces grated Gruyère cheese

ONION
1 large onion, chopped very fine and sautéed lightly in butter

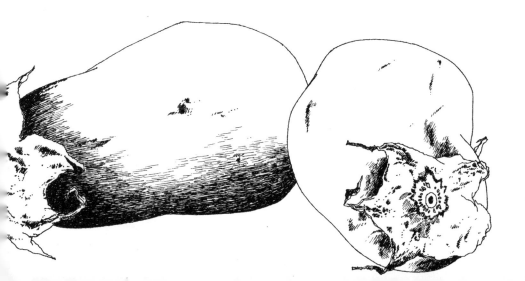

Suggestions for Sweet Soufflés

In each of the following, combine the flavorings first and then stir into
the soufflé batter.

GRAND MARNIER
2 *ounces Grand Marnier*
4 *Tablespoons sugar*
  Grated peel of ½ orange

CHOCOLATE
2 *ounces semi-sweet chocolate, melted*
4 *Tablespoons sugar*

CHOCOLATE PEPPERMINT
2 *ounces semi-sweet chocolate, melted*
1 *ounce crème de menthe*
4 *Tablespoons sugar*

LEMON
  Grated rinds of 2 lemons
1 *teaspoon lemon juice*
4 *Tablespoons sugar*

ROTHSCHILD
1 *ounce assorted candied fruit, finely chopped*
4 *Tablespoons sugar*

STRAWBERRY
½ *cup fresh strawberries, chopped and drained*
4 *Tablespoons sugar*

CHERRY
½ *cup fresh cherries, pitted and coarsely chopped*
4 *Tablespoons sugar*

Vanilla Sauce for Dessert Soufflé

4 *ounces vanilla ice cream*   ¼ *cup heavy cream, whipped*
  (½ cup)   1 *ounce Grand Marnier*

Let ice cream stand at room temperature to soften (about 10 minutes)
then fold in whipped cream and Grand Marnier.

Chocolate Sauce for Dessert Soufflé

4 *ounces chocolate ice cream*   ¼ *cup heavy cream, whipped*
  (½ cup)   1 *ounce crème de cacao, dark*

Let ice cream stand at room temperature to soften (approximately 10
minutes) then fold in whipped cream and crème de cacao.

Fish
and Seafood

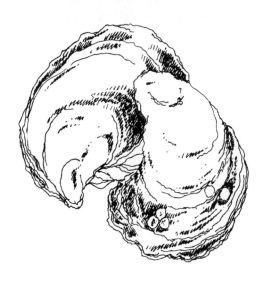

Properly cooked, fish can be the simplest and yet most delicious of all dishes. To me, the real test of a good cook or a fine restaurant is how the fish is prepared.

There are 30,000 varieties of fish, and the United States, with its fantastic miles of seacoasts, its gulfs, lakes, and rivers, enjoys perhaps more variety than any other country. Don't let this wealth of variety intimidate you. On the contrary, take advantage of it, and when you're planning to cook fish, look first for a local product and substitute it for the particular kind called for in one of the recipes that follow.

The most important point about fish is freshness. A fresh local fish, whatever it may be, will be better than the most prestigious fish frozen or flown in far from home waters several days old. If you live far from the seacoast, you can still enjoy the best fish dishes in all their glory. For many of the best salt water fish have fresh water counterparts that are not too different, such as bass, whitefish, trout, sturgeon, sole, salmon, perch, even smelts and herring.

But in substituting, remember that for cooking purposes, the fish that are classified as fatty are those that have 5% or more fat content; and lean, those that have less than 5% fat. Lean fish should be fried or sautéed and served with a richer sauce. Fatty fish should be baked or grilled and served with a non-fatty sauce.

Following is a list of the most commonly available fish in each category. If in doubt, check with your fish dealer.

Fish

Seafood

Fish

FATTY	Striped Bass	Sea Herring	Pompano	Whitefish
	Butterfish	Mackerel	Salmon	
	Catfish (or	(all kinds)	Shad	
	Bullhead)	Mullet	Lake Trout	
LEAN	Bluefish	Haddock	Rosefish	Sucker
	Buffalo	Hake	Porgy	Swordfish
	Carp	Halibut	Red Snapper	Weakfish
	Codfish	Lake Herring	Sea Bass	Whiting
	Crevalle	Ling Cod	Sea Trout	Wolf Fish
	Croaker	Pike	Sheepshead	
	Flounder	Pollack	Skate	
	Grouper	Rockfish	Spot	

There is also an in-between class, made up of fish such as smelts and perch, which can be included in either group.

The most important points about fish cookery are: never overcook the fish, and always serve and eat it immediately after it is cooked.

Trout *Bleu, Sauce Mousseline*

1 *live trout per person*
4 *quarts water*
1 *cup white vinegar*
1 *Tablespoon salt*

1 *small onion*
1 *bayleaf*
Sauce mousseline
(see page 87)

GARNISH
  Lemon wedges   *Parsley*

Stun the trout with a blow on the back of the neck. Clean and gut thoroughly, leaving on head and tail, and place in cold water.

Prepare a bouillon by bringing to a boil the water mixed with the vinegar and salt, onion and bayleaf. Place the trout in the bouillon and quickly turn off the heat or remove the pot from the heat. The trout will continue to cook. Leave it in the water for 3 minutes.

Remove the fish and serve on a hot plate immediately after it has been taken from the bouillon, with *sauce mousseline* on the side and garnished with wedges of lemon. Or if you prefer, remove the skin before serving and cover the trout with *sauce mousseline*, garnishing with wedges of lemon and sprigs of parsley.

VARIATION
Serve the trout as above, with brown butter and wedges of lemon.

Brook Trout in Beer Batter   *Serves 4*

I suggest brook trout here, but this recipe can be used for any small fish you may catch: perch, smelts, etc.

Oil for deep frying
4 *fresh brook trout*, 10 *to*12 *ounces each*
  Juice of 1 *lemon*
1 *cup flour sifted with* 1 *teaspoon salt*
  Beer batter (*see page 373*)
  Sauce Gribiche (*see page 92*)
  Lemon wedges

Start oil heating for deep frying to 375 degrees.

Clean the trout thoroughly, leaving on head and tail, and wash under running water. Sprinkle the inside of each trout with lemon juice and dredge inside and out heavily with seasoned flour. Hold the fish by the head and dip it into the beer batter, coating all around. Drop it into pre-heated oil (375 degrees) and fry until crisp and golden brown—from 6 to 8 minutes.

Serve the trout hot, garnished with wedges of lemon and individual bowls of *sauce Gribiche* on the side.

Mousse of Fresh Trout

Serves 4 to 6

1¼ *pounds of fresh trout, bones and skin removed*
½ *head Boston lettuce, blanched 1 minute in salted water*
¼ *pound butter*
½ *cup heavy cream*

2 *whole eggs*
3 *egg yolks*
1 *teaspoon salt*
　Pinch pepper
　Sauce mousseline
　(see page 87)

Preheat oven to 375 degrees.

If your fish man has not done so, with a sharp knife cut off the head and tail of the trout, and remove the skin. Wash thoroughly. Make a cut down the backbone and carefully begin to cut away the flesh from the bones, one side at a time, working from the backbone out toward the smaller bones.

Drain the lettuce and blot it dry. Grind it along with the flesh of the trout and the ¼ pound of butter, using the fine blade of the meat grinder. Transfer this mixture to the blender, add the cream, eggs, egg yolks, and seasoning, and purée until smooth. Pour the puréed mixture into an oiled mold (about 1 quart size) and place the mold in a roasting pan. Pour boiling water into the pan until it reaches one third from the top of the mold.

Bake the mousse uncovered (375 degrees) for about 30 to 35 minutes at most, or until it is firm. (Test by inserting a knife or fork in center.) If it comes out dry, the mousse is done. Turn mold over onto a warm platter. Pass the *sauce mousseline* separately.

Fish and Chips

Serves 4

THE FISH

Use cod or striped bass, halibut, perch or catfish—about 6 ounces of fish per person—cut into 2 or 3 pieces per serving. If you buy boneless fillets of any firm-fleshed white fish, which usually weigh about 8 to 10 ounces, get 3 for 4 servings.

For interesting variety use more than one type of fish at the same meal.

1½ *pounds fish*	1 *cup flour*
6 *Tablespoons lemon juice*	1 *teaspoon salt*
1 *medium onion, grated*	¼ *teaspoon pepper*
8 *medium size potatoes*	1 *teaspoon paprika*
Oil for deep frying	*Beer batter (see page 373)*

Place the fish in the lemon juice, sprinkle with grated onion, and marinate for 30 minutes.

THE CHIPS

While it is, of course, possible to serve "store bought" potato chips or to use frozen French fries, a really fine dish of fish and chips deserves freshly made French fried potatoes. Start them while the fish is marinating.

Wash and peel potatoes. Cut into strips ⅜ inch thick and three inches long (or cut with French fry cutter). Rinse in cold water and drain thoroughly.

THE FRYING

Heat deep fat fryer to 375 degrees.

First pre-fry the potatoes by filling the basket two-thirds full and immersing slowly in the hot fat. Shake the basket occasionally to keep the potatoes from sticking. Continue to deep fry until potatoes are nearly tender. (This means when a test piece yields slightly when squeezed with fingers.) Drain well and spread on a pan lined with paper towels.

Now sift the flour with the salt, pepper, and paprika onto a flat dish. Dredge the fish in the seasoned flour. Then coat the fish thoroughly in the prepared beer batter. Deep fry the coated fish in the same oil (the heat should have returned to 375 degrees) until golden brown and crisp. Place on paper towels to get rid of excess oil, and keep warm.

Allow a few minutes for oil to reach 375 degrees again. Then return the potatoes to the fry basket in small quantities and fry until golden brown. Drain again.

PRESENTATION

Serve fish and chips together, garnished, if you like, with lemon wedges.

Fresh Salmon Steak Baked in Red Wine with Grapes

Serves 4

4 *salmon steaks, 8 to 10 ounces*
  each
1 *teaspoon salt*
¼ *teaspoon pepper*
1 *Tablespoon butter, melted*
3 *Tablespoons shallots (or*
  onion), finely chopped
½ *cup dry red wine*
  Juice of ½ lemon
½ *teaspoon cornstarch dissolved*
  in 1 Tablespoon cold water
½ *cup seedless grapes*

Preheat oven to 400 degrees.

Butter an ovenproof baking dish large enough to hold the 4 salmon steaks. Season the steaks with salt and pepper and brush with the melted butter. Place in oven (400 degrees) for 5 minutes.

In the meantime, prepare the sauce by combining the shallots, red wine, and lemon juice in a small saucepan. Bring to a boil and simmer over medium heat for 5 minutes. Stir in the dissolved cornstarch to thicken sauce. Then pour the sauce over the fish.

Return to the oven for 10 minutes. Add the grapes during the last 5 minutes of baking time and serve hot.

Striped Bass Baked in White Wine and Cream

Serves 4 to 6

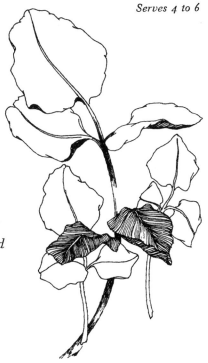

  4 *to 6 pounds striped bass*
  1 *teaspoon salt*
¼ *pound (1 stick) butter, melted*
    Juice of two lemons
  2 *cups dry white wine*
½ *onion, grated*
  1 *carrot, chopped*
  1 *stalk celery, chopped*
¼ *teaspoon thyme*
1½ *cups heavy cream*
  1 *Tablespoon chives, finely chopped*
  1 *Tablespoon parsley, finely chopped*
½ *teaspoon pepper*
  1 *Tablespoon butter*
  1 *Tablespoon flour*

Preheat oven to 375 degrees.

Clean the bass inside; leave the head on but trim off fins and tail. Scale the fish, but do not remove the skin. Do not bone. Score the outside of the bass with a sharp knife. Rub salt inside. Place the whole bass in a shallow baking pan. Pour the melted butter over the fish, covering inside and outside. Combine the lemon juice, wine, grated onion, chopped carrot and celery, and thyme, and pour over the fish. Cover the pan tightly with cooking foil. Bake (375 degrees) for 35 minutes.

Remove the foil and carefully transfer the bass to a heated serving platter and keep warm.

Strain the pan juices into a saucepan. Stir in the cream and over high heat boil to reduce by one third (to about 2½ cups). Add the chives, parsley, and pepper. Combine the butter and flour into a paste and in small bits stir into the sauce over medium heat until the sauce is thick and smooth. Pour over the fish and serve immediately.

Stuffed Baby Flounder, Oyster Sauce   *Serves 6*

Baby flounder filled with a delicate forcemeat or *quenelle* stuffing, then lightly poached and covered with a sauce of wine and oysters is a fish course for a very special dinner. Most of the preparation may be done in advance, by preparing the *quenelle* stuffing, filling the flounders, and keeping them at room temperature until time for poaching. The sauce may be made in advance and reheated over simmering water. Buy whole flounders, not the usual filets.

7 *baby flounders, 14 to 16 ounces each (5 for serving, one for quenelles)*	12 *fresh oysters*
	½ *cup heavy cream*
	White wine sauce (see page 81)
Recipe for quenelles of sole (see above), using filets of one flounder in place of sole	1 *Tablespoon parsley, finely chopped*
2 *cups dry white wine and 1 cup water or fish stock, heated*	

Preheat oven to 375 degrees.

Trim the flounders of skin, head, and tail, wash under running water and blot dry. With a sharp knife make an incision along the backbone of one side of each fish and cut the flesh away from the bone all the way to the outside edge, leaving a pocket on each side of the flounder (the bone is not removed).

Fill each pocket with as much of the *quenelle* mixture as it will hold. Lay the filled flounders flat on a baking pan. Pour the heated white wine and water or fish stock over them and poach, covered with foil, in oven (375 degrees) for 12 minutes.

In the meantime, purée in the blender the oysters and cream. Transfer flounders to a heated serving platter. Retain poaching liquid, and use as the stock in preparing the white wine sauce. Combine the puréed oysters with the white wine sauce.

Serve the flounders covered with the oyster sauce and sprinkled with finely chopped parsley.

Smelts with Fresh Asparagus, *Mornay*   *Serves 6*

6 *large smelts*
11 *stalks fresh asparagus, trimmed and cooked (If fresh is not available, use canned or frozen, cooked asparagus.)*
1 *Tablespoon unsalted butter*
3 *ounces dry white wine*

Juice of ½ lemon
2 *Tablespoons heavy cream*
2 *egg yolks*
Salt and pepper
¼ *cup bread crumbs*
¼ *cup grated Parmesan cheese*

Preheat oven to 375 degrees.

Pull out backbone of smelts or have fish man do it. Sprinkle lightly with salt and pepper. Insert one large stalk of cooked asparagus in each fish. Place in baking dish with butter, wine, and lemon juice. Bake (375 degrees) for 15 minutes or until golden brown.

Pour the juices from the baking dish into the blender. Add the heavy cream, egg yolks, remaining 5 asparagus stalks, salt, and pepper, and purée the mixture until smooth. Pour over the cooked fish. Sprinkle bread crumbs and grated Parmesan cheese on top. Place under broiler and brown lightly.

Quenelle of Sole with Sauce of White Wine and Avocado
Serves 3 to 5 (20 to 24 quenelles)

In most people's minds the *quenelle* of fish is one of those dishes to be attempted only by chefs with great culinary skill. Or if they have tried various recipes for *quenelles* they have been discouraged by finding the dough disintegrating in the water. I urge you to try again. With my recipe, these *quenelles* will hold together and float to the top of the water, feathery light. Served with my sauce of white wine, cream, and avocado, on a pile of golden rice, you will have a colorful and memorable dish.

16 *to* 18 *ounces sole, skinned*
    and boned (or flounder)
½ *head Boston lettuce*
1 *egg*
3 *egg yolks*

¼ *cup melted butter*
½ *teaspoon salt*
¼ *teaspoon pepper*
¼ *teaspoon savory*
¼ *cup heavy cream*

PREPARATION

Blot the pieces of sole until thoroughly dry. Poach the lettuce in boiling water for 1 minute; drain and blot dry. Put the sole and lettuce through the meat grinder (fine blade), then place the mixture in the blender and add the egg and egg yolks, melted butter, salt, pepper, savory, and cream. Purée until smooth, transfer to a mixing bowl and chill for at least 1 hour. This mixture may be prepared some hours in advance.

Fill a large saucepan three-quarters full of lightly salted water, and bring to a boil. Reduce the heat to simmer. Wet 2 tablespoons in the hot water, scoop out a heaping mixture of the *quenelle* mixture and use the other spoon to scrape it off into the simmering water. Wet the spoons each time. Simmer for 7 to 10 minutes, or until the *quenelles* rise to the top. Leave them in the water, but remove the pan from direct fire and keep water warm. When ready to serve, remove the *quenelles* with a slotted spoon and drain.

SAUCE

2 *cups white wine sauce*
  (see page 81)
1 *ripe avocado*

Juice of ½ *lemon*
½ *cup heavy cream*

Pour the white wine sauce (page 81) into the blender. Peel the avocado, remove the pit and cut into pieces and place in the blender. Add the lemon juice and cream and blend until smooth. Transfer to a saucepan. Reheat but do not boil.

PRESENTATION

Serve the *quenelles* either on a large heated serving platter over a bed of rice (see rice recipes pages 294–7) covered with some of the delicate sauce of white wine and avocado, or arrange two *quenelles* per person in similar fashion on individual plates. Use it as a main course—it is rather a lot for an appetizer—and pass the rest of the sauce in a sauceboat.

Rolled Filet of Sole Filled with Crabmeat   *Serves 4*

4 or 8 filets of sole, depending
    on size
½ pound crabmeat, picked over
    to remove any small shells
2 Tablespoons butter, melted
2 Tablespoons shallots (or
    onions), finely chopped
4 ounces champagne (½ cup)
    (or any dry white wine)

½ cup heavy cream
    Juice of ½ lemon
2 egg yolks
¼ cup heavy cream, for sauce
½ teaspoon cornstarch dissolved
    in 1 Tablespoon cold water

Preheat oven to 375 degrees.

Rinse the filets of sole, spread them out flat, and cover each with a layer of crabmeat. Roll the filets and fasten with a toothpick. Pour the melted butter into a shallow ovenproof dish, add the rolled filets, placing them side by side, and sprinkle the shallots over them. Pour the champagne, ½ cup of cream, and lemon juice over the fish and bake (375 degrees) for 10 minutes. Transfer the filets to a serving dish and keep warm.

Beat the egg yolks lightly with the ¼ cup heavy cream, then pour the liquid in which the filets were cooked into the egg and cream mixture. Bind with the dissolved cornstarch. Put the filets back into the baking dish, pour the sauce over them, and return to the oven for 10 minutes.

Filet of Sole Poached in White Wine with Lobster Sauce

Serves 4

Combining the fragile texture of sole with the distinctive flavor and aroma of lobster produces an elegant fish course. If you have already made lobster sauce and have stored or frozen it (as suggested on page 146), this delicious fish course is quickly and easily prepared.

4 *filets of sole or flounder*	½ *cup heavy cream*
3 *Tablespoons melted butter*	1½ *cups lobster sauce*
1 *Tablespoon grated onion*	*(see page 146)*
1 *cup dry white wine*	

Preheat oven to 450 degrees.

Wash the filets and blot them dry. Fold them from each end to the center and place them in a small, shallow ovenproof dish. Pour the melted butter and sprinkle the grated onion over the filets; add the white wine and stir in the cream. Cover the casserole with cooking foil and bake (375 degrees) for 15 minutes.

Carefully remove the poached filets to a serving dish and keep warm in the oven. Pour the pan juices into a small saucepan and, over high heat, reduce the liquid to one third its original amount. Lower heat to simmer, stir in the lobster sauce and heat through. Pour the sauce over the filets and serve at once.

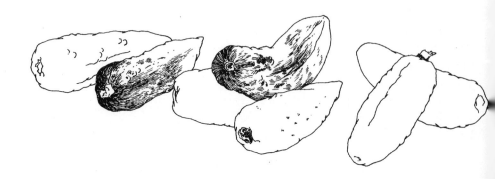

Seafood

Stewed Lobster Jennings   *Serves 4 to 6*

This hearty main course is named after a famous Long Island lobster expert. It is best made with fresh live lobster, unless you already have lobster sauce on hand.

NOTE: If you start with a live lobster, boil for 15 minutes in enough water or court bouillon to cover. Then split the lobster and clean by removing the sand sacs and intestines.

1 *pound cooked lobster meat, cut in 1-inch pieces*
½ *onion, finely chopped*
4 *Tablespoons butter*
4 *ripe tomatoes (about 1¼ pounds), peeled, seeded, and diced*
3 *Tablespoons brandy*
3 *Tablespoons dry sherry*
¼ *cup dry white wine*
½ *cup lobster sauce (see page 146) (if you use fresh lobsters,*

remove the meat and use the shells to make the sauce.)
½ *teaspoon cornstarch dissolved in 1 Tablespoon water*
¼ *cup heavy cream, whipped Dash Pernod (an anise-flavored liqueur)*

Remove meat from lobsters and prepare sauce according to lobster sauce recipe.

Sauté the onion in butter until transparent, add the tomatoes and lobster, pour in the brandy, sherry, and white wine, and the lobster sauce. Bring to a boil and simmer over medium heat for 10 minutes. Bind with the dissolved cornstarch. The recipe may be prepared to this point in advance and reheated just before serving.

Combine the whipped cream and Pernod and fold into the lobster stew just before serving. Rice is a splendid accompaniment to this rich lobster stew.

Lobster Sauce

Yield 1 pint

Lobster sauce is a wonderful way to make use of the shells when you
have had lobsters. It is called for in a number of recipes, especially
quenelles, and is excellent as a sauce on any salt water fish. The sauce
may be refrigerated for a limited time or frozen.

3 *pounds lobster shells*
4 *Tablespoons butter*
1 *Tablespoon flour*
1 *teaspoon paprika*
½ *onion, finely chopped*
2 *Tablespoons tomato purée*
⅓ *cup dry white wine*
1 *ounce brandy*
  Pinch thyme
2 *cups fish stock (see page 46) or water*
  Juice of 1 lemon

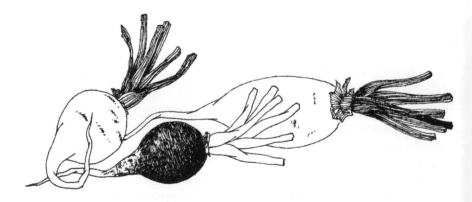

Cut up the lobster shells and put them through the coarse blade of the
meat grinder. Melt the butter in a saucepan, blend in the flour, and
add the remainder of the ingredients. Simmer, covered, for 1 hour.
Strain the sauce through a fine sieve.

Lobster Thermidor with Avocado   *Serves 4*

You may serve this colorful thermidor in two ways: in individual lobster shells, ramekins, or scallop shells, or as a main course in one large casserole.

2 *live lobsters, about 2 pounds each*
4 *Tablespoons butter*
1 *Tablespoon shallots (or onion), finely chopped*
10 *button mushroom caps, diced or chopped*
2 *ripe, medium tomatoes, peeled, seeded, and chopped*
¼ *cup dry sherry*
1 *teaspoon salt*

¼ *teaspoon pepper*
¼ *teaspoon paprika*
   Pinch dry English mustard
1 *cup* béchamel *sauce (see page 81)*
2 *Tablespoons Pernod (an anise-flavored liqueur)*
1 *avocado cut in ½-inch pieces*
½ *cup heavy cream, whipped*

Preheat oven to 450 degrees.

Drop the lobsters in boiling water and cook them for 15 minutes in enough water or court bouillon to cover.

Drain the lobsters and split them. Discard the sand sacs and intestines. Remove the coral and green and put aside. Remove all the lobster meat, including the meat from the claws, and cut into ½-inch pieces. Reserve the shells and wash them for filling later.

Melt the butter in a large frying pan, add the shallots, mushrooms, tomatoes, and sauté for 3 minutes, stirring frequently. Add the sherry, salt, pepper, paprika, mustard, only ½ cup of the *béchamel* sauce, and the lobster pieces. Mix well and simmer for another 5 minutes.

Press the coral and green through a fine sieve and mix into the sauce. Stir in the Pernod and gently fold in the avocado. Fill the lobster shells with the mixture. Combine the remaining *béchamel* sauce with the whipped cream and cover the top of each half lobster.

Place the filled lobsters in a shallow pan and bake (450 degrees) for 15 minutes or until golden brown on top. Serve at once.

Crabmeat *Impériale Gratinée*   *Serves 4 to 6*

½ cup milk

¼ cup dry sherry

1 teaspoon dry English mustard

½ Tablespoon shallots (or onion), finely minced

½ Tablespoon green pepper, finely chopped

½ Tablespoon pimiento, finely chopped

½ Tablespoon cornstarch dissolved in about 2 Tablespoons cold water

Juice of ½ lemon

2 Tablespoons hollandaise sauce (see page 86) (or 2 Tablespoons mayonnaise beaten with an egg yolk)

1 pound crabmeat, fresh or canned

¼ cup bread crumbs

Salt to taste

Preheat oven to 400 degrees.

In a saucepan over medium heat combine the milk, sherry, mustard, shallots, green pepper, and pimiento, bring to a boil and simmer for 3 minutes. Stir in the cornstarch and lemon juice. Remove from heat and add hollandaise and the crabmeat. Mix well and transfer to a buttered ovenproof baking dish.

Sprinkle the bread crumbs over the surface and bake (400 degrees) for 15 minutes, or until golden brown. Serve hot.

Baby Lobster with Crabmeat Stuffing   *Serves 4*

2 *lobsters, about* 1½ *pounds each, uncooked*
½ *cup* béchamel *sauce (see page 81)*
¼ *cup hollandaise sauce (see page 86) (or 2 Tablespoons mayonnaise)*

4 *Tablespoons butter, melted*
8 *ounces crabmeat (canned or cooked)*
½ *teaspoon dry English mustard*
Juice ½ *lemon*
1 *teaspoon salt*

Split the uncooked lobsters in half. Remove the sand sacs and intestines. Wash. Remove the coral and green, and press them through a fine sieve into a mixing bowl with the *béchamel* sauce, hollandaise sauce, melted butter, crabmeat, dry mustard, lemon juice, and salt. Mix well and fill the cavities in the four half-lobsters, heaping up with filling.

All of the foregoing may be done well in advance.

Preheat oven to 450 degrees.

Bake the stuffed lobsters (450 degrees) for 7 to 10 minutes and serve immediately.

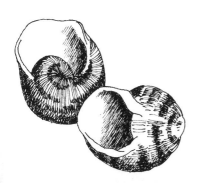

New England Seafood Casserole

Serves 4 to 6

½ *pound bay scallops*
½ *pound raw shrimp*
1 *Tablespoon butter*
2 *Tablespoons onion, finely chopped*
2 *ounces (¼ cup) dry sherry*
2 *ounces (¼ cup) clam juice*
1 *teaspoon salt*
  Pinch pepper
  Juice of ¼ lemon

1 *teaspoon paprika*
1 *teaspoon dry English mustard*
½ *pound crabmeat*
1½ *teaspoons cornstarch dissolved in about 2 Tablespoons water*
2 *egg yolks*
2 *Tablespoons heavy or light cream*
4 *Tablespoons mayonnaise*

Preheat oven to 400 degrees.

Wash the scallops thoroughly under running water to remove any sand. Peel, de-vein, and wash the shrimp. Dry the scallops and shrimp on a kitchen towel.

Melt the butter in a heated frying pan and add the scallops, shrimp, onions, sherry, clam juice, salt, pepper, and lemon juice. Stir in the paprika and dry mustard. Reduce the heat to medium and cook for 5 minutes. Remove the scallops and shrimp with a slotted spoon to a shallow ovenproof dish and add the crabmeat.

Retain the juices over medium heat and bind with the dissolved cornstarch. Remove from heat. Beat the egg yolks, stir in the cream and mayonnaise and fold into the warm sauce. Pour the thickened sauce over the scallops, shrimp, and crab, and bake (400 degrees) for about 10 minutes or until golden brown.

Baked Clams

6 to 8 fresh clams per person
Recipe for garlic butter (see
page 14), 2 teaspoons per clam

½ cup bread crumbs

Preheat oven to 450 degrees.

Open the clams and discard one shell. Pour off the liquid. Loosen the clams (but do not remove), and fill the shells around the clams with garlic butter. Sprinkle the surface lightly with bread crumbs. Place the clams on a baking sheet and bake (450 degrees) for 6 to 7 minutes or until the butter is hot but not sizzling. Serve at once.

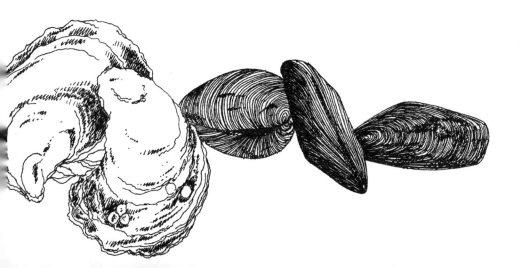

Poultry

Chicken   Turkey   Duckling   Squab

A "bird and bottle" is the traditional European and early American idea of a fine meal. But although America leads the world not only in quantity but in quality of poultry produced, our usual method for cooking birds is simply to roast or to fry them. However, our enjoyment can be greatly increased with a little more imagination in preparation and serving. Even a roasted bird can be enhanced with variations in the garniture.

Here are some of my favorites, which are also the favorites of many of my chef friends.

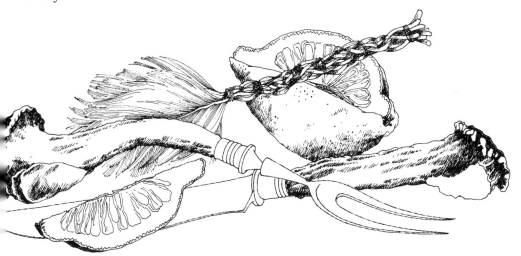

Chicken

Turkey

Duckling

Squab

Chicken

Sautéed Chicken with Tarragon *Serves 4*

While the unique flavor of fresh tarragon adds a great deal to sauces, meats, and salads, it has a special affinity for chicken. In this recipe I recommend that you make an effort to obtain fresh tarragon. It is not hard to grow in a small garden plot or even in window boxes.

  2 *frying chickens (about*
    2 pounds each)
½ *cup flour, seasoned with 1 tea-*
    spoon salt and ¼ teaspoon
    pepper
  4 *Tablespoons butter*
  4 *Tablespoons fresh tarragon,*
    finely chopped (or 2 Table-
    spoons dry)
¼ *cup dry white wine*
  2 *Tablespoons brandy*

Preheat oven to 450 degrees.

Split the chickens in half, wipe
thoroughly with damp towel, then dry.
Dredge the chickens evenly in the seasoned flour.
Melt the butter in a large frying pan and sauté
the chickens over medium heat until golden
on both sides—about 30 minutes.

    Remove the chicken from the pan and roll in the fresh tarragon. Blend wine and brandy in a small bowl. Place the chicken halves in a buttered ovenproof serving dish and bake (450 degrees) for 8 minutes, basting several times with the blended wine and brandy. Serve hot or cold.

Breast of Chicken *Paprikash*   *Serves 4*

½ cup flour
 1 teaspoon salt
 2 chicken breasts, boned and
    halved
 3 Tablespoons butter
1½ Tablespoons paprika
 2 cups heavy cream

 3 ounces dry sherry
½ clove garlic, minced
⅛ teaspoon caraway seeds
    Peel of ¼ lemon, finely
    minced
    Juice of 1 lemon

Sift flour and salt together. Dredge the chicken breasts in the flour and salt. Melt the butter in a large frying pan and sauté the chicken on both sides until light gold. Sprinkle the chicken on both sides with paprika, pour in the cream and sherry, add the minced garlic, caraway seeds and minced lemon peel, and simmer over medium heat for 25 minutes, stirring frequently.

Just before serving, add the lemon juice. Add additional salt if necessary.

Breast of Chicken Stuffed with Forcemeat and Mushrooms   *Serves 4 to 6*

2½ to 3 pound whole chicken
 2 slices crusty bread, soaked in
    milk
 6 sprigs fresh parsley
¼ pound mushrooms, sliced
 1 egg, beaten
 1 teaspoon salt
¼ teaspoon each of pepper
    and savory
 2 Tablespoons melted butter
¼ cup dry white wine

 1 cup chicken stock (see page
    43) (or use rich canned
    chicken broth)
 1 Tablespoon tomato paste
½ onion, finely diced
 1 stalk celery, finely diced
 1 carrot, finely diced
½ cup heavy or light cream
½ teaspoon cornstarch dis-
    solved in 1 Tablespoon cold
    water

Using a sharp knife, remove the skin from the chicken. Next, cut off the wings, being careful to cut through the joint at the breast. Cut off the legs at the thigh joint; cut through the rib bones to remove the back (poultry shears are best for this). Then, cut along the breast bone and carefully remove the breast meat on each side. Remove all of the meat from the other bones. Use the skin, bones, and giblets to make chicken stock.

Put the chicken meat (except the breasts) through the fine blade of the meat grinder with the bread, parsley, and one third of the mushrooms. In a large bowl combine the ground chicken mixture with the beaten egg, salt, pepper, and savory.

Preheat oven to 400 degrees.

Lay the chicken breasts out flat and carefully cut into the edge of each one to make a pocket. Fill each pocket with the forcemeat mixture leaving enough room to pull the breast over and hold stuffing in place. Transfer the stuffed chicken breasts to a buttered pan or ovenproof casserole, coat each with melted butter and bake (400 degrees) for about 35 minutes. Remove the breasts from the pan and keep warm.

SAUCE

Stir the white wine into the pan juices, add chicken stock, tomato paste, and diced vegetables. Cover and cook for 20 minutes over medium heat and then pour into the blender and purée.

Strain the sauce into a saucepan. Sauté the remaining mushrooms in a little butter until soft, about 5 minutes, and add to the sauce. Stir in the cream and bind with the dissolved cornstarch. Pour the sauce over the stuffed chicken breasts and serve.

Stuffed Breast of Chicken in Champagne *Serves 4 to 6*

A luxurious variation of Breast of Chicken with Forcemeat and Mushrooms (see page 158) is this other recipe for breasts of chicken, stuffed, then basted with champagne and served with a smooth hollandaise-flavored sauce.

Prepare the chicken breasts according to the preceding recipe, but omit mushrooms.

When the breasts are stuffed and ready for the oven, sprinkle lightly with flour.

S A U C E

2 *Tablespoons butter, melted*	1 *carrot, finely chopped*
8 *ounces (1 cup) champagne*	3 *Tablespoons hollandaise sauce*
½ *onion, finely chopped*	*(see page 86)*
1 *stalk celery, finely chopped*	

Preheat oven to 400 degrees.

Place the stuffed chicken breasts in an ovenproof casserole, cover with melted butter and pour the champagne over them. Roast (400 degrees) for about 35 minutes, basting frequently with the pan juices.

Remove the chicken breasts and keep warm. Place the casserole over medium heat, add the chopped vegetables, cover and cook for 20 minutes. Pour the contents of the casserole into a blender and purée until smooth. Strain into a saucepan and just before serving stir in the hollandaise sauce. Pour over the chicken breasts and serve hot.

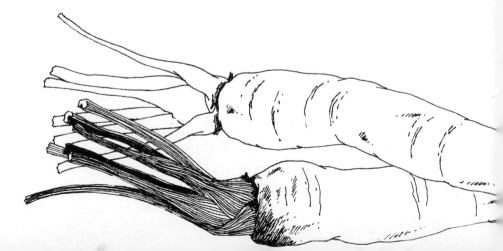

Breast of Chicken with Ham and Swiss Cheese, *Cordon Bleu*

Serves 4

2 *chicken breasts, halved*
¼ *cup flour seasoned with 1 tea-spoon salt and ¼ teaspoon pepper*
3 *Tablespoons butter*
2 *shallots (or 1 Tablespoon onion), finely chopped*

3 *Tablespoons dry white wine*
4 *slices prosciutto ham*
4 *thin slices Swiss cheese*
½ *teaspoon cornstarch dissolved in 1 Tablespoon water*
2 *egg yolks*
¼ *cup heavy cream*

Preheat oven to 375 degrees.

Dredge the chicken breasts in seasoned flour. Melt the butter in a pan (one that can go into the oven), add the chopped shallots, the wine, and the chicken breasts and sauté until golden brown on all sides—about 20 minutes.

Remove from fire and cut the breasts away from the bone carefully. Now cut a pocket into each chicken breast and put in the ham and cheese.

Return the filled chicken breasts to the pan and bake (375 degrees) for 15 minutes. Transfer the chicken breasts to a serving dish and keep warm.

Place pan with cooking juices on top of stove over medium heat and stir in the dissolved cornstarch. Beat egg yolks and cream together, and beat in a little of the hot liquid. Stir back into the pan juices and simmer until sauce is smooth and slightly thickened. Pour the sauce over the chicken breasts and serve.

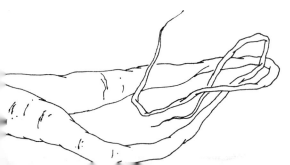

Breast of Chicken à la King

Serves 4

2 *chicken breasts, halved*
1 *cup chicken stock (see page 43) (or use rich canned chicken broth)*

½ *cup dry white wine*
½ *onion, coarsely chopped*
1 *teaspoon salt*
¼ *teaspoon pepper*

Place the chicken breasts in a saucepan, add the chicken stock, wine, chopped onion, salt, and pepper. Bring to a boil, lower heat, and simmer for 20 minutes. Remove the chicken breasts, cool and remove the bones and skin. Strain the stock and reserve for sauce.

SAUCE

1 *green pepper*
2 *Tablespoons butter*
3 *Tablespoons flour*
1 *cup chicken stock (from above —if there is not sufficient left over, add enough hot water to make 1 cup)*

2 *Tablespoons heavy cream*
1 *red pimiento, cut in ½-inch squares*
Juice of ½ lemon
¼ *cup dry sherry*
½ *cup hollandaise sauce (see page 86)*

Steam the green pepper in a colander over boiling water until tender; peel, core, and cut into ½-inch squares.

Melt the butter in the saucepan, add the flour and stir until smooth. Gradually add the hot chicken stock.

Stir in the cream, green pepper pieces, and pimiento. Return the chicken to the sauce, add the lemon juice and sherry, and just before serving fold in the hollandaise sauce.

Breast of Chicken on Spinach, *Mornay*   *Serves 4*

2 *chicken breasts, boned and*   1 *clove garlic, peeled and minced*
  halved   1 *teaspoon salt*
3 *Tablespoons butter*   ¼ *teaspoon pepper*
2 *pounds fresh spinach*
3 *Tablespoons butter*
½ *onion, finely chopped*

Preheat oven to 250 degrees.

Sauté the chicken breasts lightly in butter (about 6 minutes on each side), and slice thinly.

    Pick over the spinach, discarding yellowed leaves. Break off and discard stems and rinse several times in cold water to remove all traces of sand. Cook the spinach in a large covered saucepan with ½ cup water for 10 minutes. Drain in a colander and press out all the moisture. Chop the spinach coarsely. Melt the butter and sauté the spinach with the minced onion and garlic, stirring, for 3 minutes. Transfer the spinach to a heated ovenproof serving platter. Lay the cooked sliced chicken over the spinach, season with salt and pepper, and place in oven (250 degrees) to keep warm while you prepare the sauce.

SAUCE
1 *cup* béchamel *sauce*   3 *Tablespoons Parmesan cheese,*
  (see page 81)   *grated*
4 *Tablespoons hollandaise sauce*   1 *teaspoon paprika*
  (see page 86)
¼ *cup heavy cream, whipped*

Combine the *béchamel* sauce, hollandaise sauce, and whipped cream.

    Remove breasts of chicken from the oven. Turn the oven up to 400 degrees. Spread the sauce over the chicken, sprinkle with Parmesan cheese and paprika. Return to oven and bake (400 degrees) until the surface is golden—approximately 5 minutes.

    Serve at once.

Chicken in Red Wine

Serves 4 to 6

2½ *pound chicken, quartered*
 1 *teaspoon salt*
 ¼ *teaspoon pepper*
 1 *cup flour*
 4 *Tablespoons butter*
 8 *shallots (or ½ onion),*
    finely chopped
 ½ *pound mushrooms, thinly*
    sliced
 ¼ *pound pork belly or salt pork,*
    finely diced

   Pinch thyme
 ¼ *teaspoon peppercorns, crushed*
 1 *bayleaf*
 1 *clove garlic, minced*
1½ *cups dry red wine*
 ½ *cup gravy (to improvise*
    gravy see page xiii) or brown
    sauce (see page 79)
 1 *pound pearl onions, peeled*
    (fresh, frozen, or canned)

GARNISH
Triangles of bread sautéed in butter

Season the chicken pieces with salt and pepper, and dust with flour. Melt the butter in a frying pan and sauté the chicken until golden on both sides. Remove the chicken to paper towels to drain.

In a deep saucepan combine the chopped shallots, sliced mushrooms, and diced pork belly, and sauté for 5 minutes. Add the thyme, crushed peppercorns, bayleaf, minced garlic, the chicken pieces, red wine, and gravy, and simmer for 15 minutes. If the onions are uncooked, add them now. Simmer for an additional 45 minutes. If the onions are already cooked, add them 10 minutes before the end of cooking time.

Serve the chicken and sauce garnished with the sautéed triangles of bread.

Casserole of Chicken in Beer   *Serves 4 to 6*

3 *to* 3½ *pound whole roasting chicken*
3 *Tablespoons butter*
1 *teaspoon salt*
1 *onion, finely chopped*
2 *medium carrots, peeled and chopped*
2 *stalks celery, finely chopped*
⅛ *teaspoon marjoram*
½ *teaspoon pepper*
1 *teaspoon salt*
3 *slices bacon*
1 *can light domestic beer (12 ounces)*
  Juice of ½ *lemon*
½ *teaspoon cornstarch dissolved*
  in 1 Tablespoon cold water
  Optional: chicken giblets

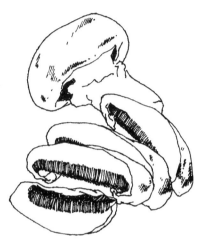

Preheat oven to 400 degrees.

Wash and dry the chicken. Rub inside and out with 1 Tablespoon butter and sprinkle with 1 teaspoon salt. Melt the remaining butter in an oven-proof casserole, add the chopped vegetables, seasonings, and chicken. Sauté over high heat until the chicken is lightly browned on all sides. Cover the breast of the chicken with bacon and roast (400 degrees), uncovered, for 15 minutes. (The giblets may be cooked with the chicken, then chopped fine and added later to the sauce.) Add the beer, cover the casserole, and return to the oven for another 25 minutes, or until the chicken is tender.

Remove the chicken and keep it warm. Strain the pan juices into a saucepan, add the lemon juice, and bind with the dissolved cornstarch. When the sauce is slightly thickened, pour it over the chicken and carve at table.

PRESENTATION
Sautéed button mushrooms and parboiled new potatoes and pearl onions make a splendid accompaniment.

Boiled Chicken in the Pot with Mustard Horseradish Sauce

Serves 4 to 6

3½ *pound whole chicken*	1 *Tablespoon salt*
1 *leek (or 3 or 4 scallions),*	¼ *teaspoon whole peppercorns,*
coarsely chopped	*crushed*
1 *onion, coarsely chopped*	1 *bayleaf*
1 *carrot, coarsely chopped*	¼ *pound fine egg noodles*
1 *stalk celery, coarsely chopped*	

GARNISH
　　1 *Tablespoon each of chives and parsley, finely chopped*

In a deep saucepan, place chicken and chopped leek, onion, carrot, and celery. Add water to cover (about 1½ quarts). Add the salt, crushed peppercorns, and bayleaf, and simmer, covered, for 50 minutes. Remove the chicken, carve into pieces, and keep warm.

　　Strain the liquid and return to the stove. Bring to a boil over high heat and cook for 10 minutes until liquid has been reduced to about half.

MUSTARD HORSERADISH SAUCE

1 *cup chicken broth*	1½ *Tablespoons prepared*
½ *teaspoon cornstarch dissolved*	*mustard*
in 1 Tablespoon cold water	1 *Tablespoon horseradish*

In a small saucepan combine the chicken broth, the dissolved cornstarch, the mustard, and horseradish, and stir until it thickens slightly.

　　Cook the noodles according to package directions, drain, and put them in a large soup tureen or deep serving dish. Pour the reduced chicken cooking liquid over the noodles, top with the chicken pieces and garnish with chopped chives and parsley.

PRESENTATION
Serve the carved chicken pieces and noodles in an individual soup plate with the broth. Serve the mustard horseradish sauce in individual bowls to season each bite of chicken.

Chicken with Truffles and Cream   *Serves 4 to 6*

Boiled chicken with a light creamy sauce is always delicious, but for this recipe I add those fabled French truffles about which so much has been written. There can be no question that these black jewel delicacies of the Périgord impart an unusual flavor. They can be obtained in any gourmet shop in your neighborhood or by mail order, and, although they are wildly expensive, they are worth the occasional treat. The French call this dish *"demi-deuil"*—Chicken in Half-Mourning—because the chicken is about half covered in black.

3½ to 4 *pound whole chicken*
  12 *thin slices black truffles*
      (2 or 3 truffles depending on
      size)
   1 *quart (4 cups) chicken stock*
      (see page 43) (or use rich
      canned chicken broth)
   1 *stalk celery, coarsely chopped*
   1 *onion, coarsely chopped*
   1 *leek, coarsely chopped*
   1 *carrot, coarsely chopped*
  ½ *cup heavy cream*
  ½ *teaspoon cornstarch dis-*
      solved in 1 Tablespoon cold
      water

Loosen the skin of the chicken with your fingers and insert slices of truffle under it on the breast and along the legs and thighs.

Place the chicken in a saucepan, add the chicken stock and chopped vegetables and simmer, covered, for 45 minutes. Remove the chicken to a heated platter and keep warm.

Strain 1 cup of the cooking liquid into a saucepan, skim off the fat, add the cream and bring to a boil. Bind with the dissolved cornstarch. Pour the sauce over the whole chicken and carve at table.

New England Chicken Pot Pie

Serves 4 to 6

3½ *pound whole chicken*
½ *onion, coarsely chopped*
1 *carrot, peeled and coarsely chopped*
1 *stalk celery, coarsely chopped*
1 *leek, white part only (or 6 scallions, white part only), coarsely chopped*
1 *teaspoon salt*
¼ *teaspoon pepper*
3 *Tablespoons butter*

6 *slices blanched bacon, drained and diced*
¼ *pound mushrooms, sliced*
4 *Tablespoons flour*
1½ *cups chicken broth*
Juice of ½ lemon
1 *heaping Tablespoon corn relish*
1 *pre-baked pie crust (see page 346), cut to the size of the top of the casserole*

Wash the chicken and place in a saucepan with the chopped vegetables and 1½ quarts of boiling water. Add salt and pepper, cover, and simmer for 40 minutes. Remove the chicken, reserving the broth. Skin and cut the meat away from the bones. Cut the larger pieces of meat into 1-inch dice and place in an ovenproof casserole.

In a frying pan melt the butter and sauté the diced bacon and sliced mushrooms together lightly, for about 5 minutes. Remove with slotted spoon and add to the chicken.

Pour the butter and bacon fat out of the frying pan into a bowl. Stir in the flour to make a smooth paste and return to the pan. Ladle out 1½ cups of the chicken broth, strain, and gradually stir into the flour. Simmer for 10 minutes, stirring frequently over medium heat until the sauce is smooth. Stir in juice of ½ lemon. Pour the sauce over the chicken mixture and add the corn relish.

Preheat oven to 375 degrees.

Cover the top of the casserole with the pre-baked pie crust, and heat (375 degrees) about 15 to 20 minutes.

Turkey

Boneless Roast Turkey

Serves 6 to 8

1 10 to 12 pound turkey
1 teaspoon each salt and pepper
1 teaspoon marjoram
1 teaspoon pepper
1 Tablespoon salt
3 eggs
1 cup dry sherry (½ cup for ground meat, ½ cup for sauce)
4 Tablespoons butter
½ onion, finely chopped

8–10 medium mushrooms, finely chopped
½ teaspoon vegetable oil
1 onion, coarsely chopped
1 carrot, coarsely chopped
1 cup rich stock (chicken, beef or veal) (see pages 43, 44, or 46) (or use rich canned chicken or beef broth)
2 teaspoons flour
1 teaspoon butter, softened

Chop the liver and gizzard finely and set aside.

Cut the legs off at the thigh joint, leaving as much loose skin on the turkey as possible. Do not remove the wings. Turn the bird over on its breast and split along one side of the backbone. Spread the turkey out and cut out the backbone and then the ribs and set them aside. Pound the meat lightly with a mallet to flatten. Sprinkle with the salt and pepper.

Bone the legs. Remove and discard all cartilage and tendons, but again reserve the bones. Cut the leg meat into small pieces and put through the fine blade of a meat grinder. Stir in the marjoram, 1 teaspoon pepper, 1 Tablespoon salt, eggs, and ½ cup of sherry.

Preheat oven to 450 degrees.

Melt the 4 Tablespoons butter and sauté the chopped half onion and mushrooms for three minutes, then add to the ground meat, making a forcemeat. Spread over the flattened breast. Fold the sides of the breast up over the forcemeat, pulling up the loose skin. Turn the stuffed breast over, place in a roasting pan, and shape neatly, tucking the wings and loose skin underneath. Rub with oil. Chop or break any large bones in half, then scatter all bones and then the onion and carrot pieces around the turkey.

Roast (450 degrees) for 45 minutes. Stir the bones and vegetables occasionally. Add the stock, the remaining sherry, and roast for another 30 minutes, basting once or twice. Remove turkey from pan and keep warm.

Bring the chopped liver and gizzard to a boil in 2 cups of water. Stir in a *roux* of the flour and softened butter blended together. When the *roux* is dissolved, pour this thickened broth gradually into the roasting pan and simmer for 15 minutes. Strain the sauce through a sieve.

Slice the turkey and stuffing and serve sauce separately.

Sliced Breast of Turkey on Broccoli, *Mornay*

Serves 4 to 6

This has become a very popular dish since I introduced it years ago in the Newarker Restaurant. Mentioning the Newarker Restaurant brings back memories. It was one of the first in the famous Restaurant Associates group that I opened, and was located at the Newark Airport. Its success illustrated two points: first, that even an airport restaurant can serve fine food, and second, that people will come from miles around to eat at an airport restaurant even when not traveling.

1 *pound broccoli*	1 *cup* Mornay *sauce*
2 *cups salted water*	*(see page 83)*
½ *teaspoon salt*	2 *Tablespoons Parmesan cheese,*
8 *thin slices cooked turkey breast*	*grated*

Preheat oven to 375 degrees.

Trim the broccoli, discarding the thick, tough stem, and cook in 2 cups of salted water until just tender, about 25 minutes. Drain the broccoli well, place on an ovenproof serving dish, and sprinkle with salt. Cover the broccoli with the turkey slices and *Mornay* sauce and sprinkle with the grated cheese. All of this may be done ahead of time.

Bake (375 degrees) for about 15 minutes, or until sauce is golden.

An unusual variation of this recipe is to place a thin slice of Swiss cheese (Emmenthaler) over the *Mornay* sauce and bake (400 degrees) for about 5 to 10 minutes, or until thoroughly browned.

Breast of Turkey Simmered with Leeks and Vegetables

Serves 6

12 *leeks*
½ *head of green cabbage or iceberg lettuce (about 1 pound)*
 1 *whole breast of turkey, uncooked, about 3 pounds*
 2 *quarts (8 cups) chicken stock (see page 43) (or use rich canned chicken broth)*

⅛ *teaspoon ginger*
 1 *teaspoon salt*
½ *teaspoon peppercorns, freshly cracked*
 1 *cup dry white wine*

SAUCE

 2 *Tablespoons butter*
 3 *Tablespoons flour*
 2 *cups stock in which turkey cooked*

 1 *Tablespoon prepared mustard*
 1 *Tablespoon mayonnaise*
 3 *Tablespoons fine bread crumbs*

Trim the leeks, leaving an inch or two of the crisp green part, and spread the leaves. Place the leeks in a deep saucepan, add the cabbage, the breast of turkey, the chicken stock, the ginger, salt, cracked peppercorns, and wine. Cover the saucepan tightly (or use foil) and simmer for 1 hour.

Preheat oven to 300 degrees.

Lift out the turkey breast, cabbage, and leeks. Cut the turkey into thin slices; cut the cabbage and leeks into serving pieces. Place vegetables on an ovenproof serving platter. Cover the vegetables with sliced turkey and keep warm in a low oven.

To prepare the sauce, melt the butter in a saucepan, stir in the flour to make a smooth paste. Gradually pour in 2 cups of turkey stock and stir until smooth. Add the mustard and mayonnaise. Remove the turkey and vegetables from the oven, then raise temperature to 400 degrees. Pour sauce over turkey and sprinkle with bread crumbs. Return turkey to the oven and bake (400 degrees) for 7 to 10 minutes or until the top is lightly colored.

Duckling

Basic Roast Duckling and Sauce *Serves 3 to 4*

4 to 5 *pound duckling*
   1 *teaspoon salt*
  ¼ *teaspoon pepper*
  ½ *teaspoon rosemary*
     Giblets, chopped
   1 *stalk celery, coarsely chopped*

1 *carrot, coarsely chopped*
1 *onion, coarsely chopped*
1 *tomato, coarsely chopped*
1 *cup brown stock (see page 45) (or use rich canned beef broth)*

Preheat oven to 450 degrees.

Trim the duckling of excess fat at the base of the tail and inside. Rub inside and out with salt, pepper, and rosemary. Prick the skin on the thighs and breast to allow the fat to drain. Place duckling and chopped giblets in a pan and roast (450 degrees) for 1½ hours. Remove the duckling and keep warm.

Pour off all but about 2 tablespoons of fat from the roasting pan. Add the chopped vegetables and sauté for 10 minutes, stirring constantly. Add the brown stock. Stir the pan and scrape up the brown bits, then strain the contents into a saucepan. This basic sauce is now ready for additional flavoring or may be served as is. (See following recipes.)

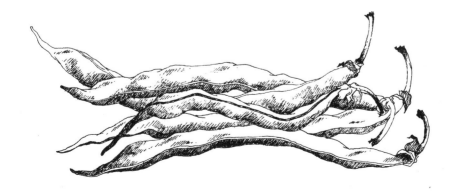

Roast Duckling with Elderberry and Ginger Sauce

Serves 4

3 *Tablespoons sugar*
1 *Tablespoon butter*
⅓ *cup cider vinegar*
8 *ounce jar of elderberry*
  preserves
  Basic roast duckling and sauce
  (see page 173)

3 *Tablespoons brandy*
1 *teaspoon ground fresh ginger,*
  or ½ teaspoon powdered
  Salt to taste

Melt the sugar and butter in a saucepan and cook, stirring, until the mixture is brown. Add the vinegar and continue to cook over high heat until the mixture is reduced by half. Stir in the elderberry preserves, the basic duck sauce, brandy, and ginger. Lower heat and simmer for 10 minutes. Taste and add salt if necessary.

PRESENTATION
Cut the duck into quarters (use poultry shears), pour the sauce over it and serve.

Roast Duckling with Brandied Peaches

Serves 3 to 4

4 *fresh peach halves, peeled (or use canned)*
¼ *cup brandy*
3 *Tablespoons sugar*
1 *Tablespoon butter*
⅓ *cup cider vinegar*
  Basic roast duckling and sauce
  (see page 173)
1 *cup canned liquid peach nectar*
  (or fresh peaches puréed in blender)
½ *teaspoon cornstarch dis-*
  solved in 1 Tablespoon cold water

Marinate peach halves in brandy. Melt the sugar and butter together in a saucepan and cook, stirring, until the mixture is brown. Add the vinegar and continue to cook over high heat until the mixture is reduced by half. Pour in the basic duck sauce, reduce heat to simmer. Add the peach nectar, bind with dissolved cornstarch and simmer for 10 minutes. Five minutes before the end of the cooking period, add the marinated peach halves and brandy.

P R E S E N T A T I O N
Cut the duck into quarters (use poultry shears), pour the sauce over it and garnish with the peach halves.

Roast Duckling with Orange Sauce   *Serves 4*

3 *Tablespoons sugar*	*Zest (rind with white mem-*
1 *Tablespoon butter*	*brane removed) of* ½ *orange*
⅓ *cup cider vinegar*	*and* ½ *lemon, cut into thin*
Basic roast duckling and sauce	*strips*
(see page 173)	2 *Tablespoons Grand Marnier*
1 *cup orange juice*	½ *orange, peeled, cut in thin slices*
1 *teaspoon dry English mustard*	
½ *teaspoon cornstarch, dis-*	
solved in 1 *teaspoon cold water*	

Melt the sugar and butter together in a saucepan and cook, stirring, until the mixture is brown. Add the vinegar and continue to cook over high heat until the mixture is reduced by half. Pour in the basic duck sauce, and reduce heat to simmer. Add the orange juice, dry mustard, and dissolved cornstarch.

Blanch the orange and lemon zest for 3 minutes. Drain and add to the sauce. Add the Grand Marnier and simmer for 10 minutes.

P R E S E N T A T I O N
Cut the duck into quarters (use poultry shears), cover with orange slices, pour the sauce over it and serve immediately.

Squab

Baked Squab with Fresh Herbs, Viennese Style

Serves 4

4 *squabs or squab chickens*
1 *teaspoon salt*
½ *teaspoon pepper*
 1 *egg*
2 *Tablespoons milk*
1 *cup flour*
2 *cups fine bread crumbs*
  Oil for deep frying

1 *Tablespoon prepared mustard*
1 *Tablespoon bottled chili sauce*
2 *Tablespoons hollandaise sauce*
  (see page 86)
1 *Tablespoon each: chives,*
  chervil, parsley, finely chopped
  (if dried use half the amount)

Wipe the squabs inside and out with a damp cloth and season with salt and pepper. Beat egg and milk together. Dredge the squabs thoroughly with flour, then roll them in the egg and milk mixture and then the bread crumbs, until they are fully coated.

Preheat oven to 400 degrees.

Heat the oil to 375 degrees and fry the squabs until golden brown—about 15 minutes. Transfer the squabs to a baking pan and bake (400 degrees) for an additional 15 minutes.

Combine the mustard, chili, and hollandaise sauce and keep warm.

Mix herbs together, sprinkle over squabs, and serve with the sauce on the side.

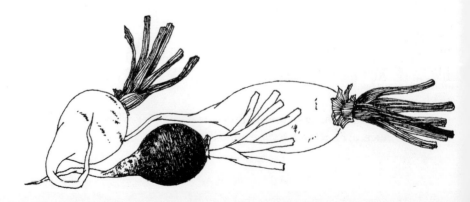

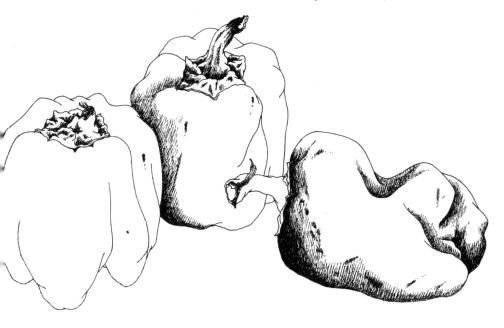

Squab Stuffed with Apple *Roësti*

Serves 4

Double recipe apple roësti
(see page 286) (½ for stuffing
the squabs, ½ for serving
with squabs)
¼ *cup (2 ounces) Calvados*
or applejack

4 *squabs or squab chickens*
2 *Tablespoons butter*
1 *teaspoon salt*
½ *teaspoon pepper*

Preheat oven to 450 degrees.

Double the recipe for apple *roësti* and then add the Calvados but do not cook.

Wipe the squabs inside and out with a damp towel, rub with butter, sprinkle with salt and pepper, and stuff each squab with one eighth of the Calvados-flavored apple *roësti*. Place the squabs in a pan and roast (450 degrees) for 45 minutes. About 10 minutes before the squabs are done, place the rest of the apple *roësti* in the pan around the birds and bake until crisp and browned.

Serve one squab per person on a bed of apple *roësti* immediately from the oven.

Squab Stuffed with Sausages   *Serves 4*

This method of cooking, and the stuffing, may be used not only for the small chicken squab but for game birds such as partridge or quail as well. It is the pungent and penetrating flavor of Calvados, distilled from the apples of Normandy, that transforms the stuffed, roasted bird into a memorable entrée. If you are unable to get Calvados, applejack may be substituted.

1 *pound cooked pork sausages*
  (skin removed)
1 *egg, beaten*
2 *cloves garlic, minced*
2 *Tablespoons parsley, finely*
  chopped
1 *onion, finely chopped*
2 *Tablespoons pistachio nuts,*
  coarsely chopped
4 *squabs or squab chickens*

Salt and pepper
4 *slices bacon*
4 *rectangles of bread, trimmed*
  of crust (or English muffins,
  cut in half)
  Enough slices of raw apple
  to cover bread
¼ *cup (2 ounces) Calvados or*
  applejack

Preheat oven to 400 degrees.

Combine the sausage meat, beaten egg, minced garlic, and chopped parsley, onion, and pistachio nuts.

Wipe the squabs with a damp towel, dry them, and rub the insides lightly with salt and pepper. Fill each squab with the sausage mixture.

Light trussing is sufficient to keep them in shape while roasting: using white string, tie the wings across the back and the two legs together over the tail. Cover the breast of each squab with a slice of bacon and roast (400 degrees) for about 40 minutes. At the end of that time prick the thigh joint and if the juice runs clear the birds are done.

While the squabs are cooking, toast the rectangles of bread, or sauté them slightly in butter; cover with sliced apple. Place a bird on each and pour the Calvados over them. Serve at once.

Deviled Squab

Serves 4

4 *squabs (or pigeons)*
1 *teaspoon salt*
½ *teaspoon pepper*
4 *Tablespoons prepared mustard*

1 *cup fine bread crumbs*
4 *Tablespoons parsley, finely chopped*

Preheat broiler.

Cut the squabs along their backs; split in half and season them with salt and pepper, then spread with mustard. Place them under the broiler, 6 inches from the flames, and broil for about 15 minutes on each side, turning once.

Combine the bread crumbs and chopped parsley.

Remove the squabs from the broiler and turn the oven down to 400 degrees.

Coat the squabs with the bread crumb mixture, place them in a buttered baking dish and bake (400 degrees) for 10 minutes.

Serve at once.

Game

Feathered   *The Noble Deer*
Game of the Plains

The term "game" is usually applied to the products of the hunt or chase and refers to wild birds and animals. In ancient times, before domesticated herds, the only meat available was from wild game. More recently in many countries royalty and nobility reserved game for themselves by imposing severe penalties on poachers. Thus game, which was once a peasant dish, became an aristocratic favorite.

In the United States today, wild game is rarely available in the big cities except in a few expensive markets. But in many parts of the country in small towns and farm areas, game birds, venison, etc., can be found. Many people hunt and often return home with game to spare. My advice is if you are not a hunter, cultivate the friendship of one!

Typically, game dishes are among the most expensive items on the menus of fine restaurants, but this is due in part to the luxurious preparation devoted to these dishes.

With freshly killed game, freshness is not necessarily the key to superior quality. On the contrary, it is often poor tasting and indigestible. Freshly killed game should be hung for one or two weeks, depending on the type of game and age, before being marinated or frozen for future use. For this reason, commercial frozen game items, which are more readily available around the country, can be used with excellent results.

Feathered

The Noble Deer

Game of the Plains

Feathered

Native Pheasant with Purée of Chestnuts   *Serves 4*

2 2½- to 3-pound whole
   pheasants
½ *teaspoon salt*
¼ *teaspoon pepper*
1 *teaspoon dried rosemary*
2 *pounds cooked and peeled*
   chestnuts, cooled (or canned)
4 *slices bacon*
1 *small onion, cut coarsely*

1 *stalk celery, cut coarsely*
¼ *cup dry sherry*
½ *cup heavy cream*
1 *ounce Cointreau*
½ *teaspoon powdered cocoa*

GARNISH
½ *cup currant jelly*

Preheat oven to 450 degrees.

Rub outside of pheasants with salt, pepper, and dried rosemary. Fill the pheasants with as many chestnuts as the birds will hold and reserve the remaining chestnuts. Place the pheasants in a roasting pan. Cover the breasts with the bacon strips. Roast (450 degrees) for 15 minutes. Add the onion, celery, and the remaining chestnuts, and roast for another 30 minutes.

Place the roasting pan on top of stove, add sherry and heavy cream, and bring to a boil.

Remove the pheasants and keep warm. Spoon the chestnut stuffing out of the birds, and add to the cooked ingredients in the roasting pan. Simmer for 3 to 5 minutes, then remove from fire. Put the contents of the roasting pan in the blender with the Cointreau and cocoa, and blend until smooth.

Spread this chestnut purée on a platter. Cut each pheasant in half and place on top of chestnut purée. Serve with currant jelly.

Roast Native Cock Pheasant *en Plumage*   *Serves 4*

The cock pheasant is called for here because, although the female is just as good to eat, she does not have the handsome plumage to display on the serving platter. The handsome plumage of the pheasant provides for a truly elegant presentation of this dish. Although it requires some additional time for the careful removal of the head, wings, and tail-feather section, I think you will find that it is well worth the effort.

You will need for the presentation:

1   A base consisting of an oval of bread large enough to hold two roasted pheasants, end to end. Use a large round loaf and cut off the top, leaving a 1½-inch-thick base. Trim to an oval shape and fry in oil until lightly browned. The bread must be fried firm in order to hold the plumage in place.

2   Four 3-inch-long thin sticks of wood.

3   The plumage—consisting of head and neck section, wings, and tail-feather section of one cock pheasant. At the base of the neck, close to the body, cut off the head and neck of the pheasant in one piece. Cut off the entire wing sections, close to the body. Cut off the entire tail section in one piece, also close to the body. (Plumage can be stored unassembled in refrigerator.)

Pluck and clean the pheasant and prepare for roasting as directed below.

R O A S T I N G   T H E   P H E A S A N T

2 2½- to 3-pound pheasants	1 onion, finely chopped
1 teaspoon salt	1 Tablespoon flour
1 Tablespoon softened butter	1 cup beef or chicken stock (see
½ teaspoon marjoram	pages 43 and 44) (or use rich
½ teaspoon pepper	canned beef or chicken broth)
10 juniper berries, crushed	¼ cup dry sherry
1 carrot, finely chopped	

Preheat oven to 450 degrees.

Rub pheasants with salt and softened butter inside and out. Sprinkle with marjoram, pepper, and crushed juniper berries.

Roast (450 degrees) for 50 minutes. In the meantime prepare the plumage as directed below. When pheasants are done, remove to a heated platter and keep warm.

Place the roasting pan on top of the stove, add the chopped carrot, onion, flour, stock, and dry sherry to the pan juices, and stir quickly to dissolve the flour. Simmer 5 minutes. Strain the gravy through a sieve and pour into a sauceboat.

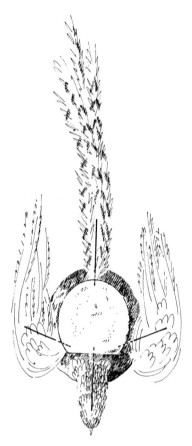

The illustration shows only one particularly plump pheasant in the frame, but as you are more likely to want to serve two pheasants, I have written my recipe accordingly.

ASSEMBLING THE PLUMAGE

Place the oval of bread in the middle of a large, attractive serving platter. Insert one 3-inch-long stick halfway into the cut-off end at the base of the neck and head section of the plumage, then insert the other end of the stick into the larger end of the oval-shaped bread frame, to resemble the front of the bird. Insert another stick halfway into the cut-off end of the right wing section, and then insert the other half of the stick firmly into the right side of the bread to resemble the right side of the pheasant. Repeat the same procedure for the left wing section. Finally insert the last stick halfway into the cut-off end of the tail-feather section, and the other half of the stick firmly into the smaller end of the oval to resemble the tail section of the pheasant. The frame is now complete. When ready to serve the roasted pheasants, place them end to end inside the plumage on the bread and fit them close together.

Bring your pheasant *en plumage* to the table. To serve, lift out the roasted pheasants and place on a serving platter. Split each pheasant in half. Serve gravy separately in a sauceboat.

Pot Pie of Ring Neck Pheasant in Champagne

Serves 4

1 flat piece baked puff pastry crust the size of a chafing dish (see page 346), or use wafer-thin slices of white bread, toasted and buttered
2 3- to 3½-pound pheasants
4 Tablespoons softened butter
1 carrot, coarsely chopped, for simmering
1 onion, chopped
2 cups champagne
1 cup clear chicken stock (see page 43) (or use rich canned chicken broth)

4 Tablespoons butter
½ medium onion, coarsely chopped for sauté
1 cup sliced fresh mushrooms
4 slices bacon, cut in julienne strips
½ teaspoon pepper
1 small truffle, chopped coarsely
1 cup small white onions, blanched
2 Tablespoons flour
3 cups pheasant stock
3 egg yolks, beaten
1½ cups heavy cream

Preheat oven to 425 degrees.

Prepare the pastry crust according to directions on page 346 (this may be done well ahead).

Rub pheasants with soft butter and roast (425 degrees) for 10 minutes.

Remove from oven and place in a larger casserole with chopped carrot, 1 chopped onion, champagne, and chicken stock. Cover, return to oven, and simmer for 30 minutes.

Melt the 4 Tablespoons butter in a large saucepan and add ½ chopped onion, sliced mushrooms, bacon, pepper, and truffle. Sauté until onion is soft and transparent. Add small white onions. Stir flour into the saucepan mixture to bind. Add 3 cups of the pheasant stock from casserole, and boil until the amount of liquid is reduced by one quarter.

In a small bowl combine egg yolks with heavy cream and mix well. Beat a little of the hot pheasant stock into the egg-cream mixture, and stir back into the saucepan. Then return all to the casserole and stir well. Keep warm but do not boil.

Bone the pheasants and place in a chafing dish. Pour the hot sauce over the boned meat and cover with the baked pastry crust. Warm in the chafing dish and serve.

Casserole of Pheasant with Wild Mushrooms

Serves 4

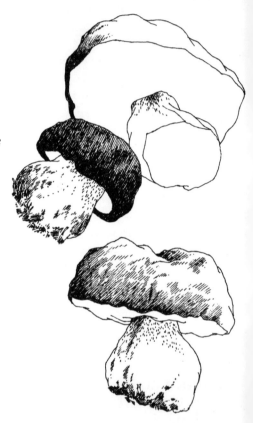

2 2¾-pound pheasants,
  each cut in half
1 Tablespoon salt
1 teaspoon oregano
2 Tablespoons butter
½ onion, finely chopped
1 teaspoon basil
6 slices bacon, cut in small dice
1 ounce dried imported
  mushrooms (or 5 ounces
  canned wild mushrooms)
¼ cup dry red wine
1½ ounces brandy
1 cup brown gravy, any kind
  (to improvise gravy see page
  xiii)
1 cup pearl onions,
  peeled and blanched
1 cup fresh mushrooms, halved
2 Tablespoons chopped raw
  chicken livers

Sprinkle pheasants with salt and oregano. In large skillet, melt butter and sauté pheasants until golden brown. Remove pheasants from skillet and place in a flame-proof casserole.

In the skillet with the sautéeing butter, add chopped onion, basil, bacon, dried or canned mushrooms, red wine, brandy, brown gravy, pearl onions, and halved fresh mushrooms. Mix thoroughly and pour over the meat in the casserole. Cover and simmer for 35 minutes.

Five minutes before casserole is finished simmering, add chopped chicken livers.

Pheasant with Champagne Sauerkraut   *Serves 4*

1 *pound sauerkraut*
1 *medium onion, minced*
4 *slices bacon, diced*
2½ *cups champagne*
   (Reserve ¼ cup for later
   addition. Leftover cham-
   pagne which has lost its
   sparkle may be used because
   it loses its sparkle in cooking
   anyway.)
1 *teaspoon salt*
2 *2½- or 3-pound pheasants*
1 *teaspoon fresh sage or ½*
   teaspoon dried
2 *Tablespoons butter*
1 *teaspoon raw grated potato*
½ *ounce brandy*

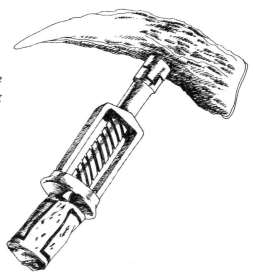

Rinse the sauerkraut with cold water and drain. In a large saucepan, sauté onion and bacon lightly until soft and transparent. Put sauerkraut over this and add 2¼ cups of champagne. Cover and simmer for 1 hour.

Preheat oven to 450 degrees.

While sauerkraut is cooking, sprinkle salt on pheasants, rub skin with sage and butter. Place in shallow roasting pan and roast (450 degrees) for 20 minutes.

Remove from oven, split the pheasants, which are only partly cooked, and cool slightly. Place on top of the sauerkraut and cover saucepan. Simmer for another 20 minutes. Add to the sauerkraut the grated potato, reserved ¼ cup champagne, brandy, and, with long fork, stir well. Simmer 3 minutes longer for the potatoes to bind the sauerkraut. Serve the pheasants on a bed of sauerkraut.

Pheasant Stewed in Red Wine

Serves 4

2 *3-pound pheasants*	12 *peppercorns, crushed*
½ *cup flour for dusting*	1 *Tablespoon currant jelly*
1 *teaspoon salt*	1 *cup brown sauce*
½ *teaspoon pepper*	*(see page 79) (or to improvise*
¼ *cup butter (for sautéing)*	*gravy see page xiii)*
1 *Tablespoon butter (for sauce)*	10 *mushrooms, cut in quarters*
¼ *cup shallots (or onions),*	1 *carrot* — *Cut in pieces,*
chopped	1 *white turnip* *and trimmed to*
½ *teaspoon dried marjoram*	*the size of clove*
1 *cup dry red wine*	*of garlic.*
1 *Tablespoon vinegar*	

Cut the pheasants into 16 pieces: each breast in two pieces and each leg in 2 pieces. Dust in flour and sprinkle with salt and pepper.

In a large skillet, melt ¼ cup butter and sauté the pheasant meat until golden brown.

In a saucepan, melt 1 Tablespoon of butter, add chopped shallots and marjoram, and sauté lightly. Add red wine, vinegar, peppercorns, currant jelly, brown sauce, and simmer uncovered for 20 minutes. Strain through a sieve over the pheasant. Add the mushrooms, carrot, and turnip, and simmer covered for 30 minutes.

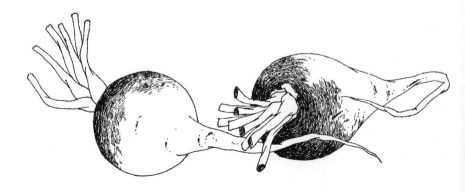

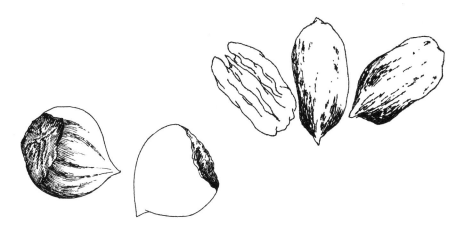

Casserole of Pheasant, Madeira

Serves 4

2 *3-pound pheasants*	1 *teaspoon dry English mustard*
6 *ounces Madeira wine*	1 *egg*
1 *Tablespoon butter*	¼ *cup milk*
Sprig parsley	½ *cup bread crumbs*
1 *Tablespoon shallots (or onions), chopped*	1 *Tablespoon parsley, chopped*
	1 *clove garlic, crushed*
1 *teaspoon salt*	¼ *cup mustard seeds*

Preheat oven to 400 degrees.

Split each pheasant into quarters. Marinate the pheasants in Madeira, uncovered, for 2 hours at room temperature. Remove the meat, drain, wipe dry and reserve marinade. Lightly flatten each piece with the side of a large knife or a pounder.

Melt butter in a large skillet and sauté the meat with sprig of parsley, shallots, salt, and dry mustard until golden brown, approximately 20 minutes. Remove meat from pan and keep warm. Add the Madeira marinade and simmer to reduce to half the amount of liquid in the pan.

In a separate bowl, beat egg with milk, and mix in the bread crumbs, chopped parsley, crushed garlic, and mustard seeds. Place the meat back in the pan with the Madeira sauce. Cover meat thoroughly with the bread crumb–egg mixture. Bake (400 degrees) until golden brown, about 5 to 10 minutes.

Salmi of Pheasant *Printanier*

Serves 4

2 *3-pound pheasants*
½ *cup flour for dusting*
1 *teaspoon salt*
2 *Tablespoons butter*
¼ *cup shallots (or onions),
    finely chopped*
12 *medium mushrooms, cut in
    quarters*
4 *slices bacon, cut in thin strips,
    and blanched in ¼ cup hot
    water for 2 minutes*
1 *cup dry red wine*
1 *cup brown stock (see page 45)
    (or use rich canned beef broth)*
2 *small carrots, 2 small white
    turnips, and 1 stalk celery, cut
    in pieces the size of a match-
    stick about 1 inch long
    and ⅛ inch thick*
1 *cup blanched pearl onions*

1 *sprig fresh rosemary
    (or ½ teaspoon dried)*
½ *pound of cooked frozen peas (or
    1 pound can)*

Cut the pheasants into 16 pieces: each breast in two pieces and each leg in 2 pieces. Dust lightly in flour, sprinkle with salt.

In a large heated skillet, melt butter and sauté the pheasant pieces until golden brown. Add chopped shallots, mushrooms, bacon, red wine, brown stock, and simmer uncovered for 20 minutes.

In enough water to cover bring the carrots, turnips, celery, onions, and rosemary to a boil, then reduce heat and simmer for 5 minutes. Drain vegetables and spread over pheasant. Cover and simmer 10 minutes longer.

To serve, spread warm peas over the top.

Quenelle of Pheasant with Brandied Crabapples

Serves 4

1 *3-pound pheasant*
½ *pound pork shoulder*
1 *teaspoon salt*
   Pinch of pepper
2 *ounces brandy*
3 *ounces dry white wine*
¼ *pound butter, softened at*
   room temperature

¼ *cup heavy cream*
3 *egg yolks*
½ *teaspoon salt*
½ *teaspoon poultry seasoning*
1 *teaspoon pepper*
8 *canned crabapples*

SAUCE
2 *ounces brandy*
¼ *cup dry red wine*

¼ *cup beef gravy (to improvise*
   gravy see page xiii)

Remove all pheasant meat from the bones. Put through medium blade of meat grinder with pork shoulder, salt, and pepper. Marinate in brandy and white wine for 1 hour uncovered, at room temperature. Mix the pheasant meat and the marinade with the softened butter, heavy cream, egg yolks, salt, poultry seasoning, and pepper. Blend in blender until smooth.

To make *quenelles*, first bring to a boil in a 10-inch saucepan two inches of well-salted water. Wet two tablespoons in the hot water, take a tablespoon of the blended mixture and use the other tablespoon to scrape it off into the boiling water. You should have enough dough to make 8 *quenelles*. Spoon them one by one into the boiling water, wetting the spoons each time, and simmer for 15 minutes until they rise to the surface of the water.

Preheat oven to 400 degrees.

Remove the *quenelles* with a slotted spoon, drain, and transfer to an ovenproof platter and garnish with crabapples.

Make a sauce of brandy, red wine, and beef gravy; pour it over the *quenelles* and roast (400 degrees) for 10 minutes.

Breast of Pheasant *Grandmère*   *Serves 4*

  2 3- to 3½-*pound pheasants*
  1 *teaspoon salt*
     Pinch of rosemary
  ½ *cup flour for dusting*
  2 *Tablespoons butter*
  8 *slices bacon, coarsely cut*

 12 *mushrooms, cut in quarters*
  1 *cup dry white wine*
  2 *medium potatoes, cooked and*
     cooled, cut in ⅛-inch cubes
  ½ *cup cooked pearl onions*
  1 *Tablespoon parsley, chopped*

Remove the four breasts from the two pheasants, sprinkle with salt and rosemary. Dust lightly in flour.

In a heated skillet, melt butter and sauté the pheasant breasts for 10 minutes until golden brown. Add bacon and mushrooms and sauté a few minutes longer, until bacon is cooked through but not crisp. Add wine, potatoes, and onions. Cover and simmer slowly for 25 minutes. Sprinkle with chopped parsley, and serve.

The remaining pheasant meat and bones can be used for soup, sauce, or one of the other recipes, such as the *quenelle* of pheasant, which follows.

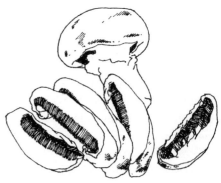

Partridge *au Chartreuse*   *Serves 4*

Chartreuse is a famous liqueur named after a French monastery, but it is also a term used for a dish of game or fish combined with a variety of vegetables.

2 *partridges (approximately*
  1½ pounds each)
2 *Tablespoons butter, for*
  roasting
1 *teaspoon salt*
½ *teaspoon dried rosemary*
½ *teaspoon dried marjoram*
8 *large green cabbage leaves*
1 *teaspoon melted butter for*
  baking dish
6 *slices bacon*
¼ *pound Bauernwurst or Kielbasa*
  (cut in ⅛-inch slices)

1 *peeled and cooked carrot*
  (cut in ⅛-inch thin slices)
¼ *cup chicken broth (see page*
  43) (or used rich canned
  chicken broth)
¼ *cup white wine*
  Pinch of salt

Preheat oven to 450 degrees.

Rub partridges with butter, salt, rosemary, and marjoram. Put in roasting pan and roast (450 degrees) for 15 minutes. Reduce oven heat to 400 degrees and roast for 10 minutes more. Remove from oven and cool to room temperature.

Blanch the 8 cabbage leaves in hot water for 6 minutes. Reserve 4 whole leaves. Chop 4 leaves very fine, put in a cheesecloth and press out all the water. Put aside.

Butter the inside of a large baking dish 2½ inches high (or soufflé mold) with melted butter. Arrange bacon and sliced sausages on bottom of the mold. Stand the carrot slices on end around the edges of the mold. Line the bottom and sides of the mold with the cabbage leaves, laying these over the bacon, sausage, and carrots. Cut each partridge in quarters and place in layers on top of the cabbage leaves. Pour the chicken broth and wine over the meat and sprinkle with salt. Then fill any space left in the mold with the chopped cabbage. Fold protruding top ends of the cabbage leaf lining over the chopped cabbage.

Cover tightly with aluminum foil and bake (450 degrees) for 40 minutes.

To serve, invert the mold onto an attractive serving platter and spoon the pan juices over it.

The Noble Deer

Venison

Venison is the collective term for a variety of game meat, especially deer, elk, etc. It makes a memorable and festive dish.

For both texture and flavor venison should be marinated and the following basic marinade is suggested:

BASIC MARINADE FOR VENISON *(for 4 pounds of meat)*

2 *cups dry red wine*
1 *cup wine vinegar*
1 *cup water*
1 *carrot, coarsely chopped*
1 *stalk celery, coarsely chopped*

1 *large onion, coarsely chopped*
2 *cloves garlic*
3 *teaspoons pickling spices*
1 *teaspoon peppercorns,*
   freshly crushed

Use any container (except one made of copper or silver) large enough to hold the meat, the liquid, and spices. Combine all above ingredients in the container and marinate uncovered in the refrigerator 3 to 5 days for stew meats or small cuts, 5 to 10 days for roast saddle, leg, or larger quantities of meat.

Suggested cuts of venison for marinating:

Leg or shoulder for stew: Cut in 2-inch cubes.
Saddle: Cut and trim into servings for four persons, half of each side
   of saddle per person (approximately 5 inches long).
   Marinate with bone in.
Filet: Leave whole.

Cut other meats according to directions in recipe.
All venison should be marinated with bone in.

NOTE: If more or less than 4 pounds of meat is called for, increase or decrease proportionately only the liquid called for. Amounts specified for other ingredients should remain as above.

Venison Stew

Serves 6

2 *pounds marinated venison, cut into 2-inch cubes (see basic marinade above)*
3 *Tablespoons oil or butter*
1 *teaspoon salt*
¼ *teaspoon pepper*
1 *onion, coarsely chopped*
1 *carrot, coarsely chopped*
1 *stalk celery, coarsely chopped*
2 *Tablespoons tomato purée*
1 *cup marinade, strained*

½ *cup dry red wine*
1 *cup beef gravy (to improvise gravy see page xiii)*
1 *Tablespoon red currant jelly*
1 *Tablespoon heavy cream*

GARNISH
2 *slices blanched bacon, diced*
¼ *pound mushrooms, coarsely sliced*
12 *pearl onions, preboiled until tender*

1 *cup croutons (tiny cubes of bread toasted in the oven)*

Drain the cubes of venison and pat dry. Strain and reserve the marinade. Sauté the venison in a skillet in oil or butter until brown—about 10 minutes. Transfer to a casserole. Add salt, pepper, the vegetables, tomato purée, the cup of strained marinade, the red wine, the beef gravy, and simmer, covered, for 1½ hours.

Prepare the garnish while the venison is cooking. Sauté the diced bacon for 2 minutes, add the mushrooms and onions, and sauté until the mushrooms are soft—about 3 minutes. Add the toasted croutons and mix well. Set aside and keep warm.

Remove the pieces of venison to a serving dish and keep warm. Strain the liquid remaining in the casserole through a sieve, then return to casserole. Stir in the red currant jelly and cream. Reheat, but do not allow to boil.

To serve, pour this sauce over the venison, then cover with garnish mixture.

Venison Cutlet Sauté *Grand Veneur*   *Serves 4*

4 *1-inch slices of filet of venison, marinated (see basic marinade page 196)*

2 *Tablespoons butter*

Remove the venison from marinade, drain and pat dry. Drain the marinade and reserve the sauce.

SAUCE GRAND VENEUR

1 *Tablespoon onion (or chives), finely chopped*

1 *Tablespoon butter*

1 *cup marinade, strained*

1 *cup beef gravy (to improvise gravy see page xiii)*

1 *Tablespoon beef blood (or ¼ cup heavy cream)*

1 *teaspoon dill, chopped*

1 *Tablespoon Cassis (a Burgundian black currant liqueur)*

To prepare *sauce Grand Veneur,* simmer onion, butter, 1 cup strained marinade, and the beef gravy until liquid is reduced to one-half the original amount, or to 1 cup of liquid. Stir in the beef blood, dill, and Cassis. Remove immediately from fire. Additional cooking may curdle the blood.

Pound the slices of venison flat. In a heated skillet, melt the 2 Tablespoons butter and sauté the filets over high heat for not more than 1 minute on each side. (Overcooking will dry and toughen meat.)

Pour the sauce over the filets and serve.

Roast Saddle of Venison　　　　*Serves 4 to 6*

As in other venison recipes this must be started a few days ahead in order to flavor and tenderize the venison with the marinade.

5 to 6 *pound saddle of venison (consisting of the entire loin with backbone, tenderloins, kidneys, and flanks), marinated (see basic marinade, page 196). Marinate the saddle with filet on bottom and bone ends up.*	1 *carrot, coarsely chopped*
	1 *stalk celery, coarsely chopped*
	2 *Tablespoons tomato purée*
	4 *cups marinade, strained*
	½ *cup dry red wine*
	1 *cup brown gravy, any kind (or to improvise gravy see page xiii)*
1 *teaspoon salt*	1 *Tablespoon red currant jelly, melted*
½ *teaspoon pepper*	
3 *Tablespoons oil or butter*	1 *Tablespoon heavy cream*
1 *onion, coarsely chopped*	

Preheat oven to 450 degrees.

Remove the saddle from the marinade, drain, and pat dry. Strain the marinade and reserve for the sauce. Sprinkle the saddle with salt and pepper. Heat the oil or butter in a roasting pan over medium heat. Place the saddle in the pan, surround the meat with the vegetables and roast (450 degrees) for 40 minutes.

Remove the saddle to a serving platter and keep warm.

Over low heat on top of the stove, scrape the bottom and sides of the roasting pan to loosen all brown bits, stir in the tomato purée, the reserved marinade, red wine, beef gravy or stock, and simmer over medium heat for 10 to 15 minutes. Using a sieve, strain this mixture into a saucepan. Let it settle for about 5 minutes; remove any fat that rises to the top. Return to the top of the stove and, over medium heat, stir in the red currant jelly and cream. Bring to a boil and immediately remove from the fire. Do not continue to boil.

Carve the saddle at table and serve the sauce separately.

Game of the Plains

Despite popular misconceptions, the only significant difference between the European hare and the American rabbit is one of size. However, with all the various species of each, even that distinction has become ignored in popular usage. In Europe the hare is most popular, especially the large Belgian hare, and Europeans cannot understand the prejudice of many Americans who will not eat this delicate meat. But American rabbit is even milder and more delicate than the European hare and tastes like a more flavorful chicken or veal. I am convinced that once you try hare or rabbit in one of my recipes, you will gladly add it to your menus.

Ragoût of Hare in Red Wine and Vegetables

Serves 4

6 *pound hare, cleaned*

BASIC HARE MARINADE

2 *cups dry red wine*
1 *cup wine vinegar*
1 *cup water*
1 *onion, cut in one-eighths*
1 *leek, cut in large pieces*

1 *celery stalk, cut in large pieces*
1 *carrot, cut in large pieces*
1 *Tablespoon pickling spice*
1 *clove garlic, crushed*

Place all the above ingredients in any large vessel, except one of copper or silver. Cut the back, legs, and shoulder of the hare into 2-inch-thick pieces. Place hare in marinade and refrigerate uncovered for one week. Remove meat, drain and pat dry. Strain the marinade and reserve.

PREPARATION

½ *cup flour for dusting*
1 *teaspoon salt*
½ *cup corn oil*
1 *teaspoon cornstarch dissolved in 2 Tablespoons water*
1 *Tablespoon red currant jelly*

or ¼ *cup Cassis (Cassis is a Burgundian black currant liqueur)*
1 *Tablespoon fresh dill, chopped (or 1½ teaspoons dried)*

Dip the meat in flour, sprinkle with salt. Brown in corn oil until golden —7 to 8 minutes. Put in a deep casserole and pour the strained marinade over the meat. Cover tightly and simmer for 1½ hours until tender.

Remove the meat to a heated serving platter. Add to the liquid in the casserole the cornstarch dissolved in water, and bring to a boil. Add currant jelly or Cassis. Strain the liquid through a sieve and serve over the meat. Flavor with chopped dill.

Roast Saddle of Hare in Cream   *Serves 2 to 3*

3 *pound saddle of hare, larded and marinated (see basic hare marinade, preceding recipe)**
1 *teaspoon dried thyme*
1 *teaspoon salt*
1 *teaspoon pepper (for roasting)*
1 *cup marinade, strained (or ½ cup dry red wine)*
1 *Tablespoon vinegar*
½ *teaspoon coriander*

1 *Tablespoon shallots (or onions), finely chopped*
½ *cup thick brown gravy (to improvise gravy see page xiii)*
1 *Tablespoon currant jelly*
1 *teaspoon pepper (for sauce)*
½ *cup heavy cream*
1 *teaspoon cornstarch dissolved in 2 Tablespoons cold water*

Remove the saddle from the marinade, drain, and pat dry. Strain the marinade and reserve for the sauce.

Preheat oven to 450 degrees.

Rub the larded and marinated hare with thyme, salt, and pepper and roast (450 degrees) for 25 to 30 minutes. The meat should be pink and not overcooked. Remove from oven and keep warm.

Place the roasting pan on top of the stove over medium heat, scrape the pan of drippings, add 1 cup of strained marinade, vinegar, coriander, chopped shallots, brown gravy, and simmer for 10 minutes. Add currant jelly, pepper, and heavy cream. Bind quickly with dissolved cornstarch. Strain through a sieve into a sauce bowl.

To carve, cut along the backbone, loosen meat around rib. Remove the whole piece from the bone and slice. Serve the sauce over the meat.

* *If butcher will not lard meat, marinate and cover top with thin slices of pork belly while roasting.*

Beef

The Roasts   Steaks
The Ragoûts

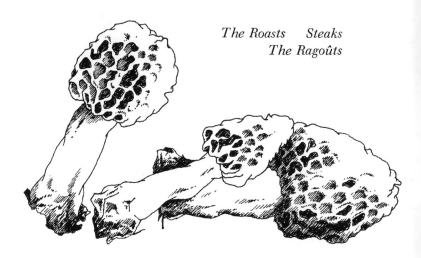

Beef is by far the most popular American meat, at least for those who can afford it, and there is little disagreement with my opinion that American beef is generally much better than the European quality, with possibly a few local exceptions.

Beef is generally regarded even by gourmets as the best of all meats, but I cannot fully agree. To me, beef is the cliché among meats—sometimes excellent but mostly obvious, and more of a challenge to the cattle raiser, the butcher, and the meat buyer than to the chef.

To most Americans, beef means steaks and roasts, and the rest of the products which make up by far the greater part of the beef supply are largely neglected. Yet the steaks and roasts are not the most flavorful cuts of beef, only the most tender. Square shoulder cuts, top sirloin and hip, for example, are much more flavorful. That is why I have selected in several instances recipes which make use of some of these neglected cuts of beef.

The Roasts

Steaks

The Ragoûts

The Roasts

Sirloin of Beef with *Sauce Bordelaise*   *Serves 6*

3 *pounds boneless sirloin strip (one piece)*
Pepper to taste
½ *cup shallots (or onion), finely chopped*
1 *cup dry red wine*

1 *cup beef or veal gravy (to improvise gravy see page xiii)*
½ *teaspoon cornstarch dissolved in 1 Tablespoon water*
2 *Tablespoons butter softened to room temperature*

Preheat oven to 500 degrees.

Remove sirloin from refrigerator 1 hour before roasting.

Sprinkle beef with pepper and place on a rack in a shallow roasting pan. Roast (500 degrees) for 20 minutes; reduce heat to 400 degrees and roast for 15 minutes more for rare. (Allow an additional 7 minutes for medium and an additional 10 minutes for well done.)

Remove sirloin to a heated serving platter and keep warm. Drain off all but 1 Tablespoon fat from roasting pan and add the shallots or onion, wine, and beef or veal gravy.

Boil on top of stove for about 10 minutes, or until liquid is reduced by one quarter. Reduce heat, add dissolved cornstarch and stir for about 1 minute, or until sauce is thickened. Add 2 Tablespoons softened butter and mix in lightly.

Slice sirloin and serve on heated platter. Serve sauce separately.

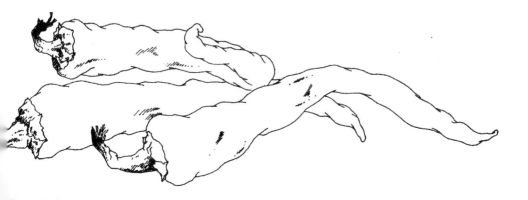

Sliced Roast Beef or Braised Beef with Horseradish *Mousseline* Sauce

Serves 4

This is an excellent recipe for using cooked roast beef or braised beef. Or, you can obtain sliced roast beef in any delicatessen. Select rare and fairly thick slices. The preparation can be done in advance and heated in minutes before serving. The combination of delightful flavors in this dish brings back fond memories of my childhood in Switzerland.

1 *Tablespoon flour*
4 *slices roast beef or braised beef*
1 *cup coarsely grated bread crumbs (day-old bread)*

4 *Tablespoons butter*
1 *cup horseradish* mousseline *sauce (see page 87)*

MUSTARD DRESSING

Mix together:

4 *teaspoons prepared mustard*
½ *teaspoon Worcestershire sauce*
½ *teaspoon salt*

Pinch pepper
2 *egg yolks blended with*
1 *teaspoon dry English mustard*

Sprinkle and press flour on beef slices on both sides. Coat both sides with some of the mustard dressing. Dredge both sides with bread crumbs.

In a large frying pan, melt butter and sauté beef quickly for about one minute, or until golden brown on each side. Arrange on a heated serving platter and spoon on the remaining mustard dressing and then the horseradish *mousseline* sauce over the beef slices. Recipe may be prepared in advance to this point.

When ready to serve, place under preheated broiler until sauce is golden brown.

Steaks

Filet Mignon, *Cordon Bleu* *Serves 4*

4 *filets mignon, trimmed*
   (1 inch thick, approximately
   8 ounces each)
8 *thin slices prosciutto ham*

8 *thin slices Gruyère cheese*
¼ *cup* Béarnaise *sauce*
   (see page 85)

Preheat broiler.

Broil filets for 1 minute on each side.

Remove from broiler; make a side slice three quarters through each filet, like a butterfly opening. Lift top part and place ham and cheese inside, alternating two slices of ham and two slices of cheese in each filet. Fold back top part over ham and cheese and return to the broiler for another 2 minutes on each side for a rare filet. (Broil 3 minutes longer for medium or 5 minutes longer for well done.)

Spoon *Béarnaise* sauce over each filet and place under broiler again for a few seconds.

Filet Beefsteak *Tartare* *Serves 1*

1 *egg separated*
8 *ounces bottom round,*
   ground once
1 *teaspoon capers, chopped*
4 *anchovy filets, chopped*
¼ *medium onion, minced*

⅛ *teaspoon pepper*
½ *teaspoon salt*
   Dash Worcestershire sauce
6 *Tablespoons dry red wine*
   A pinch of dry English mustard
½ *teaspoon brandy*

Mix egg white with ground meat. Grind once again. Mix in remaining ingredients, except egg yolk. Form into a patty, make a well in the center and place egg yolk there. Serve at room temperature.

Before eating, break the egg yolk with a fork and mix into the meat.

Minute Steak *Roquefort*

When you plan a main course of steak, this recipe will give it a flourish and the dashing flavor of really fine Roquefort. Fine restaurants serve sirloin in this manner frequently, but I seldom see it in homes. Try it, and don't overcook the steak; the combined flavors are so much better when the steak is rare or at least still pink inside.

1 *clove garlic, minced*
6 *ounces Roquefort cheese,*
   crumbled
2 *Tablespoons butter softened*
   to room temperature
1 *ounce dry sherry*

1 *ounce brandy*
1 *teaspoon tomato purée*
1 *teaspoon pepper*
4 *sirloin steaks (7 or 8 ounces*
   each)

Preheat broiler.

Prepare the cheese topping in a bowl by combining the garlic, Roquefort cheese, butter, sherry, brandy, tomato purée, and pepper. Using a wooden spoon, blend all ingredients into a smooth paste.

Broil the steaks for 1 minute on each side for rare steaks. (For medium, broil 2 minutes on each side.) Remove the steaks from the broiler; place on a large ovenproof platter, cover the top of each steak with the cheese mixture. Place under broiler again for another two minutes. Serve immediately.

Black Pepper Steak (*Steak au Poivre*)

Steak au Poivre, as it is called on the continent, is more frequently served there than in America. I have often wondered why, since American beef is far superior. And it is a splendid way to serve a thick steak cooked rare and highly seasoned with freshly crushed pepper. Try my version and I am sure your family will ask for it again. Do not overcook the beef—the fresh peppery flavor is more appetizing when the steak is rare in the center.

2 *Tablespoons peppercorns, crushed*	3 *ounces brandy*
4 *sirloin steaks (about 8 ounces each)*	¼ *cup beef gravy (to improvise gravy see page xiii)*
1 *teaspoon salt*	½ *teaspoon prepared mustard*
1 *Tablespoon oil, for sautéing*	½ *teaspoon Worcestershire sauce*

Using a rolling pin, crush the peppercorns into tiny bits. Sprinkle the steaks with salt and lightly press the steaks in the crushed pepper on each side, until well covered.

In a large, heated frying pan, sauté steaks in oil for 2 minutes on each side. Remove the steaks and keep warm. To the pan juices, add the brandy, beef gravy, mustard, and Worcestershire sauce, stir and simmer until it bubbles. Place steaks on heated dinner plates, pour the sauce over the meat, and serve immediately.

Chopped Sirloin Steak *Roquefort*   *Serves 4*

¼ *medium onion, finely chopped*	1½ *pounds chopped sirloin of beef, freshly ground*
½ *teaspoon salt*	½ *pound Roquefort cheese, crumbled*
1 *pinch black pepper*	
1 *teaspoon prepared mustard*	

Preheat broiler.

Mix onion, salt, pepper, mustard thoroughly into the meat. Form into 1½-inch round patties. For a rare chopped steak, broil ½ minute on each side. Sprinkle Roquefort cheese on top and broil quickly until cheese melts.

Beef Tenderloin in Fresh Herbs with Mushrooms

Serves 4

Oil for deep frying onion
(at least 1 quart)
1 medium onion, thinly sliced
4 beef tenderloin slices
(approximately 6 ounces each)
1 teaspoon pepper, freshly
ground
10 Tablespoons butter
(6 Tablespoons for sautéing,
4 Tablespoons for sauce)
1 4-ounce can of imported
chanterelles or other canned
wild mushrooms

½ teaspoon chopped fresh
tarragon (or ¼ teaspoon dried)
½ teaspoon fresh basil
(or ¼ teaspoon dried)
½ teaspoon fresh oregano
(or ¼ teaspoon dried)
¼ cup dry sherry
½ teaspoon salt
2 Tablespoons beef gravy (to
improvise gravy see page xiii)
Chopped chives or parsley

Heat oil in a deep-fryer to about 375 degrees. Deep fry sliced onions until dark brown and crisp. Drain on brown paper and keep warm.

Sprinkle meat with pepper and sauté quickly in 6 Tablespoons of butter about 2 minutes. Remove to heated platter and keep warm.

In another saucepan, melt 4 Tablespoons of butter and lightly sauté chanterelles with tarragon, basil, oregano, sherry, salt, and beef gravy. Pour sauce over meat and arrange onions on top. Garnish with chopped chives or chopped parsley.

Beef Tenderloin with Morels

Serves 4

You will notice that I have included morels or other wild mushrooms in a number of meat recipes. Morels are common enough on the continent, the finest ones being the smaller, black pointed morels that grow high in the Alps of Switzerland. I can remember going out to pick them as a young boy. We would use them in a variety of ways. Their flavor is more intense and I recommend you keep a supply on hand. They are now easily found in cans, ready for use. Dried morels are also available and are equally flavorful after they have been soaked in water and cooked lightly in butter. They have a mushroom flavor but are more pungent and add a very special tang to sauces.

3 *Tablespoons butter (2 Table-*
  spoons for sautéing, 1 Table-
  spoon for sauce)
8 *beef tenderloin slices (2 ounces*
  each)
1 *Tablespoon shallots (or onions),*
  finely chopped
1 *teaspoon chives, finely chopped*
½ *teaspoon dry English mustard*
2 *ounces dry sherry*
⅓ *cup beef gravy (to improvise*
  gravy see page xiii)
4 *ounces morels, cooked and*
  cut into bite-size pieces

In a heavy-bottomed frying pan over high heat melt 2 Tablespoons butter and sauté the tenderloin slices no more than 1 minute on each side. Remove the beef to a heated serving dish and keep warm.

Add to the frying pan the remaining 1 Tablespoon butter, shallots, chives, mustard, sherry, beef gravy, and morels. Simmer over medium heat for 2 minutes. Pour the sauce over the beef, and serve at once.

Roulade of Beef with Mustard Fruit, Braised in Beer

Serves 4

STUFFING

4 *slices bread, soaked in ½ cup milk*

¼ *pound ground pork*

¼ *pound ground beef*

½ *medium onion*

1 *stalk celery*

6 *sprigs parsley*

¼ *teaspoon each: thyme, marjoram, savory, salt, pepper*

2 *eggs, beaten*

4 *cube steaks, about 6 ounces each, pounded thin (ask your butcher to do this)*

2 *slices lean bacon, cut in half*

½ *cup Italian mustard fruit (Italian:* Frutta di Cremona *or Swiss:* Genf Fruechte*), coarsely chopped and drained*

12 *ounces light domestic beer*

½ *cup beef stock (see page 44) (or use rich canned beef broth)*

¼ *cup tomato purée*

¼ *cup prepared mustard*

¼ *cup chili sauce*

¼ *cup hollandaise sauce (see page 86)*

1 *Tablespoon parsley, finely chopped*

Preheat oven to 400 degrees.

First prepare the stuffing. Put the bread, pork, beef, onion, celery, and parsley through the fine blade of the meat grinder. Add the thyme, marjoram, savory, salt, and pepper. Stir in the beaten eggs. Mix thoroughly.

Spread the steaks out, side by side, and lay a piece of bacon in the center of each. Spread the stuffing equally and evenly over each steak, leaving an uncovered border. Place equal amounts of drained mustard fruit in the center of each. Fold in the edges and roll steaks over to a loose but firm *roulade*. Place *roulades* in a roasting pan, closely, but loosely packed. Pour the beer and beef stock over *roulades*, cover, and roast (400 degrees) for about 1¾ hours, or until the beef is tender and nicely browned.

Remove *roulades* to a heated ovenproof casserole or chafing dish. Place the roasting pan over medium heat, stir the pan juices, and mix in the tomato purée. Pour this sauce over the *roulades*.

In a bowl, combine the mustard, chili sauce, and hollandaise. Pour this mixture over the *roulades*. Put back in oven for 5 minutes. Sprinkle with chopped parsley and serve.

Beef Tenderloin with Garden Herbs and Marrow

Serves 4

8 *beef tenderloin slices*
 (approximately 3 *ounces each)*
½ *teaspoon pepper, freshly*
 ground
3 *Tablespoons butter*
¼ *teaspoon marjoram*
¼ *teaspoon coriander*
¼ *teaspoon dry English mustard*

1 *teaspoon shallots (or onions),*
 chopped
½ *teaspoon chives, chopped*
½ *cup dry sherry*
5 *ounces or about* ¾ *cup beef*
 marrow, thinly sliced
 Salt to taste

Preheat oven to 400 *degrees.*

Sprinkle meat with freshly ground pepper and sauté in butter very quickly on both sides—about 1 minute. Arrange each slice separately on an overproof platter. Set aside.

Mix remaining ingredients thoroughly and spread a thin layer on top of each filet. Sprinkle filets lightly with salt to taste. Place platter in preheated oven for 2 to 2½ minutes, until heated through.

Beef Tenderloin Stroganoff

Serves 4

Tenderloin of beef lightly sautéed and served in a smooth sauce richly flavored with sherry, brandy, and cream, is an entrée of distinction and elegance. With this version of Stroganoff, it is important to choose accompanying foods to balance the meal. Rice goes well with Stroganoff. Contrast the deep color of the sauce with a bright green vegetable, a green salad, and a fresh, zesty dessert; perhaps a lemon soufflé, poached fresh pears, or just a basket of fresh fruit.

2 *Tablespoons butter*	½ *cup beef gravy (to improvise*
8 *beef tenderloin slices*	*gravy see page xiii)*
(about 2½ ounces each)	2 *ounces dry sherry*
1 *Tablespoon shallots (or*	1 *ounce brandy*
scallions, white part only),	⅓ *cup heavy cream*
finely chopped	¼ *teaspoon salt*
1 *teaspoon paprika*	
¼ *teaspoon crushed mustard seed*	
Juice of ½ lemon	

OPTIONAL

¼ *pound mushrooms, thinly*	1 *Tablespoon butter*
sliced	

Mushrooms may be added if desired. Wipe clean, trim and discard stems. Slice the mushrooms thin, sauté in butter and add to sauce just before serving.

Heat a heavy-bottomed skillet. Melt the butter, and immediately sauté the tenderloin slices over high heat only 1 minute on each side.

Remove beef slices and keep warm. Add the shallots and paprika to the pan and sauté for 1 minute, stirring constantly. Add the crushed mustard seed, lemon juice, beef gravy, sherry, brandy, cream, and salt, and simmer over medium heat for 2 minutes. Return the beef to the sauce. Heat only to a quick boil and serve at once.

The Ragoûts

Filet Beef Goulash

Serves 4 to 6

½ *pound mushrooms, thinly*
  sliced
  Juice of 1 lemon
2 *Tablespoons butter*
½ *medium-size onion, minced*
1 *Tablespoon paprika*
1 *teaspoon fresh summer savory*
  (or ¼ teaspoon dried)

1½ *pounds ends or tips of beef*
  tenderloin (cut into approxi-
  mately 1-inch cubes)
½ *teaspoon salt*
½ *cup dry red wine*
1 *cup beef gravy (to improvise*
  gravy see page xiii)

Trim off hard edge of mushroom stems and discard. Slice rest of mushrooms very thin, and sprinkle with lemon juice. Set aside.

Melt the butter in a large saucepan, add the onion, paprika, and savory, and sauté until the onion takes on a light color. Add the mushrooms, beef, and salt. Continue to sauté until the beef is lightly sautéed on all sides. Be careful not to overcook the beef.

Add the red wine and simmer for 2 to 3 minutes. If you prefer the meat well done, cut one piece of beef in half to see if longer simmering is required. Add the beef gravy and bring to a light boil.

PRESENTATION
A chafing dish or well heated casserole on the table is the most appropriate way to serve this goulash. As an accompaniment, I would suggest *roësti* potatoes (see page 285), a fresh vegetable in season, and a crisp green salad.

Beef Stew in Red Wine and Mushrooms   *Serves 4*

4 *Tablespoons butter*
2 *pounds beef (shoulder) cut*
  in 1-inch cubes
1½ *teaspoons salt*
3 *medium onions (approxi-*
  mately 1 pound), thinly sliced
1 *clove garlic, crushed*
1 *teaspoon fresh basil, chopped*
  (or ½ teaspoon dried)

Grated peel of ½ lemon
1 *teaspoon paprika*
1½ *Tablespoons flour*
1 *cup dry red wine*
1 *cup beef stock (see page 44),*
  (or use rich canned beef broth)
½ *pound raw mushrooms,*
  coarsely chopped
Chopped parsley

Melt butter in a large heat-proof casserole and brown beef lightly. Add salt, onions, garlic, basil, grated lemon peel, and paprika. Cover and simmer for 30 minutes.

Sprinkle flour over the beef and mix well. Add wine and beef stock, cover, and simmer for 1 hour.

Mix in the chopped mushrooms, cover, and simmer 15 minutes longer, or until beef is tender. Sprinkle with chopped parsley.

Stonehenge Braised Beef   *Serves 4 to 6*
with Tiny Dumplings *Gratinées*

2½ *pounds lean brisket of beef*
  Salt and pepper
¼ *cup vegetable oil*
3 *medium onions, thinly sliced*
1 *Tablespoon vinegar*
1 *cup dry red wine*
1 *teaspoon prepared mustard*
1½ *Tablespoons chili sauce*

1½ *Tablespoons tomato purée*
1 *cup beef stock (see page 44)*
  (or use rich canned beef
  broth)
1 *teaspoon cornstarch dissolved*
  in 2 Tablespoons water
Chopped parsley

DUMPLINGS

½ *pound (1 cup) pâte à choux*
  (see page 373)

1 *Tablespoon cheddar cheese,*
  grated

Sprinkle beef with salt and pepper. Heat oil in a deep saucepan and brown the beef. Add to the saucepan the sliced onions, vinegar, red wine, mustard, chili sauce, tomato purée, and beef broth. Cover and simmer for 2¾ hours, or until tender.

Remove meat from saucepan, slice and arrange on a heated platter and keep warm.

Prepare *pâte à choux* according to recipe on page 373, adding grated cheese to the *pâte à choux* batter. Heat the broth left in the saucepan, and drop in teaspoonfuls of batter to make tiny dumplings. Simmer the dumplings until they rise to the top. Remove dumplings with slotted spoon and arrange over the sliced beef. Add dissolved cornstarch to the broth and stir until thickened. Pour this over the beef. Sprinkle with chopped parsley and serve.

Braised Beef in Red Wine and Wild Mushrooms

Serves 4 to 6

2 *Tablespoons butter*
2 *pounds square shoulder of beef,*
   cut into 8 4-ounce slices
1 *teaspoon paprika*
1 *teaspoon salt*
½ *pound blanched bacon*
   (drained and diced)
3 *medium onions, diced*

5 *ounces dried wild mushrooms,*
   rinsed
2 *cups dry red wine*
1 *cup beef stock (see page 44)*
   (or use rich canned beef
   broth)
1½ *cups fresh white bread crumbs*
½ *teaspoon dried rosemary*

Melt butter in a large ovenproof casserole and brown well the pieces of beef a few at a time until golden. Return them all to the casserole and add paprika, salt, bacon, onion, mushrooms, wine, and beef stock. Cover and simmer for 2 hours, or until beef is tender. Remove meat to a heated platter and keep warm.

Add the bread crumbs and rosemary to the casserole and cook for 2 to 3 minutes, or until thickened. Pour sauce into a blender for ½ minute. Return sauce to casserole. Slice the beef on a heated serving platter. Bring sauce to a boil and pour over the sliced beef. Serve immediately.

Stonehenge Braised Beef with Cauliflower Mousse and Mustard Fruit

Serves 6 to 8

4 *Tablespoons butter*
2 *pounds shoulder of beef (in 1 or 2 pieces)*
2 *cloves garlic, crushed*
2 *leeks (or 5 scallions), chopped*
1 *large onion, diced*
12 *ounces light domestic beer*
1 *Tablespoon tomato purée*
1 *Tablespoon butter, softened*
1 *Tablespoon flour*
1 8–10 *ounce jar mustard fruit (Italian:* Frutta di Cremona *or Swiss:* Genf Fruechte) *(Reserve ½ jar for garnish.)*

1 *cup brown stock (see page 45) (or use rich canned beef broth)*
2 *Tablespoons prepared mustard*
½ *cup chili sauce*
1 *cup mayonnaise*
1 *teaspoon fresh thyme (or ¼ teaspoon dried)*
4 *cups cauliflower mousse (see page 15)*

Heat butter in a large saucepan and brown the beef. Add the garlic, chopped leeks, onion, beer, and tomato purée. Cover and simmer for 3 hours or until tender.

Preheat oven to 450 degrees.

Remove beef from saucepan and place on a heated platter and keep warm. Mix softened butter with flour and add to mixture in saucepan. Boil for 3 to 5 minutes, or until reduced to one-half. Strain the mixture, return to the saucepan and simmer for 15 minutes.

Meanwhile, dice coarsely ½ jar of the mustard fruit, and combine with the brown stock, prepared mustard, chili sauce, mayonnaise, and thyme. Mix thoroughly and add to contents of saucepan.

Spread the cauliflower mousse on an ovenproof serving platter. Slice the beef and arrange over the cauliflower mousse. Pour sauce from the saucepan over the beef. Slice remaining ½ jar of the mustard fruit and arrange over the beef slices and sauce. Place platter in the hot oven (450 degrees) for about 10 minutes, or until heated through and nicely browned. Serve immediately.

Rigi Sauerbraten with Gingersnaps and Dill

Serves 6

3 *pound piece of square
   shoulder of beef, at least 4–5
   inches in diameter*
4 *Tablespoons butter*
1 *teaspoon salt*
1 *cup brown sauce (see page
   79) (to improvise gravy see
   page xiii)*
1 *fresh pig's knuckle,
   split in half*
1 *cup gingersnaps, crushed*

1½ *Tablespoons homogenized
   beef blood (optional)
   See Note**
1 *Tablespoon fresh dill, finely
   chopped (or ¼ teaspoon
   dried)*
   Pinch cayenne pepper

MARINADE

1 *large carrot, diced*
1 *large onion, diced*
1 *Tablespoon pickling spice*
1 *stalk celery, diced*

1 *cup red wine vinegar*
2 *cups dry red wine*
1 *cup water*

Marinate the beef in the above mixture, uncovered, in the refrigerator for five days.

Remove beef from marinade and dry meat thoroughly, reserving marinade and vegetables.

In a casserole (large enough to hold meat, marinade, and vegetables) brown the meat in butter. Add marinade with the vegetables and salt. Cover and simmer slowly for 1½ hours. Add brown sauce and pig's knuckle, cover and simmer slowly for 2¼ hours, or until tender. Remove meat to heated serving platter and keep warm. Add gingersnaps to casserole and simmer for ten minutes. Strain all remaining ingredients in the casserole to make a sauce. Return the sauce to the casserole and add beef blood (optional), dill, and cayenne pepper. Pour over the beef and serve.

* *Note:* If beef blood is added, do not simmer sauce again, as the blood will curdle the sauce. Homogenized beef blood can be obtained in most butcher shops.

Beef Pyramids in Beer Sauce

Serves 6

3½ *pounds boneless beef,*
    about 2 inches thick (lean
    rump, hip, top or bottom
    round)
    Salt and pepper
    Flour for dredging meat
2 *Tablespoons butter*
2 *large onions, thinly sliced*
2 *large sweet red peppers,*
    seeded and sliced or
1 *pimiento, sliced*
12 *mushrooms, coarsely chopped*
12 *ounces domestic light beer*
1½ *Tablespoons catsup*
1 *Tablespoon prepared mustard*

Trim all fat off meat. With a sharp knife, slice meat lengthwise into 2 strips about 3 inches wide. Cut a diagonal slice off one end. Starting at point, cut diagonally in opposite direction to make thick triangular pieces of meat. Continue until whole roast is cut in triangles or "pyramids."

Sprinkle each piece of meat with a pinch of salt and pepper and dredge in flour on all sides. Melt butter in a large frying pan or skillet, and brown meat lightly, turning carefully to retain the pyramid shapes. Add the onions, peppers, and mushrooms to pan and brown lightly. Pour beer over all. Stir in catsup and mustard. Cover tightly and simmer slowly for 1 to 1½ hours, or until meat is tender. If more sauce is desired, add another 6 ounces of beer during cooking.

To serve, stand pyramids of meat up on a warm platter and pour sauce and vegetables over all.

Boiled Beef

Serves 4 to 5

3 *pounds chuck or shortribs*
  of beef (in one piece)
1 *teaspoon peppercorns*
1 *Tablespoon salt*
2 *leeks (or 6 scallions), sliced*
  once lengthwise, then in half

3 *medium carrots, cut in half*
¼ *head cabbage, cut in eighths*
1 *stalk celery, cut in half*

Place beef in a pot. Pour over it enough boiling water to cover. Add peppercorns and salt. Simmer uncovered for 1½ hours. While beef is simmering, add boiling water if needed to keep meat covered. Add leeks, carrots, cabbage, and celery, and simmer for 1 hour longer.

PRESENTATION
To serve, slice the beef and place slices in the center of a soup plate. Arrange vegetables around the slices and ladle the broth over them.

Beef *en Daube* in a Sauce of Red Wine and Olives

Serves 4

Daube is really a method of slow cooking, which used to be widely used in Europe. In fact, the cooking time was so lengthy that very old *daubiers* had deeply indented covers in which hot coals were placed. A feature of this method was to thoroughly seal the pot during the slow cooking. Here I propose a *daube* equal in flavor to the old romantic method but with the cooking time diminished considerably, thanks to our blender. Beef and red wine have a wonderful affinity and, like old violins and some women, improve with age. By this I mean that the *daube* may be made the day before and reheated, or even kept for days. Be sure to cool the *daube* before you refrigerate; sauces tend to sour with sudden changes of temperature from stove to refrigerator.

RED WINE AND OLIVE SAUCE

Combine in the blender and blend until smooth:

½ cup green olives, pitted and coarsely chopped	2 cloves garlic, peeled and cut in pieces
½ cup fresh orange juice	1 Tablespoon shallots (or onions), coarsely chopped
15 anchovy filets, coarsely chopped	1 cup tomato juice
½ cup pimientos, coarsely chopped	1 cup dry red wine

4 Tablespoons olive oil	1 teaspoon salt
2 pounds of lean shoulder of beef (or 1½ pounds of hip beef) cut in 1-inch pieces	¼ teaspoon pepper
	½ teaspoon oregano
	Chopped parsley

The *daube* may be made on top of the stove or in the oven. Preheat oven to 375 degrees if you prefer this method of cooking.

Select a large, heavy, heatproof casserole, heat the olive oil until it begins to sizzle. Put the beef in hot oil and sauté all sides until lightly brown. Cover the beef with the wine-olive sauce. Mix in salt, pepper, and oregano.

Cover and put in oven (375 degrees) for 2 to 2½ hours, or over low simmering heat on top of the stove for the same period of time. When the meat is tender, skim off the fat from the top of the sauce. One advantage of making this some time in advance is that the fat rises to the top and is more easily removed when cold. Serve it generously sprinkled with chopped parsley.

PRESENTATION

Bring it to the table in the casserole over low heat. Rice or potatoes are fine with this *daube,* but I prefer several freshly cooked vegetables of the season and a green salad, leaving the starch for dessert.

Lamb

The Roasts   *The Chops and Steaks*
The Ragoûts

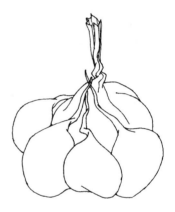

Lamb is more popular in many European countries than it is in the United States. One reason is that real baby lamb, the best of all, is not usually available in the United States due to agricultural laws, and even the so-called spring lamb, which is less than three months old, is more generally available in Europe.

Again, in this country too often we ignore the dozens of available cuts and concentrate on the prestigious parts—lamb chops and legs of lamb. Yet these are not the most flavorful parts of the lamb.

One of the most magnificent dishes of all is a crown roast (double rack) of lamb, and properly cooked roast lamb, rare and pink, is to me as good, if not better, than the best roast beef. You can get it that way in just a very few restaurants—only the very best—but there is no reason why you should not be able to enjoy it that way at home.

In deference to the average American taste, I have soft-pedaled the use of garlic with lamb, but this is one meat that has the greatest affinity for garlic and I recommend you try using a little garlic in seasoning your lamb dishes.

The Roasts

The Chops and Steaks

The Ragoûts

The Roasts

Roast Rack of Lamb with Herbs and Garlic Bread Crumbs

Serves 4

3¾–4 *pound rack of lamb*
    (8 chops)
  1 *Tablespoon salt*
  2 *Tablespoons* fines herbes
    (½ Tablespoon each fresh
    tarragon, chives, shallots,
    parsley, all finely chopped—
    if dried use half the amount.)
 ½ *cup bread crumbs*
  1 *Tablespoon parsley, finely*
    chopped
  2 *cloves garlic, peeled and*
    finely chopped

Preheat oven to 450 degrees.

Ask your butcher to trim the fat from the ends of the chop bones, or do it yourself by cutting down each rib bone about halfway toward the base, removing the rectangle of fat.

Rub the meat all over with salt. Score the fat and rub in the *fines herbes* on all surfaces. Roast (450 degrees) with fat side down for 25 minutes. The outside curve of the ribs has a thick coat of fat. Cut from the top, pull away this coating and discard.

Combine the bread crumbs with the finely chopped parsley and garlic. Sprinkle the outside surfaces of the rack of lamb with the bread crumbs and return to the oven for 5 minutes for rare or 10 minutes for medium, or 15 minutes for well done.

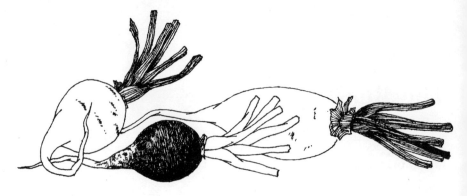

Rack of Lamb Stuffed with Avocado, Tomatoes and Herbs

Serves 4 to 6

4 *pounds rack of lamb (consist-*
  ing of 2 racks, each about 2
  pounds, with chine bone
  cracked)
1 *tomato, sliced into 6 slices*
1 *avocado, peeled and sliced*
  into 6 slices

1 *teaspoon salt*
¼ *teaspoon pepper*
¼ *teaspoon thyme*
1 *clove garlic, finely chopped*

Preheat oven to 500 degrees.

Remove lamb from refrigerator one hour before roasting.

Trim all but a thin layer of fat from the lamb. Place the racks on a table, with curved bone side standing up, and the "eye" or "filet" on the bottom. With a sharp knife, cut the tissue from the bones along the ribs of the loin all the way down to the "eye" to make a pocket. (Stop about ¼-inch from the eye, do not cut into it.) Into this open pocket, insert alternate slices of tomato and avocado along the length of the filet. Tie pocket loosely back into place with butcher's twine along the ribs, making sure the tomato and avocado are secure inside. Sprinkle the racks with salt, pepper, thyme, and chopped garlic.

Place racks in a shallow roasting pan and roast (500 degrees) for 20 minutes. Reduce heat to 400 degrees and roast for 15 minutes more for medium rare, 22 minutes for medium, and 25 minutes for well done. Slice each rack in half at the center between two ribs. This will yield 4 servings from the 2 racks of lamb.

Roast Shoulder of Lamb with Minted Turnips

Serves 4

4 *pounds shoulder of lamb, boned*
12 *sprigs of fresh mint*
1 *teaspoon salt*
¼ *teaspoon pepper*
1 *Tablespoon butter*
1 *onion, diced*
2 *pounds white turnips, peeled*
  and diced

½ *cup beef stock (see page 44)*
  (or use rich canned beef broth)
  Fresh mint, finely chopped

Preheat oven to 450 degrees.

Spread the shoulder of lamb out flat, cover the surface with fresh mint, sprinkle with salt and pepper. Roll the shoulder and tie with strings every 2 inches along the length. Place in a roasting pan, rub the lamb with butter, and roast (450 degrees) for 30 minutes. Add the diced onion, turnips, and beef stock, and roast for another 30 minutes. Remove the onion and turnip with a slotted spoon and put them through the meat grinder or purée in a blender.

PRESENTATION
Spread the purée on a serving platter. Slice the roast and place on top of the purée. Sprinkle with chopped mint and serve at once.

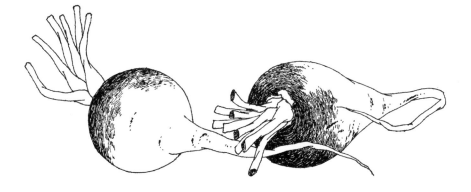

The Chops and Steaks

Curried Lamb Chops Javanese

Serves 4

¼ *cup flour*
1 *Tablespoon curry powder*
8 *lamb chops, French cut (the eye of the chop trimmed of all fat)*
1 *Tablespoon butter*
¼ *cup mangoes, fresh or canned*
1 *Tablespoon kumquats, finely chopped*

1 *cup basic curry sauce (see page 99)*
Juice of 1 lemon
¼ *cup shredded coconut, lightly toasted in oven*

Sift flour with curry powder. Dust the lamb chops in the flour. Melt butter in a large skillet, and sauté the lamb chops for about 2 minutes on each side. Add the mango, chopped kumquat, curry sauce, and lemon juice. Simmer for 3 minutes to warm thoroughly. Transfer to a serving dish and garnish with toasted coconut.

Casserole of Lamb Chops with Puréed Mushrooms

Serves 4

¾ *pound raw mushrooms,*
  washed and drained
1 *Tablespoon butter*
½ *teaspoon salt*
  Pinch of pepper
6 *Tablespoons dry red wine*
½ *teaspoon prepared mustard*
6 *Tablespoons beef gravy (to im-*
  provise gravy see page xiii)

8 *lamb chops, French cut (the*
  eye of the chop trimmed of
  all fat)
  Butter or corn oil for sautéing
2 *Tablespoons ground nuts*
  (any kind)

Preheat oven to 450 degrees.

Put the mushrooms through the fine blade of the meat grinder and then into a saucepan. Add the butter, salt, pepper, wine, mustard, and beef gravy. Bring to a boil, lower heat, and simmer for 10 minutes.

Sauté the lamb chops in butter or oil for 1 minute on each side. Transfer the chops to a shallow, ovenproof dish. Pour the sautéed mushrooms over chops, sprinkle with ground nuts and bake (450 degrees) for 10 minutes.

Serve from the casserole.

Kebab of Lamb *Orientale*   Serves 4

3 *pounds lean lamb from the leg,
    cut into 1-inch cubes*
½ *cup oil*
3 *cloves garlic, peeled*
1 *teaspoon thyme
    Juice of 1 lemon and rind cut
    into strips*
1 *green pepper, cut in 1-inch
    pieces*
2 *tomatoes, thickly sliced and
    halved*
1 *onion, thickly sliced and halved
    Pinch salt*

Marinate the meat in oil, garlic, thyme, lemon juice, and lemon rind for 24 hours uncovered in the refrigerator, turning over the meat several times during this period.

Preheat broiler.

Skewer the cubes of lamb, alternating with a slice of green pepper, another cube of lamb, a slice of tomato, another cube of lamb, a slice of onion, and so on until the lamb is used up. Sprinkle with salt and place the skewers under very hot broiler for 2 minutes. Turn the skewers over and cook 1 minute longer. Serve at once.

Sautéed Lamb Chops with Tomatoes *Provençale*

Serves 4

8 *lamb chops (loin or rib)*
½ *onion, sliced paper thin*
4 *tomatoes (about 1 pound),
    peeled, seeded, and diced*
1 *clove garlic, minced*

¼ *teaspoon each thyme, oregano,
    basil*
4 *Tablespoons tomato juice*
¼ *cup pitted black olives, chopped*

While the lamb chops are sautéing or broiling to your taste, prepare the sauce. In a saucepan combine the sliced onion, the diced tomatoes, the minced garlic and seasoning, and tomato juice, and simmer for 10 minutes.

PRESENTATION
Pour the sauce over the lamb chops, and garnish the top with the chopped olives.

Spring Lamb Steak with Cauliflower Mousse

Serves 4

2 *pound head of cauliflower (trimmed of its core)*
1 *Tablespoon butter*
½ *Tablespoon flour*
½ *cup heavy cream (¼ cup for flour blend, ¼ cup for egg yolk thickening)*
1 *teaspoon salt*
¼ *teaspoon pepper*
2 *egg yolks*
1 *Tablespoon grated Parmesan cheese*
  Oil or butter for sautéing
4 *lamb steaks, ½ to ¾ inches thick*

Trim the core off the cauliflower and cook in water to cover until just tender and slightly underdone. Drain and put the cauliflower through the fine blade of the meat grinder. Set aside.

Combine the butter, flour, and ¼ cup cream in a saucepan and simmer for 3 minutes, stirring constantly. Stir in the ground cauliflower, add salt and pepper.

Beat the egg yolks with the remaining ¼ cup heavy cream, then add to the cauliflower and stir in the grated cheese.

Melt the oil or butter in a large frying pan and sauté the lamb steaks for 2 minutes on each side, turning once. This will be rare. If you prefer them well done, sauté longer. Place the steaks on a baking sheet, cover each one with the cauliflower mousse, and put under the broiler until golden brown. Serve at once.

Curried Lamb Steak

Serves 4

2 *Tablespoons butter*
4 *lamb steaks,* 10 *ounces each*
1 *cup basic curry sauce*
   (see page 99)
1 *teaspoon prepared mustard*

1 *Tablespoon chili sauce*
2 *bananas, peeled and cut in*
   half lengthwise
1 *Tablespoon sugar*
   Juice of one half lemon

Melt the butter in a large skillet and sauté the lamb steaks no longer than 3 minutes on each side. Transfer the lamb steaks to an ovenproof serving dish, side by side.

Combine the curry sauce with the mustard and chili sauce, and pour over the steaks. Sprinkle the banana halves with sugar and lemon juice, place on top of the steaks, and put under the broiler until golden brown. Serve at once.

The Ragoûts

Irish Lamb Stew

2 *Tablespoons butter*
1 *medium onion, finely chopped*
1 *clove garlic, peeled, minced*
2 *pounds shoulder of lamb, cut into 1-inch pieces*
3 *cups beef, chicken, or veal stock (see pages 43, 44, 46) (or use rich canned beef or chicken broth), or water*
1½ *teaspoons salt*
½ *teaspoon pepper*
1 *small bayleaf*
1 *clove*
Pinch each of thyme, oregano, marjoram
3 *stalks celery, scraped, cut into 1-inch strips*

4 *medium carrots (about 8 ounces), peeled, cut into 1-inch strips*
½ *pound white cabbage, coarsely chopped*
1 *large leek (or 2 large scallions), green and white parts, coarsely chopped*
2 *small turnips, peeled and quartered*
1 *pound raw potatoes, peeled and diced*
1 *Tablespoon parsley, finely chopped*

Melt the butter in a large saucepan. Add half of the chopped onion and the minced garlic and sauté for 3 minutes, stirring constantly. Add the lamb, the water or stock, salt, pepper, bayleaf, clove, thyme, oregano, and marjoram. Bring to a boil, cover and simmer for 1 hour. Add the celery strips and carrots, chopped cabbage and leek, quartered turnips, and the rest of the chopped onion, cover, and simmer for 20 minutes. Add the diced potatoes, cover, and simmer for another 10 minutes. Serve the Irish Stew in a large heated casserole sprinkled generously with chopped parsley.

With this delicious stew, I suggest you serve herb dumplings (see page 279).

Lamb Stew with Fresh Vegetables and Red Wine

Serves 4 to 6

2 *Tablespoons butter*
2 *pounds shoulder of lamb, cut into 1-inch pieces*
1½ *teaspoons salt*
½ *teaspoon pepper*
  Pinch each of savory, marjoram, thyme, basil, oregano, rosemary
1 *teaspoon parsley, finely chopped*
1 *medium onion, coarsely chopped*

1 *clove garlic, peeled and minced*
1 *heaping Tablespoon tomato purée*
½ *cup dry red wine*
2 *cups brown stock (see page 45) (or use rich canned beef broth)*
4 *medium carrots cut into 1-inch strips*
3 *stalks celery, scraped and cut into 1-inch strips*

Melt the butter in a large skillet and sauté the lamb until each piece is lightly colored (about 5 or 6 minutes.) Combine the seasonings and sprinkle them over the lamb. Put meat in large saucepan. Combine the chopped onion, minced garlic, and tomato purée, mix thoroughly and add to meat. Add the red wine, bring to a boil, and simmer for 5 minutes. Add the stock, bring to a boil, cover, and simmer for 20 minutes. Add the carrot and celery strips, cover, and simmer for another 40 minutes.

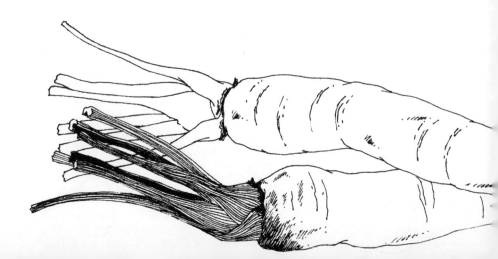

Navarin of Lamb

Serves 4 to 6

3 *pounds shoulder of lamb (bone in) or leg (boned)*

⅓ *cup flour seasoned with* 1½ *teaspoons salt,* ½ *teaspoon pepper*

3 *Tablespoons butter or oil for roasting*
   Pinch powdered sugar

2 *cups dry red wine combined with* 1 *cup water*

3 *Tablespoons tomato purée*
   Bouquet garni *(8 sprigs parsley,* 1 *bayleaf, sprig each of*

thyme and basil, tied together, wrapped in cheesecloth. If dried herbs are used, use half the amount.)

1 *clove garlic, peeled and chopped*

2 *Tablespoons butter (for sautéing)*

½ *pound pearl onions, peeled*

1 *pound tiny new potatoes, peeled*

1 *Tablespoon parsley, finely chopped*

Preheat oven to 400 *degrees.*

Trim off as much fat as possible from the lamb and cut into 2-inch pieces. Dust the pieces of lamb in seasoned flour. Melt 3 Tablespoons of butter in an ovenproof casserole, add the meat, sugar, wine, tomato purée, *bouquet garni*, and garlic. Cover and bake (400 degrees) for 1 hour. Remove from oven and skim off the grease from the top with a large spoon.

Melt 2 Tablespoons of butter in a skillet and sauté the onions and potatoes for 5 minutes. Add them to the casserole, cover, put back in oven for about 35 minutes, or until the potatoes are tender.

Remove any grease that comes to the top. Just before serving, sprinkle with chopped parsley.

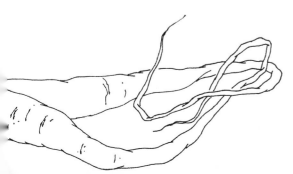

Veal

The Roasts   *The Chops and Cutlets*
The Ragoûts   *Sweetbreads and Liver*

Veal is meat from calves less than three months old, and the best is from ones which have been milk fed. This meat is much more popular in Europe than in the United States and I must admit that the veal available in Europe is better than what we get here. Europe does not have the vast cattle grazing areas of the United States and feed is so expensive in winter that calves are sent to market rather than kept to be developed as beef animals.

However, excellent veal can be obtained in many parts of the United States, and it offers a delicious and welcome change from the too frequent beef and pork dishes. I feel that if people keep asking for veal in their markets, the demand will eventually increase the supply.

Veal is a delicately flavored meat with very little fat. In buying it, a good guide is that the whitest meat is likely to be the best and most tender. It lends itself especially to the use of sauces because it absorbs and blends with other flavors so readily.

The Roasts

The Chops and Cutlets

The Ragoûts

Sweetbreads and Liver

The Roasts

Roast Loin of Veal with Cream, *Paprikash* *Serves 4*

2 *pounds boneless loin of veal,*
  untied
1 *teaspoon salt, for roasting*
¼ *teaspoon pepper, for roasting*
1 *medium carrot, finely chopped*
1 *medium onion, finely chopped*
1 *Tablespoon paprika*
6 *Tablespoons butter*
2 *Tablespoons flour*
2 *ounces dry white wine*

Juice of ½ *lemon*
1 *teaspoon salt*
½ *teaspoon pepper*
2 *ounces dry sherry*
1 *cup chicken stock (see page*
  45) (or use rich canned
  chicken broth)
½ *teaspoon paprika*
2 *Tablespoons heavy cream*

Remove veal from refrigerator one hour before roasting.

Preheat oven to 450 degrees.

Sprinkle veal with 1 teaspoon salt and ¼ teaspoon pepper. Place in a shallow roasting pan without a rack and roast uncovered (450 degrees) for 45 minutes. Add chopped carrot and onion, paprika and the butter, and roast for 10 minutes more.

Remove roasting pan to the top of the stove, stir the pan juices and mix in flour until smooth and the flour is well absorbed. Add the white wine, lemon juice, 1 teaspoon salt, ½ teaspoon pepper, sherry, and chicken stock and simmer over low heat for 3 minutes.

Remove veal to a heated serving platter and keep warm. Strain the sauce through a fine sieve into a saucepan. Over medium heat, stir in ½ teaspoon paprika and the heavy cream. Slice the veal and place on a heated serving platter. Serve the sauce over the meat.

Breast of Veal with Pistachio Stuffing   *Serves 6*

One of the least expensive cuts of veal is the breast. Filled with a savory stuffing and pistachio nuts, it becomes a very special meat course. Tell the butcher to carefully remove the bones and make a pocket of the outer skin. Or, with a small sharp knife and a bit of time, you can do it yourself. The cooked breast, sliced and served cold, is an excellent luncheon dish—perhaps even more flavorsome, as herbs become more piquant the following day.

BREAST OF VEAL
(2½ pounds, after boning)
Once the bones have been removed, turn the breast over with the outer skin up. Trim off any bits of fat or meat to make a neat rectangle. With a small sharp kitchen knife, make an incision on the right edge of the meat to separate the outer skin from the body of the roast. The purpose is to make a pocket the entire width of the roast into which you will place the stuffing. Cut the whitish membrane right on through to the left side but leave it attached on that end as well as top and bottom. Run your hand inside to loosen the membrane until you have a large pocket.

FILLING
4 *slices bacon, coarsely chopped, blanched in 1 cup water for 2 minutes, and drained*
1 *stalk celery, coarsely chopped*
½ *medium onion, coarsely chopped*
1 *clove garlic, minced*
6 *springs parsley, coarsely chopped*
¾ *pound veal, cut in small pieces*
6 *slices bread (5 ounces) soaked in ½ cup milk*
2 *eggs*

1 *teaspoon salt*
¼ *teaspoon pepper*
  Pinch each of savory, rosemary, oregano, thyme
½ *cup pistachio nuts, coarsely chopped*

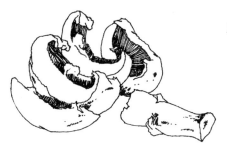

MUSHROOM SAUCE

Base of pan juices

¼ cup dry white wine

1 teaspoon cornstarch dissolved in 2 teaspoons water

½ cup veal stock, or a combination

of beef and chicken (see page 46), (or rich canned beef and chicken broth)

¼ pound mushrooms, finely sliced

Salt and pepper to taste

Preheat oven to 450 degrees.

Sauté the blanched bacon, celery, onion, garlic, and parsley in a frying pan over high heat for 5 minutes. Remove from the fire, mix with the veal and bread, and put through the meat grinder, using the finest blade.

Add to the ground meat mixture the eggs, salt and pepper, savory, rosemary, oregano, thyme, pistachio nuts.

Carefully fill the pocket, separating the outer skin from the meat, distributing the filling evenly. Seal the opening of the pocket either by sewing with a needle and thread or with skewers. If you have made any holes, be sure to close them as well.

Place the breast of veal, filled side up, in a roasting pan and bake (450 degrees) for 1½ hours, or until golden brown. Baste with the pan juices every 15 minutes or so.

SAUCE

Remove the roast from the pan and keep warm. Place the roasting pan over medium heat on top of the stove, scrape the pan and stir in the white wine and dissolved cornstarch. Add stock and simmer to reach the consistency of light cream. Add the sliced mushrooms, simmer until the mushrooms are soft—about 5 minutes. Taste and correct the seasoning with salt and pepper.

PRESENTATION

This is an excellent roast to carve at table. Cut slices thick enough so that the dressing remains intact and cover the individual serving with the mushroom sauce.

Roast Loin of Veal with Purée of Mushrooms and Onions

Serves 4

1 *pound boneless loin of veal, untied*

1 *teaspoon salt (for roasting)*

1 *teaspoon fresh rosemary (or ½ teaspoon dried)*

6 *Tablespoons butter (4 Tablespoons cut in pieces for roasting, 2 Tablespoons for sauce)*

1½ *teaspoons flour*

2 *ripe, whole tomatoes, peeled and coarsely chopped*

¼ *cup dry white wine*

¼ *cup beef gravy (to improvise gravy see page xiii)*

½ *pound onions, coarsely chopped*

1 *pound mushrooms, coarsely chopped*

1 *pint water*

¼ *teaspoon lemon juice*

1 *teaspoon salt*

¼ *cup* béchamel *sauce (see page 81)*

Pinch of cayenne pepper

Remove veal from refrigerator one hour before roasting.

Preheat oven to 400 degrees.

Sprinkle veal lightly with salt and rosemary and distribute 4 Tablespoons butter pieces on top of meat. Put in a shallow roasting pan, without a rack, and roast for 25 minutes (400 degrees).

Stir the flour into the pan juices, mix in the chopped tomatoes, white wine, and beef gravy and roast for 25 minutes more.

While the veal is roasting, simmer the onions, mushrooms, water, lemon juice, and salt for 25 minutes in a saucepan. Pour mixture into a sieve and drain. Purée the drained onions and mushrooms in a blender with the ¼ cup *béchamel* sauce. Pour the purée back into the saucepan and bring to a boil. Add remaining 2 Tablespoons of butter, pinch of cayenne, and remove from the fire.

Remove the veal from the oven (juices should run clear after 50 minutes of roasting), carve into eight slices, and arrange on a heated serving platter. Spoon the purée over the veal slices. Strain the sauce from the roasting pan into a sauce boat and serve separately.

The Chops and Cutlets

Veal Cutlet Hungarian Style

Serves 4

This recipe shows how readily, despite its lack of color and rather mild flavor, veal can be transformed into an exciting, colorful dish, with the appropriate use of herbs and spices. Hungarians have created many great dishes and this one illustrates their effective use of paprika to add color and taste. It makes an easily prepared main course, served with noodles and a freshly cooked vegetable.

½ teaspoon salt
¼ teaspoon pepper
1½ teaspoons paprika
   (1 teaspoon for dusting,
   ½ teaspoon for sauce)
4 veal cutlets (about 4 ounces
   each), pounded thin
   Flour (for dredging)
2 Tablespoons butter

1 Tablespoon shallots (or
   onion), finely chopped
¼ cup dry white wine
½ cup beef stock (see page 44)
   (or use a rich canned beef
   broth)
   Grated rind of ½ lemon
¼ cup heavy cream

GARNISH
1 teaspoon dill, chopped

Watercress or parsley

Sprinkle salt, pepper, and 1 teaspoon of paprika on both sides of the cutlets and dredge thoroughly in flour. Shake off the excess.

Melt the butter in a large skillet and sauté the cutlets over medium heat until golden brown on both sides. Remove cutlets and keep warm.

To the pan juices add the shallots, white wine, beef stock, lemon rind, and ½ teaspoon paprika. Simmer and stir constantly for about 5 minutes, or until the sauce thickens slightly. Then add the ¼ cup of heavy cream, mix well and heat through.

PRESENTATION
Pour the sauce over the cutlets, sprinkle with dill, and serve garnished with bouquets of watercress or parsley.

Medallions of Veal with Hearts of Artichoke

Serves 4

4 *Tablespoons butter*
8 *medallions of veal,*
  2 ounces each
1 *teaspoon salt*
½ *teaspoon marjoram*
8 *cooked artichoke hearts (frozen*
  or canned)
1 *Tablespoon shallots (or*
  onions), chopped

6 *anchovy filets, finely chopped*
  Juice of ½ lemon
2 *Tablespoons veal gravy (to im-*
  provise gravy see page xiii)
¼ *cup black and green olives,*
  diced
1 *Tablespoon Parmesan cheese*

Melt butter in a large skillet and sauté veal over medium heat for 3 minutes on each side, until golden brown. Add to the pan the salt, marjoram, artichoke hearts, shallots, anchovy filets, lemon juice, veal gravy, chopped olives, and Parmesan cheese, and stir until veal is coated.

PRESENTATION
Arrange the sauced medallions on a heated serving platter and serve.

Veal Cutlet, Julienne of Vegetables and Cheese

Serves 4

1 *cup each (cut in julienne*
  strips 3 inches long): carrots,
  leeks, cabbage, and celery
4 *3-ounce veal cutlets, thinly*
  sliced
½ *cup flour*
½ *teaspoon salt*
6 *Tablespoons butter (4 Table-*
  spoons for sautéing, 2 Table-
  spoons for sauce)

Pinch marjoram
1 *Tablespoon tomato sauce (see*
  page 93) (or use canned)
½ *teaspoon salt*
4 *slices Swiss (Emmenthaler)*
  cheese
  Paprika

Preheat oven to 400 degrees.

Blanch the julienne vegetable strips in boiling salted water for 5 to 8 minutes.

   While they are cooking, pound the cutlets thin. Dust with flour, shake off excess, sprinkle each cutlet with salt. Melt 4 Tablespoons butter in a large frying pan and over high heat sauté cutlets quickly—about ½ minute on each side—until golden brown. Arrange side by side on an ovenproof serving platter and keep warm. Drain the julienne vegetables and add marjoram, 2 Tablespoons butter, tomato sauce, and ½ teaspoon salt to them. Heap the julienne strips with their sauce in a mound on each cutlet. Cover each with thinly sliced cheese. Sprinkle with a little paprika. Put in oven (400 degrees) for 5 minutes, or until cheese starts to melt. Serve.

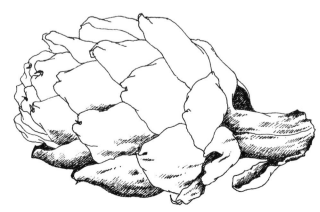

Paprika Veal Schnitzel

Serves 4

8 *thin slices veal scallopine*
  (about 1½ ounces each),
  pounded thin
½ *cup flour*
½ *teaspoon salt*
4 *Tablespoons butter*
1 *Tablespoon shallots (or*
  onions), finely chopped

1 *Tablespoon paprika*
1½ *ounces dry sherry*
¼ *cup heavy cream*
¼ *cup rich veal gravy (to im-*
  provise gravy see page xiii)
½ *teaspoon salt*
  Grated peel of ½ lemon

Dust veal slices with flour, then sprinkle with ½ teaspoon salt.

Melt the butter in a saucepan and sauté scallopine quickly on both sides, until golden brown—about 2 minutes. Add the shallots and paprika and stir until the veal slices are coated with the paprika. Add sherry and cream and simmer for 5 minutes. Add the veal gravy to the pan, sprinkle with the remaining ½ teaspoon salt and simmer for 5 to 8 minutes more.

Remove to heated serving platter. Sprinkle grated lemon peel over all and serve.

Breaded Veal Parmesan

Serves 4

4 *scallops of veal (about*
  3 ounces each), pounded thin
¼ *cup flour*
1 *cup fine bread crumbs*
⅔ *cup grated Parmesan cheese*
  Grated rind of 2 lemons

1 *Tablespoon salt*
¼ *teaspoon pepper*
1 *egg*
3 *Tablespoons butter*
1 *lemon, cut in quarters*

Pound the scallops of veal very thin or have your butcher do it.

Sift the flour onto a flat plate. In a shallow bowl, combine the bread crumbs, cheese, lemon rind, salt, and pepper. Lightly beat the egg in another small shallow bowl.

Dust each scallop thoroughly with flour, shake off excess, dip and coat well in beaten egg, and then coat with the bread crumb mixture.

Melt the butter in a skillet large enough to hold the 4 scallops and sauté 2 minutes on each side or until golden brown. Serve with wedges of lemon.

Veal Cutlet in White Wine, Cream, and Morels

Serves 4

Morels, a variety of European mushroom, are becoming increasingly popular in this country and are available in two forms—dried or in cans. Morels provide a much stronger and more pungent flavor than our own domestic mushroom and combined with white wine and cream create a delicious sauce for veal.

1 *teaspoon salt*
½ *teaspoon pepper*
8 *veal cutlets, about* 2 *ounces each, pounded thin*
½ *cup flour*
4 *Tablespoons butter*
2 *ounces morels, drained and cut in halves*
¼ *cup dry white wine*

¼ *cup heavy cream*
¼ *cup brown sauce (see page 79) (to improvise gravy see page xiii)*
1 *teaspoon cornstarch dissolved in 2 Tablespoons water*
1 *Tablespoon parsley, finely chopped*

Sprinkle salt and pepper on each cutlet, and dust lightly with flour.

Melt the butter in a large skillet and sauté the cutlets over high heat about 2 minutes, until golden brown on each side. Reduce the heat to medium and add the morels. Stir in the white wine, heavy cream, and brown sauce. Mix in the dissolved cornstarch and simmer for 5 minutes.

PRESENTATION
Place the cutlets on heated platter, serve sauce over meat, and sprinkle chopped parsley on top.

Veal Pojarsky

Serves 6

1 *pound veal shoulder*
4 *Tablespoons (½ stick) softened*
   butter
½ *cup heavy cream (for mousse)*
1 *Tablespoon salt*

½ *teaspoon pepper*
½ *teaspoon rosemary*
½ *teaspoon marjoram*
3 *whole eggs*

SAUCE

¼ *cup heavy cream*
½ *cup veal or beef gravy (to im-*
   provise gravy see page xiii)

3 *ounces dry sherry*
1 *Tablespoon paprika*

Remove the gristle and veins and put veal through a meat grinder. Then blend in a blender with the butter, ½ cup heavy cream, salt, pepper, rosemary, marjoram, and eggs, until it is a fine mousse. Put in a bowl and set aside for 1½ hours in a cool place.

Preheat oven to 375 degrees.

Form veal mixture into the shape of a large chop or 6 small chops and place on a buttered cookie sheet. Roast (375 degrees) for 15 minutes. Remove from oven and arrange in a chafing dish.

SAUCE

In a saucepan, combine ¼ cup heavy cream, gravy, sherry, and paprika. Simmer for 5 minutes. Pour over the veal cutlet and serve.

Cold Veal with Tuna Fish and Sour Cream   *Serves 4*

(This dish is a version of the Italian Vitello Tonnato.)

¼ cup cooking oil
2 pound piece of veal, preferably leg or shoulder, free of veins and gristle
1 cup dry white wine
½ cup tomato juice
1 Tablespoon flour
2 cloves garlic, crushed
1 Tablespoon paprika
1 teaspoon salt
8 ounces tuna fish
3 anchovy filets, chopped
1 medium onion, coarsely chopped
1 teaspoon oregano

1 calf's foot, split in half, or ¼ teaspoon unflavored gelatin dissolved in 1 Tablespoon boiling water
½ cup sour cream
Juice of ½ lemon

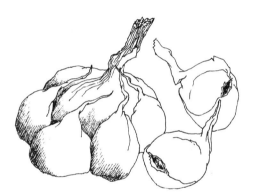

GARNISH
1 Tablespoon capers, chopped

1 Tablespoon chives, chopped

Heat cooking oil in heavy-bottomed pot and brown the veal. Add wine, tomato juice, flour, garlic, paprika, salt, tuna fish, chopped anchovy, onion, oregano, and calf's foot. Simmer uncovered for one hour.

Remove veal, cool, and refrigerate. Discard calf's foot.

Turn the contents of the pot into the blender and add the sour cream and lemon juice. Blend until smooth. Then strain the sauce through a sieve into a bowl.

PRESENTATION
When ready to serve, slice the veal thin and spoon the sauce over the veal. Sprinkle with capers and chives and serve cold.

The Ragoûts

Scallops of Veal in White Wine and Mushrooms

Serves 4

This combination of tender veal, mushrooms, and white wine is a particularly good way to serve veal properly. In Switzerland it is very popular. This richly flavored dish, which is so easily and quickly prepared, should be accompanied by a delicately seasoned risotto (or *roësti*) potatoes (see page 285).

6 *slices of prosciutto ham, thinly sliced (or dried chipped beef)*
1 *teaspoon salt*
¼ *teaspoon pepper*
½ *teaspoon paprika*
1 *pound veal, cut in 1½ ounce scallops*
2 *Tablespoons butter*
½ *pound mushrooms, thinly sliced*
1 *Tablespoon shallots (or scallion, white part only), finely chopped*

½ *cup dry white wine*
½ *cup brown sauce (see page 79) (or to improvise beef gravy see page xiii)*
1 *Tablespoon cornstarch dissolved in 3 Tablespoons water*
1 *cup heavy cream*
Juice of ¼ lemon
1 *Tablespoon parsley, finely chopped*

Slice the prosciutto very thin and set aside.

Sprinkle the salt, pepper, and paprika on each scallop. Melt the butter in a large frying pan over high heat. Add the seasoned veal and sauté until golden brown on both sides.

Reduce heat to medium, add the mushrooms, shallots, white wine, and brown sauce, and simmer for 5 minutes, stirring frequently.

Mix in the dissolved cornstarch and cream and simmer for another 5 minutes, stirring frequently.

Add lemon juice and prosciutto. Sprinkle with chopped parsley and serve.

Scallops of Veal with Mousse of Fresh Asparagus, *Mornay*

Serves 4

MOUSSE

1 *pound fresh or frozen asparagus*

3 *shallots (or ½ onion), finely chopped*

¼ *teaspoon salt*

¼ *cup hollandaise sauce (see page 86)*

Wash the fresh asparagus thoroughly under running water, scrape off the stem skin and cut off and discard the tough white part at the base. Cut asparagus into small 1-inch pieces and cook in a saucepan with the shallots and salt for 15 to 20 minutes (if frozen, 12 to 15 minutes will be sufficient) or until they are tender. Drain thoroughly and chop fine. In a mixing bowl combine the asparagus with the hollandaise sauce. Keep warm.

8 *scallops of veal, pounded thin to the width of a silver dollar*

½ *teaspoon salt*

½ *cup flour*

4 *Tablespoons butter*

¼ *cup dry white wine*

¼ *cup Parmesan cheese, grated*

Sprinkle the scallops of veal with salt and dust them lightly with flour on both sides.

Melt butter in a large sauté pan over high heat and sauté the scallops about 1 minute on each side, until golden brown. Do not overcook the veal.

Add white wine to the sauté pan and scrape up all the browned pieces from the bottom.

Preheat broiler.

Arrange the sautéed veal scallops in a large, shallow, ovenproof casserole. Cover with the white wine and scrapings. Put an even amount of the mousse of asparagus in the center of each scallop. Sprinkle Parmesan cheese over the mousse and place under the broiler 2 to 3 minutes until the cheese is golden. Serve at once.

Paupiettes of Veal *en Brochette*   *Serves 4*

  4 *ounces cooked ham (or use canned)*
 16 *thinly sliced veal scallops, 1 ounce each*
  2 *calomandin, diced (or 4 kumquats diced) (Calomandin is a small, sour Philippine orange.)*

 ¼ *teaspoon paprika*
  1 *egg yolk, beaten*
 ¼ *teaspoon salt*
  2 *Tablespoons butter*

Put the ham through the fine blade of a meat grinder to purée.

Pound the scallops until paper thin. Combine ground ham, diced calomandin, paprika, beaten egg yolk, and salt.

Spread thinly on each veal scallop, and roll up. Skewer 4 rolled scallops together per serving.

Sauté in butter, or broil until golden brown all over.

Veal in Cream *à la Suisse*   *Serves 4*

  4 *Tablespoons butter*
  1 *pound veal, in julienne strips*
  1 *teaspoon salt*
 ¼ *teaspoon pepper*
 ½ *teaspoon paprika*
 ½ *pound mushrooms, thinly sliced*
  3 *Tablespoons shallots (or onions), finely chopped*

 ¼ *cup dry white wine*
 ⅔ *cup heavy cream*
  1 *cup beef gravy (to improvise gravy see page xiii)*
  1 *Tablespoon cornstarch dissolved in 3 Tablespoons cold water*
 Juice of ¼ lemon

Melt the butter in a large skillet over high heat. Sauté the veal for 5 minutes, stirring frequently. Sprinkle with salt, pepper, and paprika.

Add mushrooms and shallots and sauté for 3 minutes, stirring constantly. Pour in the wine, cream, and gravy. Simmer for 5 minutes.

Stir the dissolved cornstarch into the veal to thicken the sauce. Add the lemon juice and serve.

Sweetbreads and Liver

Calf's Liver Slices with Avocado

8 *thin 1½ ounce slices
  calf's liver*
2 *medium avocados, peeled,
  each divided in four*
½ *cup flour*
2 *teaspoons salt*
12 *Tablespoons butter (8 Tablespoons for sauté, 4 Tablespoons
  for sauce)*

1 *Tablespoon chives, chopped
  Juice of 1 lemon*
1 *Tablespoon Parmesan cheese,
  grated*

Ask your butcher for thin (1½ ounce) slices of calf's liver.

Peel the avocados and cut each one into quarters. Dust liver slices and avocado slices with flour and sprinkle them lightly with salt. Heat two sauté or frying pans, melt 4 Tablespoons of butter in each; in one pan quickly sauté the liver slices and in the other sauté the avocado slices, about ½ minute on each side.

Arrange the liver slices on a heated serving platter, alternating each liver slice with a slice of avocado.

To the pan in which the liver was sautéed, add 4 Tablespoons butter, chopped chives, lemon juice, and Parmesan cheese. Sauté and stir until the butter is nicely browned. Pour the sauce over the liver and avocado slices and serve.

Fresh Calf's Sweetbreads on a Purée of Garden Peas

Serves 6

1 *teaspoon salt*	½ *teaspoon salt*
½ *medium onion, in one piece*	*Pinch of pepper*
1 *clove (stuck into the onion)*	*Pinch of sugar*
1 *bayleaf*	½ *cup flour*
2 *pair calf's sweetbreads (about 3 pounds)*	4 *Tablespoons butter*
1 *pound fresh peas*	½ *cup mushrooms, cut into thin strips*
3 *Tablespoons heavy cream*	¼ *cup beef gravy (to improvise gravy see page xiii)*
1 *Tablespoon butter, softened at room temperature*	1 *Tablespoon dry sherry*

GARNISH
½ *cup cooked or Westphalian ham, cut into strips*

Fill a 2 quart saucepan about half full with water (it should cover the sweetbreads when you add them). Add the salt, the onion with the clove, and the bayleaf. When the water comes to a boil, add sweetbreads, reduce heat and simmer for 20 minutes. Remove the sweetbreads, reserving the cooking liquid, and plunge them into cold water. Carefully remove all filaments, skin, and gristle from the sweetbreads and cut them into half-inch slices. Remove (and discard) the onion with clove and the bayleaf from the liquid.

Put the peas into the cooking liquid and cook until they are soft. Drain the peas, then purée them in a blender or press them through a sieve. Mix the purée with 2 Tablespoons of the cooking liquid, the cream, 1 Tablespoon butter, salt, pepper, and sugar, and keep hot.

Dust the sliced sweetbreads with flour. Melt the remaining butter in a saucepan and sauté the sweetbreads for about 2½ minutes each side, until golden. Add the mushrooms to the sweetbreads and sauté until just cooked through. Add the beef gravy and sherry to heat through.

PRESENTATION
On a heated serving platter, make a bed of the purée of peas, place sweetbreads on top, spoon the sauce over the sweetbreads and garnish with the strips of ham.

Queen's *Bouchée* of Calf's Sweetbreads   *Serves 4*

1 *pair calf's sweetbreads,*
  1¼–1½ pounds
4 *Tablespoons butter*
1 *Tablespoon onion, finely*
  minced
½ *cup mushrooms, diced*
1 *Tablespoon flour*
1 *cup veal or chicken stock (see*
  pages 43 or 46) (or use rich
  canned chicken broth)

¼ *cup dry sherry*
¼ *cup dry white wine*
½ *cup heavy cream*
1 *teaspoon salt*
¼ *cup hollandaise sauce*
  (see page 86)
4 *puff paste pastry shells*
  (obtain from a pastry shop)

Simmer sweetbreads uncovered in a pan with enough water to cover meat for 20 minutes. Cool off under cold running water. Remove all filaments, gristle, and skin. Dice the sweetbreads in ⅛-inch cubes.

In a large saucepan, melt the butter and add the minced onion and mushrooms. Sauté until onions are soft and clear. Stir in flour and mix well. Set aside.

In another saucepan, bring to a boil the veal or chicken stock, sherry, white wine, and heavy cream. Add to the onion and mushroom mixture.

Return to heat, add salt, stir in, and simmer for 10 minutes, stirring often. Add the diced sweetbreads and remove from fire. Fold in hollandaise, pour into pastry shells and serve.

Pork

The Roasts   The Chops
Ham and Sausages

Pork is by far the most versatile of all meats, and the proof is that all over Europe even today there are special pork stores that sell only the great variety of fresh, smoked, cured, and salted pork products in addition to the pork sausage products called *charcuterie*.

We enjoy great quantities of pork in the United States but, unfortunately, we are not as adventurous as Europeans. As a result, bacon, ham, ham steaks, pork loins, and chops, and a few other items represent the extent of our interest, while we leave to our European friends the enjoyment of pig's feet and knuckles, pork livers, head, hocks, joints, etc. Lard (pork fat) is somewhat out of fashion in this country, but it is excellent for every kind of cooking and is especially ideal for flaky pie crust baking.

Pork as a hearty meat lends itself particularly well to some of the dishes you will find in the "accompaniments" section, especially those using cabbage, fruits, pungent salads, and vegetables.

One final note concerning the cooking times specified in my pork recipes. Most Americans cook pork far too long and hurt both the texture and flavor. Follow the timing of my recipes and you will find them both safe and delicious.

The Roasts

The Chops

Ham and Sausages

The Roasts

Curried Pork Loin

Serves 4 to 6

1 *cup basic curry sauce*
  (see page 99)
1 *teaspoon salt*
¼ *teaspoon pepper*
1 *Tablespoon curry powder*
4 *pound loin of pork, backbone*
  removed, rolled and tied
1 *Tablespoon chili sauce*

1 *clove garlic, peeled and finely*
  chopped
  Juice of ½ lemon
2 *Tablespoons butter*
1 *onion, thinly sliced*
¼ *cup seedless raisins (3 ounces)*
1 *cup cider*
2 *Tablespoons prepared mustard*

Prepare basic curry sauce.

Preheat oven to 450 degrees.

Combine the salt, pepper, and curry powder, and rub the entire surface of the loin. In a bowl, combine the curry sauce, chili sauce, garlic, and lemon juice. Cover the loin with the sauce and roast (450 degrees) for 40 minutes.

During the roasting time, melt the butter in a skillet and sauté the sliced onion until slightly colored, add the raisins, cider, and mustard, and simmer for 10 minutes.

Remove the loin from the roasting pan, scrape the pan juices and strain them through a sieve into the sauce in the skillet. Return the loin to the roasting pan, pour the sauce over it, and roast for another 10 minutes, basting frequently.

Slice the pork loin on a heated platter and serve with the sauce over the meat.

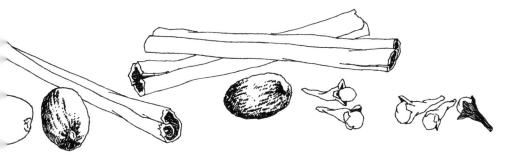

Loin of Pork with Pistachios on Apple Brown Betty

Serves 6

4 *pounds boneless loin of pork*
2 *teaspoons salt*
1 *teaspoon pepper*
1 *teaspoon powdered ginger*
1 *cup onion, finely chopped*
1 *cup dry white wine*

3 *apples, peeled, cored, and diced*
4 *cups stale white bread, diced*
4 *eggs*
1 *cup milk*
2 *Tablespoons pistachio nuts, finely chopped*

Remove pork from refrigerator 1 hour before roasting.

Preheat oven to 450 degrees.

Trim the loin of all excess fat and rub surface with salt, pepper, and ginger. Place in a shallow roasting pan, without a rack, and roast for 25 minutes (450 degrees). Add chopped onion and roast for 5 to 10 minutes more, until onions are lightly browned. Stir in the white wine, diced apple, and bread cubes to the onions in the pan and roast for another 25 minutes. Beat eggs and milk together and stir into the roasting pan mixture. Sprinkle chopped pistachio nuts all around and stir lightly into mixture. Roast for an additional 25 minutes, or until pork is golden and tender.

PRESENTATION
Slice pork and arrange on heated platter over the pistachio and apple brown Betty mixture.

Roast Smoked Pork Loin with Pistachios, Chestnut Purée

Serves 6

Chestnut purée (see page 314)
4 *pound smoked loin of pork*
½ *cup grenadine*
¼ *cup powdered sugar*
¼ *cup pistachio nuts, finely chopped*

Prepare chestnut purée.

In a large pot, cover the loin with boiling water and slowly simmer, uncovered, for 45 minutes. Be careful not to allow the water to boil after the loin is in it.

Preheat oven to 450 degrees.

Transfer the loin to a roasting pan. Pour the grenadine over the meat, sprinkle with powdered sugar and roast (450 degrees) for 25 minutes, basting frequently.

PRESENTATION

Slice the loin thin, sprinkle with pistachio nuts. Pour the sauce over the meat and serve with chestnut purée on the side.

Roast Loin of Pork with Apple Charlotte　　*Serves 6*

3½ *pound loin of pork, boned*	2 *Tablespoons sugar*
1 *Tablespoon salt (for pork)*	8 *Tablespoons butter*
½ *teaspoon pepper*	3 *cups bread cubes (tightly*
3 *cups apples, peeled, cored, and*	*packed) cut into 1-inch*
diced	*squares*
Grated rind of 1 lemon	½ *cup apple sauce*
Pinch each of ginger, cin-	1 *teaspoon salt (for apples)*
namon, cloves	3 *egg yolks*

Preheat oven to 450 degrees.

Place pork in a shallow roasting pan, fat side up. Rub fat with 1 Tablespoon salt and the pepper and roast (450 degrees) for 40 minutes.

Add the apples, lemon rind, ginger, cinnamon, cloves, and sugar and put back in oven for 15 minutes, or until apples are tender. Stir in the butter and bread cubes and roast 5 minutes longer. Mix apple sauce, the remaining teaspoon of salt, and egg yolks, and pour over the apples. Bake 15 minutes longer, or until golden brown.

PRESENTATION

Place apple charlotte on a heated serving platter, arrange sliced pork on top, and serve.

The Chops

Pork Medallions in Buckwheat *Crêpes*   Serves 4

4 *large* crêpes *(see basic*
  crêpes *recipe, page 109)*

12 *pork cutlets cut very thin*
  (about 1½ ounces each)

¼ *cup flour*

1 *teaspoon salt*

¼ *teaspoon pepper*

3 *Tablespoons butter*

1 *ounce applejack (or Calvados)*

½ *apple, peeled and grated*

¼ *cup brown gravy (to improvise*
  gravy see page xiii)

1 *Tablespoon walnuts, chopped*

1 *cup* béarnaise *sauce*
  (see page 85)

Preheat oven to 400 degrees.

Prepare *crêpes*.

Dust the pork cutlets with flour seasoned with salt and pepper. Melt the butter in a skillet and sauté the cutlets over medium heat until brown on both sides. Add the applejack, grated apple, and brown gravy, and mix thoroughly.

Spread the *crêpes* out flat and place 3 cutlets in the center of each with a little of the sauce. Sprinkle chopped walnuts over the sauce. Roll the *crêpes* and place them in a buttered ovenproof serving dish. Cover each *crêpe* with *sauce Béarnaise* and bake (400 degrees) for 5 minutes.

Pork Chops with Sauerkraut

Serves 4

1 *teaspoon salt*
¼ *teaspoon pepper*
8 *pork chops, cut medium thick (about ½ inch)*
1 *pound sauerkraut (imported wine kraut, if possible), drained*

1 *green apple, peeled, cored, and grated*
1 *teaspoon raw potato, finely grated*
Dry white wine, about 1 pint, depending on casserole

Preheat oven to 400 degrees.

Sprinkle salt and pepper on pork chops and place them overlapping in the bottom of a casserole. Combine sauerkraut, grated apple, grated potato, and spread over the chops. Pour in enough white wine just to cover the chops and sauerkraut. Put a cover on the casserole and roast (400 degrees) for 1 hour.

Breaded Pork Cutlet

Serves 4

8 *pork chops, cut thin (about ¼ inch)*
½ *cup flour*
1 *teaspoon salt*
¼ *teaspoon pepper*

3 *eggs, beaten*
1 *Tablespoon water*
1 *teaspoon prepared mustard*
1 *cup fine bread crumbs*
4 *Tablespoons butter or oil*

GARNISH
2 *cups apple sauce with 1 teaspoon cinnamon (canned or freshly made)*

Dust the pork chops with flour, sprinkle salt and pepper over them. In a mixing bowl, combine eggs with the water and mustard. Dip each cutlet in the egg and then into the bread crumbs.

Melt the butter or oil in a large skillet and sauté the cutlets until golden brown on both sides—about 15 minutes.

PRESENTATION
Serve garnished with cinnamon apple sauce.

Casserole of Pork Chops Pot Boy   *Serves 4*

8 *pork chops, cut thin (about*   3 *eggs*
  ¼ inch) and trimmed of   ½ *pound cream cheese,*
  some fat   *cut into small pieces*
1 *teaspoon salt*   1 *cup milk*
¼ *teaspoon pepper*   ¾ *cup brown sauce, (to improvise*
2 *Tablespoons butter or oil*   *gravy see page xiii)*
½ *pound wide egg noodles*   ½ *cup Gruyère cheese, grated*

Preheat oven to 450 degrees.

Sprinkle pork chops with salt and pepper. Melt the butter or oil in a large skillet and sauté the chops until golden—approximately 3 minutes on each side.

Cook the noodles according to package directions and drain. In the bowl of the electric mixer, combine the eggs, cream cheese, milk, brown sauce, and Gruyère cheese. Beat until well mixed. Stir the noodles into the egg–milk mixture. Place four of the chops on the bottom of a 2-quart casserole, cover with half of the noodles. Place the remaining chops on top and cover with the rest of the noodles. Sprinkle with grated cheese and bake (450 degrees) for 25 minutes and serve at once.

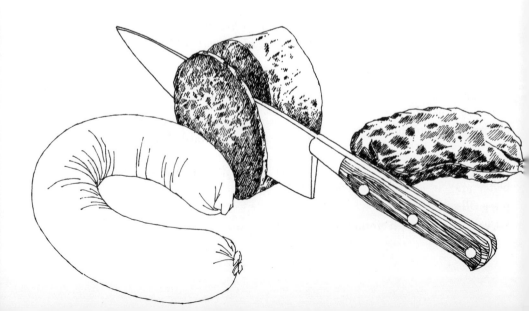

Ham and Sausages

Mousse of Ham with Fruit Sauce
Serves 4

¾ *pound cooked ham, or ham*
  shanks, or smoked butt, diced
¼ *cup heavy cream*
 3 *egg yolks*
¼ *cup piñon nuts (pine nuts)*
½ *teaspoon salt*
  Pinch turmeric

1½ *Tablespoons candied*
   red cherries, diced
½ *teaspoon Worcestershire sauce*

Preheat oven to 450 degrees.

Put diced ham, heavy cream, egg yolks, pine nuts, and salt in a blender and purée.

Remove and place in a mixing bowl. Add turmeric, diced candied cherries, and Worcestershire sauce. Mix thoroughly.

Pour into a 1-quart savarin mold or individual molds and set in a pan of hot water. Bake (450 degrees) for 40 minutes.

Meanwhile prepare fruit sauce. When the mousse is done remove it from the mold or molds by turning it over quickly. Cover lightly with fruit sauce and serve.

FRUIT SAUCE

6–8 *dried apricots,*
    depending on size
 1 *Tablespoon honey*
¼ *cup lemon juice*

Pinch salt
1 *Tablespoon sesame seeds*

Boil apricots in enough water to cover for 20 minutes. Remove from water and let dry. Chop, then blend in blender with honey and lemon juice. Place in saucepan, add salt and sesame seeds; warm slightly and serve.

Baked Smoked Ham with Mustard and Brown Sugar

Serves 8

8 *to* 10 *pound smoked ham with*
  bone in (Ask butcher to
  remove skin and excess fat.)
1 *cup prepared mustard*
1 *pound brown sugar*
30–40 *whole cloves*

2 *cups hard cider*
  (or sweet cider mixed with 2
  ounces applejack)
1½ *teaspoons cornstarch dissolved*
  in 2 Tablespoons cold water
1 *Tablespoon red currant jelly*

Slowly simmer ham, uncovered, in enough water to cover for 1½ hours. Remove, drain, and wipe dry.

Preheat oven to 450 degrees.

Coat ham first with the mustard and then the brown sugar. Stick cloves into the ham all around and place in an ovenproof casserole. Bake (450 degrees) uncovered for 30 minutes or until a golden brown.

Remove ham to a heated serving platter and keep warm. Place casserole over medium heat, add cider, cornstarch, and currant jelly, and stir quickly to dissolve cornstarch and to thicken slightly. Remove sauce and strain through a fine sieve. Serve separately in a sauceboat.

Excellent accompaniments are sweet potatoes or baked squash.

Baked Ham in Champagne Sauce

Serves 12

6 *to* 8 *pound smoked ham*
½ *bottle champagne (14 ounces)*
½ *cup ham broth*

¼ *cup prepared mustard*
3 *Tablespoons brown sugar*
½ *cup raisins*

Preheat oven to 450 degrees.

Place the ham in a saucepan with enough water to cover. Bring to a boil, reduce heat and simmer, uncovered, for 1 hour.

Remove the ham to a large ovenproof casserole. Pour champagne and ½ cup ham broth over meat, spread mustard over the ham, sprinkle with brown sugar, and add the raisins to the pan.

Bake (450 degrees) for 20 minutes or until golden brown.

PRESENTATION
Serve with sauce on the side. (Save any leftover sauce to reheat leftover ham.)

Roulade of Ham Stuffed with Calomandin

Serves 4

Calomandin is a Philippine small sour orange, somewhat like a kumquat.

¼ cup cooked ham (may be from ends), diced

¼ cup calomandin (or kumquats), chopped

1 teaspoon prepared mustard, for blending

1 Tablespoon mayonnaise

1 egg yolk

¼ cup walnuts, chopped

½ teaspoon turmeric

¼ cup pickled watermelon rind, sliced

½ teaspoon salt

8 1½-ounce large, thin slices of canned or smoked ham

1 teaspoon prepared mustard for baking

¼ cup maple syrup

1 teaspoon vinegar

1 teaspoon curry powder

Preheat oven to 450 degrees.

In a blender, put diced ham, calomandin, 1 teaspoon mustard, mayonnaise, and egg yolk, and blend until smooth.

Place in a mixing bowl. Add walnuts, turmeric, watermelon rind, and salt. Mix thoroughly.

Spread on the ham slices. Roll up and place the rolled pieces close together in a shallow baking dish. Brush lightly with 1 teaspoon mustard. Mix maple syrup and vinegar and pour over *roulades*. Sprinkle with curry powder, and bake (450 degrees) for 15 minutes.

Pork and Sauerkraut Platter

Serves 6

1 *smoked pork butt,*
  1½–2 pounds
1 *pound piece of lean*
  smoked bacon

8 *frankfurters, cut into chunks*
1½ *pounds sauerkraut, fresh or*
  canned, drained

Bring a large saucepan of water to a boil; add the pork butt, and simmer for 15 minutes. Add the bacon and simmer uncovered another 45 minutes. Remove from fire and put frankfurters into the hot liquid with pork and bacon. Leave all meats in hot liquid.

Place the sauerkraut in another saucepan, fill saucepan with enough broth from the pork meats to cover kraut, and simmer, uncovered, for 30 minutes. Drain through a sieve, pressing out all liquid, and spread out on a hot serving platter. Remove the pork butt and bacon from the liquid, cut into slices, and arrange on the sauerkraut with the frankfurters.

Serve with boiled potatoes.

Swiss Ham with Fresh Asparagus *Gratinée*

Serves 4

 1 *pound fresh asparagus*
 1 *teaspoon salt*
20 *paper-thin slices Swiss*
   mountain ham or Italian
   prosciutto
 1 *Tablespoon Parmesan cheese,*
   grated

½ *cup* béchamel *sauce*
  (see page 81)
½ *cup hollandaise sauce*
  (see page 86)
¼ *cup grated Gruyère cheese*

Cut off the tough end of each asparagus stalk and peel 2 inches of skin off the remaining bottom. Wash under running water and cook in salted water until tender—about 15 minutes. The best way to cook asparagus is to tie the stalks together with kitchen string and cook them standing upright in a tightly covered tall pot, with water not quite to the top of the tips.

Preheat oven to 450 degrees.

Drain the cooked asparagus well. Place in an ovenproof serving dish.

Cover the tips and half of the stalks with the thinly sliced ham. Sprinkle evenly with the grated Parmesan. Mix together the *béchamel* and hollandaise and spread evenly over the ham. Sprinkle with grated Gruyère and bake (450 degrees) 10 to 15 minutes, until golden brown. Serve at once.

Leaves of Cabbage Filled with Smoked Sausage

Serves 4

1 *whole cabbage (about* 1½ *pounds)*
1 *cup* béchamel *sauce (see page 81)*
½ *teaspoon salt*
  Pinch pepper

¼ *teaspoon savory*
4 *smoked sausages (bratwurst, knockwurst, or beerwurst)*
1 *Tablespoon prepared mustard*
¼ *cup light colored cheddar cheese, grated*

Trim the cabbage of damaged outer leaves. Carefully remove 6 of the outer leaves (4 for wrapping and the 2 additional may be used for patching). Trim off the thick white base and poach the leaves in boiling water for 7 minutes. Remove the leaves to drain.

Cut the remaining head of cabbage into pieces, removing the hard core. Place in the boiling water and cook for 20 minutes.

Preheat oven to 450 degrees.

Drain the poached cabbage pieces and put through the fine blade of the meat grinder. To remove excess liquid put the ground cabbage in a sieve or strainer and press water out. Mix the ground cabbage together with the *béchamel* sauce, add the salt, pepper, and savory.

Heat the sausages in boiling water for 3 minutes. Drain.

Spread out the poached cabbage leaves and cover them lightly with mustard. Make a deep incision in each sausage cutting almost through. Place 1 sausage in the center of each cabbage leaf. Fill and cover each sausage generously with the creamed cabbage, reserving about one-third for topping. Roll the filled cabbage leaves and place them side by side in a shallow ovenproof casserole. Spread the remaining creamed cabbage over; sprinkle with cheese. Bake (450 degrees) for about 30 minutes, or until the cheese is golden brown.

Boiled Smoked Pork Dinner   *Serves 8*

1¼–1½ *pounds smoked pork butt*
  2 *pounds beef tongue, pickled*
    or fresh
  8 *small raw potatoes, peeled and*
    quartered
  1 *head (1–1¼ pounds) green*
    cabbage, cut in eighths

½ *teaspoon caraway seed*
  1 *Tablespoon vinegar*
  1 *teaspoon sugar*
  1 *teaspoon salt*
  1 *smoked sausage (Polish*
    kielbasa *or German*
    bauernwurst*)*

Simmer, uncovered, the smoked pork butt and beef tongue in enough water to cover 1 inch above meat. After 1½ hours, remove the pork butt and continue simmering the beef tongue 45 minutes longer. Remove beef tongue.

Add potatoes, cabbage, caraway seed, vinegar, sugar, and salt, and simmer for 30 minutes. Return the meats to the pot, cover and simmer for 10 minutes.

PRESENTATION
Place vegetables in center of heated platter with sliced meats around.

Sauerkraut and Pork in White Wine   *Serves 4 to 6*

1 *can (1 pound 4 ounces)*
    fresh or canned sauerkraut
  1 *medium onion stuck with 1*
    clove
  1 *pound pork belly, trimmed*
    of skin and sliced (or you may
    substitute fresh bacon)

1 *pound smoked pork butt,*
    cut in ¼-inch slices
    Dry white wine to cover sauer-
    kraut (about 1½ cups)
  1 *medium-size raw potato,*
    peeled and grated
  ½ *cup milk*

Preheat oven to 400 degrees.

Rinse and drain sauerkraut. Place layer in ovenproof casserole. Place onion stuck with clove and sliced pork belly and butt over sauerkraut.

Top with remaining kraut and pour in enough white wine to cover. Place lid on casserole and bake (400 degrees) for 2½ hours.

Meanwhile peel and grate potato. Add milk to it. After 2½ hours remove the casserole from oven, remove and discard the onion. Add potato mixture, stirring it in with the other ingredients. Cover, return to oven and bake for another 20 minutes.

Pork Sausage Meat

Serves 4

1 *pound lean pork meat from*	½ *teaspoon salt*
neck or shoulder	¼ *teaspoon crushed black*
¼ *teaspoon marjoram*	*peppercorns*
¼ *teaspoon sage*	¼ *cup water*

Force the pork meat through the finest blade of the meat grinder into a mixing bowl. Add the marjoram, sage, salt, pepper, and water, and put through the fine blade of the meat grinder once more. Shape into patties and broil or sauté.

Pork Sausage and Lentils

Serves 6

¾ *pound lentils, pre-soaked in*	½ *cup corn oil*
water 4 or 5 hours, then	2 *Tablespoons vinegar*
drained	1 *Tablespoon prepared mustard*
¼ *teaspoon turmeric*	1 *pound sweet smoked sausages,*
2 *tomatoes, peeled and diced*	*Swiss or Italian, cut into*
½ *onion, finely chopped*	*chunks*
4 *slices bacon*	*Garnish of sliced tomatoes*

Place the drained lentils in a saucepan with boiling water to cover. Add the turmeric, tomatoes, onion, bacon, oil, vinegar, and mustard, and simmer, uncovered, for about 1½ hours, or until the lentils are tender. Add more water when necessary. Then add the sausages and cook for another 25 minutes. Serve garnished with sliced tomatoes.

Accompaniments

The Starches   The Vegetables

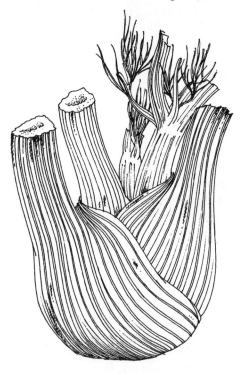

One of the greatest opportunities for improving the quality of even the simplest meal is the selection of an imaginative, unexpected accompaniment to the main dish. Too often, housewives and even experienced restaurateurs repeat the inevitable tired combinations of meat and potatoes, chicken and rice, etc. Historically, side dishes were widely varied, even including sweets, but today we have gotten into a rut.

In the class of "cereal" accompaniments, which includes the usual potatoes and rice and noodles, there is a whole range of different, flavorful dishes—dumplings, polenta, barley, kasha, cracked wheat, and lentils. Moreover, even old standbys can be transformed and made fresh with creative variations. For example, you can add mango and almond to rice, spinach or broccoli to noodles, herbs or cheese to dumplings.

The same idea can be applied to vegetable and salad side dishes as well: pear in potato salad, tomatoes and oysters instead of plain stewed tomatoes, cauliflower or broccoli or zucchini or eggplant in a beer batter, to give a few examples.

I have selected some of my own innovations and offer them in this section, as well as suggestions for suitable combinations, but you will find most rewarding your own efforts at experimentation and innovation.

I have included stuffing in this section because it is a mistake to limit our use of these delicious combinations to stuffing the cavity of a bird. Stuffing can be baked in the oven and served as a side dish; can be rolled in beef or veal filets; can be used as a topping on slices of meat, etc.

The Starches

The Vegetables

The Starches

It is much easier for me to cook dumplings than to tell you what they are. Each country has its own version and although dumplings are probably very ancient in origin, in modern cuisine they are identified most with Germanic cooking. There are so many variations that no single definition can be accurate or complete. In general a dumpling is a cooked lump of dough—but there agreement ends.

The dough can be ordinary flour, or biscuit dough, or corn flour, etc. A dumpling may be merely flavored dough, as in my herb dumpling recipe, or it can be filled with anything from meat to fruit. It may be used in soups or stews or as a garnish or accompaniment, as an appetizer or even as a dessert, when fruit-filled and baked.

A dumpling might be boiled, steamed, fried, or baked. French *quenelles*, Italian *gnocchi* or ravioli, Jewish *kreplach* or matzoh balls, chinese *won ton*, Spanish *albondigas* and Austrian or German *knodel*, *spaetzli*, *klosse*, and *nocherln* are all forms of dumplings. The rich choice of materials and treatment makes monotony totally unnecessary.

Herb Dumplings

Serves 7 to 8

Light, freshly made dumplings make a splendid accompaniment to a variety of meat dishes—especially boiled beef. Herb dumplings are one of my favorites, but it is essential in this case that you use fresh herbs and that the dumplings be served the moment they are removed from the simmering water. The herb-flavored *pâte à choux* may be made well ahead of time. I find the easiest way to make dumplings—the way I do it in my kitchen—is to use two spoons, the size of the spoon depending upon what size dumpling I plan to serve. I first wet the spoons in the hot water, then fill one spoon with the dough and use the other spoon to scoop off the dough into simmering, lightly salted water, wetting the spoons each time.

2 *cups* pâte à choux *(see page 373)*   *Chervil*

1 *Tablespoon each, fresh, finely chopped:* *Chives*   *If dried use half*

   Shallot or onion   *Savory*   *the amount.*

                                             Basil

Stir the chopped herbs into the cooled *pâte à choux* until thoroughly mixed. Make dumplings as described above, dropping them into a 2-quart saucepan with 1½ quarts of simmering, lightly salted water. The dumplings should be cooked when they rise to the surface—about 10 to 15 minutes. Open the first dumpling to see that it is cooked through—the inside should look like fine white bread. If it has not reached that stage, allow the other dumplings to remain on the surface a bit longer. Do not cook too many at once as they tend to stick together. Keep the dumplings in a covered dish in a warm oven until the dough is used up.

Cheese Dumplings

Serves 4

1 *cup* pâte à choux
  (see page 373)
  Oil for deep frying

3 *ounces cheese, grated (Gruyère,*
  cheddar, Emmenthal, or any
  hard cheese)

½ *teaspoon salt*

¼ *teaspoon pepper*

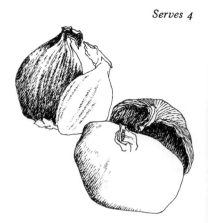

Prepare *pâte à choux.*

    Heat oil in deep frying pan to 350–375 degrees.

    Meanwhile combine the *pâte à choux,* grated cheese, salt and pepper in a bowl, and beat to form a smooth dough. Fill 1 teaspoon with the dough and use another spoon to scoop the dough off into the hot oil. Fry until golden brown. This amount of dough will make 20 walnut-sized dumplings.

Apricot Dumplings

Serves 4 to 6

The Viennese serve these feather-light dumplings, which are crisp and golden on the outside and have a bittersweet center of fresh apricot, to accompany dark roasts of pork, pungent ragoûts, or chicken.

1½　cups pâte à choux
　　(see page 373)
　1　*cup potatoes (about 2
　　　medium-sized), boiled*
　1　*teaspoon sugar*
　¼　*teaspoon baking powder*
　¼　*cup flour (for dough)
　　　Flour for dusting*
　8　*small fresh apricots, pitted
　　　(or 8 canned whole apricots)*

¼　*cup fine bread crumbs*
2　*Tablespoons melted butter*

Prepare *pâte à choux.*

Mash potatoes and put through ricer. Combine *pâte à choux* and mashed potatoes in a mixing bowl and beat until smooth. Mix in the sugar, baking powder, and ¼ cup flour.

Spread a clean kitchen towel on a flat surface, dust heavily with flour and roll out the dough as thin as possible. Cut the dough into 2-inch squares, place an apricot in the center of each, dust with flour, and form into a ball. This preparation may be done well in advance, dumplings set aside, and kept at room temperature.

Preheat oven to 375 degrees.

Carefully lower the dumplings into 2 quarts of simmering water and allow them to simmer about 8 minutes, or until they rise to the top. Remove with slotted spoon and drain.

Pour the bread crumbs onto a plate, stir in the melted butter and carefully roll each dumpling in the bread crumb mixture. Butter a shallow, ovenproof dish, arrange dumplings in one layer, and bake them (375 degrees) for about 15 minutes or until they are golden brown. Serve at once.

French Dumplings *Gratinées*

These light-textured dumplings are another example of the versatility of *pâte à choux*. The dumplings and the sauce may be prepared ahead of time, allowing about 30 minutes before serving to make them golden brown in the oven.

2 *cups* pâte à choux
  (see page 373)
2 *Tablespoons butter*
3 *Tablespoons flour*
1 *cup milk*
½ *teaspoon salt*

1 *Tablespoon chicken stock (see page 43) (or use rich canned chicken broth)*
½ *cup Gruyère cheese, grated (¼ cup for sprinkling, ¼ cup for sauce)*

Prepare *pâte à choux*.

Fill a large saucepan with water, salt lightly and bring to a boil, then reduce heat to simmer. Wet two teaspoons, take small bits of *pâte à choux* on the end of one teaspoon and use the other to scoop the dough off into the simmering water. Drop them one by one into the water, and simmer for no more than 5 minutes. Remove the dumplings from the water with a slotted spoon, placing them to dry on a kitchen towel.

Butter a large shallow ovenproof serving dish and arrange the dumplings, allowing space for them to double in size. Use two dishes if necessary.

Preheat oven to 350 degrees.

Melt the butter in a small saucepan, stir in the flour to make a thick paste. Gradually stir in the milk, add the salt, chicken stock, and ¼ cup grated cheese, and simmer until the sauce is smooth and not too thick. The sauce must be light enough to allow the dumplings to rise in the oven.

Pour the sauce over the dumplings, sprinkle them with remaining ¼ cup grated cheese and bake (350 degrees) until puffed and golden—about 30 minutes. Serve them as quickly as possible as they will deflate with change of temperature.

Stuffed Baked Potatoes

Serves 4 to 6

America is blessed with the finest potatoes in the world—those "apples of the earth," as the French call them. Maine and Long Island potatoes and others are excellent, but the Idaho variety is the best for baking. An Idaho baked in the oven and served hot and fluffy with butter and/or sour cream goes well with almost any main course. My suggestion here adds another dimension to the baked potato, with the addition of cheese and crisp bits of bacon.

4 *medium Idaho potatoes*
3 *Tablespoons butter*
2 *slices bacon, cooked crisp and*
  crumbled
1 *Tablespoon Gruyère cheese,*
  finely grated

1 *teaspoon salt*
1 *Tablespoon onion (or scallion),*
  finely chopped
  Paprika

Preheat oven to 375 degrees.

Scrub the potatoes, pierce the skins of each with a fork and bake them (375 degrees) for 40 to 45 minutes or until soft. Holding each potato lengthwise, carefully cut a long thin slice off the potato and scoop out the insides into a mixing bowl. Mash with a fork until potato is free of lumps, add the butter, crumbled bacon, cheese, salt, and onion, and stuff back into the shells. Sprinkle the tops with paprika and place them back in the oven until heated through and golden on top. Serve immediately.

Au Gratin Potatoes

Serves 4 to 6

I prefer to use small new potatoes for this recipe, though the larger potatoes will do if the quantity of milk is reduced. If you boil the potatoes ahead of time the dish can be done in only 20 minutes.

1½ *pounds potatoes (6 large)*
    or about 1 dozen new
    potatoes, unpeeled
  1 *teaspoon salt*
  1 *cup milk (approximately)*

2 *Tablespoons butter*
¼ *cup cheese, finely grated*
    (Gruyère, cheddar, or other
    cheese)
    Paprika

Preheat oven to 375 degrees.

Boil the unpeeled potatoes in enough water to cover, until tender. Drain, peel, and cut into small cubes. Place the cubed potatoes in a shallow, ovenproof serving dish and sprinkle with salt. Add the milk and butter and bake (375 degrees) until the potatoes begin to take on a light brown color. Add the grated cheese, sprinkle liberally with paprika and return to the oven until the potatoes are golden—about 20 minutes.

Potato Puffs

Serves 4 to 6

  1 *cup* pâte à choux
    (see page 373)
1½ *cups mashed potatoes*
    (about 3 medium-size
    potatoes)

Pinch each of nutmeg and
pepper
½ *teaspoon salt*

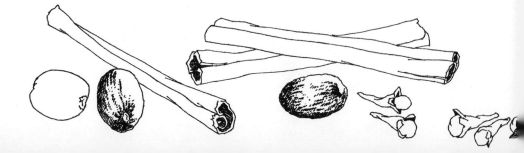

Prepare *pâte à choux.*

Heat oil to 350–375 degrees in fryer or in deep frying pan.

Meanwhile combine the mashed potatoes and *pâte à choux* and seasonings in a mixing bowl to make a smooth dough. With a tablespoon scoop out a spoonful of the dough, and use another spoon to slide it off into hot oil. Fry until golden brown.

This recipe will make 15 egg-sized puff balls of potatoes. Use teaspoons to make more, smaller puffs.

Roësti Potatoes

This is one of the best ways I know to serve potatoes: fried in butter, crisp and golden brown. If you like potatoes for breakfast you will find *roësti* an excellent accompaniment to eggs and bacon. They are easy to make and may be kept warm in a low oven until the eggs and bacon are ready.

4 *medium potatoes*
  (about 1 pound), unpeeled
1 *teaspoon salt*

2 *Tablespoons butter for each*
  pan load

Boil the unpeeled potatoes for about 15 minutes, drain, and chill thoroughly. Peel and make thin strips by putting potatoes through the shredding blade of an electric grater, or use the side with largest holes on a hand grater. (Leftover baked potatoes make excellent *roësti.*) Sprinkle with salt.

Melt the butter in a small frying pan and cover the bottom of the frying pan with about one quarter of the grated potato. This way you will make four flat, crisp potato cakes, which will be much easier to handle than trying to make a single large one.

Stir until potatoes are coated with butter. Press down flat with a spatula and sauté until brown and crisp. Turn over and sauté the other side.

Apple *Roësti*

Every Swiss can remember the aroma of apple *roësti* fresh from the oven, golden and crisp—a wonderful cold weather dish and a tart accompaniment to a baked ham or roast chicken or pork.

3 or 4 *hard, crusty rolls*
3 *tart, green apples (about*
   1 *pound)*
   Juice of 1 *lemon*
3 *Tablespoons butter*
½ *onion, thinly sliced*

Pinch each of salt, cinnamon,
   cloves
2 *eggs*
1 *cup milk*
½ *teaspoon sugar*

Preheat oven to 350 degrees.

Cut the rolls lengthwise into paper-thin slices, spread slices on a baking sheet and bake (350 degrees) until they are light brown in color—about 5 minutes. Remove.

Increase oven temperature to 375 degrees.

Peel and core the apples. Slice thin and sprinkle immediately with lemon juice. Melt the butter in a large frying pan, add the sliced apples and onion, the salt, cinnamon, and cloves, and sauté for 5 minutes. Add the crisp slices of rolls and mix with the apples and onion. Beat together the eggs, milk, and sugar, pour over the apple-and-bread mixture, toss lightly and transfer to a buttered ovenproof baking dish. Bake (375 degrees) until the top is crisp and golden, about 10 minutes.

Basic Recipe for Albert's Poultry Stuffing

Makes 10 cups or 2½ to 3 pounds (for large turkey)

This poultry stuffing is distinctive; I like to think of it as a "custardy" bread-and-butter pudding with vegetables. Do not hesitate to use all the milk suggested in the recipe; then you need not be concerned about it drying out.

½ *pound butter*
2 *onions, coarsely chopped*
3 *green peppers,*
   coarsely chopped
1 *stalk celery,*
   coarsely chopped
12 *slices bacon, diced into ½-inch*
   pieces
½ *pound ham butt, put through*
   coarse blade of meat grinder

½ *teaspoon each of sage,*
   thyme, rosemary, oregano
2 *loaves bread (2 pounds each),*
   diced into ½-inch cubes
2 *Tablespoons salt*
1 *teaspoon pepper*
8 *eggs*
1 *quart milk*

Preheat oven to 375 degrees.

Melt the butter in a large frying pan, add the chopped onions, green peppers, and celery, diced bacon and ground ham. Sauté until the onions are soft—about 10 minutes. Sprinkle with the sage, thyme, rosemary, oregano. Place the diced bread in a large baking pan and bake (375 degrees) until crisp and golden. Pour the sautéed vegetables over the bread; add salt and pepper. Beat the eggs and add to the stuffing. Add as much milk as you need to moisten.

To the regular roasting time of the turkey add 18 minutes for each pound of stuffing.

Any remaining stuffing may be placed in a pan and put in the oven to cook during the final 50 minutes that the bird is roasting. During this time add 4 to 5 Tablespoons of basting juices to the stuffing in the pan.

Fresh Cranberry Stuffing   *Makes 8 cups*

Follow directions for basic poultry stuffing (page 286), but for 1 quart milk substitute: 2 cups milk and 2 cups sweet cider.

Wash 1 pound cranberries, place them in a saucepan, add 4 cups water and 1 Tablespoon sugar, bring to a boil and cook for 3 minutes, or until the cranberries break open.

Add cranberries to basic stuffing at the same time as you pour sautéed vegetables over bread. Moisten with milk and cider mixture.

Chestnut Stuffing

Makes 6 to 8 servings or 8 cups

Basic recipe for Albert's poultry stuffing (see page 286), omitting 1 loaf of bread and sautéed vegetables

2 *pounds fresh peeled chestnuts, cooked and drained (or canned and drained)*

Preheat oven to 375 degrees.

If you use fresh chestnuts, make a cross on the outer skin with a sharp kitchen knife and bake in a flat pan (375 degrees) for 15 to 20 minutes, or until the skins begin to curl back. Remove the skin and dark scale and boil the chestnuts in water to cover for about 30 minutes, or until soft.

Follow directions for basic stuffing, using only 1 loaf of bread rather than 2. Add cooked chestnuts in place of sautéed vegetables.

Oyster Stuffing

Makes 10 cups (for large turkey)

Follow directions for basic poultry stuffing (page 286), adding 40 raw oysters, coarsely chopped, when you pour sautéed vegetables over bread.

Egg Noodles with Cheese and Calf's Brains

Serves 4 to 6

This recipe can be served as an hors d'oeuvres, as an accompaniment, or as a first course.

½ *pound egg noodles, cooked*
3 *Tablespoons butter*
1 *calf's brain (½ pound),*
  skinned, and blanched in
  boiling water for 5 minutes
2 *eggs*
1 *cup milk*

2½ *ounces cheese, grated*
  (1 cup)
½ *onion, grated*
1 *teaspoon salt*
½ *teaspoon pepper*
½ *bunch watercress, trimmed*
  and coarsely chopped

Preheat oven to 350 degrees.

Cook egg noodles in salted boiling water until soft but still firm; drain and mix them with the butter in a 1½ to 2 quart ovenproof casserole. Slice the blanched calf's brain into 1-inch-square pieces; add to noodles.

In a mixing bowl beat together the eggs and milk and pour over the noodles. Sprinkle with the grated cheese, and the grated onion, the salt and pepper, and toss lightly. Place the casserole in a baking pan filled with enough boiling water to come three quarters of the way up the casserole. Bake (350 degrees) for 30 minutes.

PRESENTATION
Wash and drain the watercress, trim off the stems and just toss the hot noodles and watercress together lightly. Serve hot.

Egg Noodles Magyar   *Serves 4*

½ *pound egg noodles*
3 *Tablespoons butter*
¼ *onion, finely chopped*
¼ *cup bread crumbs*

1 *Tablespoon poppy seeds*
  (or caraway seeds)
1 *teaspoon salt*
⅛ *teaspoon pepper*

Cook the egg noodles in boiling salted water until they are soft but still firm. Do not overcook them. Drain the noodles and keep them warm.

Melt the butter in a large frying pan. Add the onions and sauté until they are a light golden color. Add the bread crumbs, poppy seeds, and the noodles. Toss lightly to mix thoroughly and season with salt and pepper. Serve hot.

Buttered *Spaetzli*

Buttered *spaetzli* are not often served in this country, probably because most people are not familiar with them. *Spaetzli* are not difficult to make and can be prepared far ahead of time. All you need to do before serving is to sauté them lightly in butter and finish them off in the oven while you are having your first course.

I remember how during my early years of apprenticeship in my uncle's restaurant, I prepared great piles of *spaetzli* in advance and watched the prosperous burghers of my Swiss village arrive at midday to devour plates of them before going on to the meat course. But for the more modest appetites in this country I serve them with a meat. A yellow-gold pile of delicate *spaetzli* usually accompanies pheasant or venison with a dark, rich sauce.

3½ *cups sifted flour*	*Dash nutmeg, grated*
6 *eggs*	½ *cup water*
1 *teaspoon salt*	3 *Tablespoons butter*
¼ *teaspoon pepper*	

Place the sifted flour in a large mixing bowl, add the whole eggs, salt, pepper, nutmeg, and water. Mix well. Beating of the dough is an important step in making *spaetzli* properly. Take a firm hold on the bowl and begin beating the dough with a large wooden spoon or spatula. Scrape the dough toward you in a regular beat allowing air to get into the dough. After 5 minutes of this, allow the dough to rest. Then beat another 5 minutes (I generally try to get someone else to help) with the same regular aerating beat.

Now, strangely, the main problem is cutting the dough into the proper size for *spaetzli*. You have a number of alternatives:

1   The best solution for real *spaetzli* aficionados is to buy a *spaetzli* mill which cuts the dough to the required size in a matter of seconds.

2   Next best is to spread the dough on a board dusted with flour and cut it into ⅜-inch strips and these across into ⅜-inch squares. But you have to be awfully speedy in order to cut them and scrape them off the board into the boiling water practically all at once.

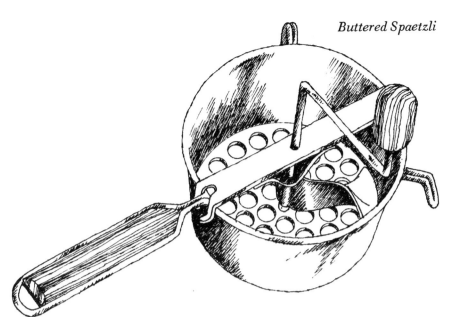

3 Another method is to use a large steamer. This is like a double boiler, but the steamer tray has perforations, preferably ⅜ inches in diameter. Fill the bottom of the steamer with salted water, bring to a boil and keep it boiling. Then hold the tray over the boiling water.

4 If you don't have a steamer you can use a large open pot for the boiling water and a sieve or colander with ⅜-inch holes to press the *spaetzli* through. As a result of the beating, the dough will have begun to form very large air bubbles. Pour the dough in a mass onto the tray of the steamer (or sieve or colander) and press the dough through the holes into the boiling water, using the back of a large spoon. Be careful not to have the tray (or sieve or colander) too close to the boiling water in the bottom of the pot. If you do, the dough will congeal before you can press it through. Hold it about 8 inches above the boiling water.

When the dough has all been pushed through, keep the *spaetzli* boiling for 5 minutes.

Remove the pot from the heat, drain the *spaetzli*, and then place them under cold running water for a minute or two.

Cover a baking sheet with a kitchen towel and spread out the *spaetzli*. Cover with a damp towel and keep in a dry place until ready to serve.

Preheat oven to 350 degrees.

Melt the butter in a hot frying pan and sauté the *spaetzli*, tossing lightly for 3 minutes. Finish them off by baking (350 degrees) for about 10 minutes. During this time they will swell slightly. Serve them golden brown.

Cheese Polenta

Polenta, a corn meal porridge, is a fine accompaniment to game or any meat course and a colorful change from the white potato. This porridge may be cooked in advance and quickly prepared for the table just before serving. I am giving you two ways of serving this nourishing and delicious form of meal.

POLENTA GRATINÉE

½ pound (1 cup) finely ground
   yellow corn meal
3 Tablespoons onion, finely
   chopped
3 Tablespoons butter
1 teaspoon salt
¼ teaspoon pepper
2 eggs, beaten

1 cup grated cheese (Parmesan,
   Gruyère) (¾ cup for polenta,
   ¼ cup for topping)

Preheat oven to 400 degrees.

Bring 3½ cups of water to simmer in a saucepan, gradually stir in the corn meal and the finely chopped onion with a wooden spoon and simmer, uncovered, for 25 minutes, stirring frequently.

Stir into the cornmeal the butter, salt, pepper, beaten eggs, and ¾ cup of cheese. Transfer the mixture to a shallow baking dish, sprinkle with remaining cheese and bake (400 degrees) until the cheese topping is melted and golden brown. Remove from the oven and serve.

SAUTÉED POLENTA

For this variation Parmesan cheese is best. Prepare the polenta as above. Pour into a buttered baking pan in an even layer, about 1 inch thick. Set aside and cool until mixture becomes firm. Cut into 1½-inch squares. Dust the pieces of cold polenta with the remaining cheese and sauté in melted butter in a frying pan until golden brown. Serve hot.

Pearl Barley and Green Butter   *Serves 4*

1 *cup pearl barley*
3 *Tablespoons butter*

1 *teaspoon each of parsley*
  and chives, finely chopped

Wash the barley in a sieve under cold running water. Simmer in 1 quart of boiling water uncovered for 45 minutes. Then drain and rinse in a sieve under cold running water.

Melt the butter in a large pan, add the barley, sprinkle with the parsley and chives and sauté lightly, stirring, until the barley is heated through.

Kasha   *Serves 4 to 6*

Kasha, a popular food in eastern Europe, is called buckwheat groats in this country. It is available in fine, medium, and coarse particles. I prefer the coarse. You will find it an excellent accompaniment for spicy lamb kebabs, roast lamb or other lamb dishes—a good change from rice and potatoes. This recipe may be prepared in advance and reheated before serving.

1½ *cups kasha (buckwheat*
    groats)
  1 *carrot, peeled*
  1 *onion*

1 *teaspoon salt*
¼ *teaspoon pepper*
3 *Tablespoons butter*
  Chopped parsley

Preheat oven to 375 degrees.

Bring 2 quarts of water to a boil, add kasha and simmer uncovered for 25 minutes. Drain in sieve under running water, and leave water running over it for a few minutes to separate the grains. Pour into a shallow buttered baking dish. Grate the raw carrot and onion onto the kasha, add the salt, pepper, and butter, and mix well. Bake (375 degrees) for 20 minutes. Just before serving sprinkle with the parsley.

Cracked Wheat *Orientale*   *Serves 4 to 6*

¼ *cup raisins*
1 *cup dry sherry*
½ *pound cracked wheat (bulgar)*
¼ *cup piñon nuts (pine nuts),*
  lightly toasted in the oven

½ *teaspoon turmeric*
½ *teaspoon salt*
  Pinch pepper

Place raisins in 1 cup dry sherry to soak for 30 minutes.

Cook cracked wheat for a few minutes in one quart boiling water until tender but firm.

Preheat oven to 350 degrees. Meanwhile lightly toast pine nuts in oven.

Place the cooked cracked wheat in a shallow buttered baking dish. Drain raisins and stir into the wheat, together with toasted pine nuts, turmeric, salt, and pepper. Bake (350 degrees) for 15 minutes and serve hot.

Basic Rice   *Serves 3 to 4*

The excellent long grain Carolina rice we have in this country provides for a great variety of rice dishes. This rice absorbs flavor readily and I prefer to cook it in stock—chicken, beef, or fish—depending upon how I plan to use it. Rice should always be dry and fluffy with each grain separate. Also, rice prepared in the way I suggest here may be cooked in advance and reheated in a tightly covered pot with a little bouillon or butter just before serving.

2 *Tablespoons butter*
¼ *onion, finely chopped*
1 *cup long grain rice*
2½ *cups of clear stock, beef,*
  chicken, or veal (see pages

43, 44, 46) (or use rich canned beef or chicken broth), or use water
1 *teaspoon salt*

Melt the butter in a saucepan and sauté the onion lightly. Stir the raw rice into the butter and onion. Pour the boiling stock or water over the rice, add salt, stir, cover and simmer for about 25 minutes. Test the rice by biting several grains. Do not overcook it.

The rice is now ready. It may be served plain or you can use one of the following variations.

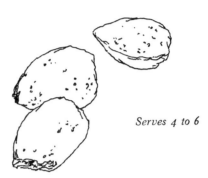

Almond Rice

Serves 4 to 6

4 *Tablespoons butter*
5 *cups cooked rice*
½ *cup slivered almonds, toasted*
   in the oven until lightly
   colored

Melt the butter in a frying pan or saucepan, add the cooked rice and the almonds. Stir until the butter is absorbed. Keep warm in low oven until ready to serve.

Mango Rice

Serves 4 to 6

3 *Tablespoons butter*
5 *cups cooked rice*

6–8 *ounces of fresh (or canned)*
     mango, seeded and chopped

In a large frying pan, melt the butter, add the cooked rice and sauté until heated through. Add the chopped mango and sauté for 3 minutes. This mango rice may be kept warm in the oven, covered, until ready to serve.

Green Rice

Serves 4 to 6

5 *cups cooked rice*
2 *Tablespoons fresh, raw spinach, finely chopped*
1 *teaspoon each fresh watercress, chives, savory, basil, finely*

chopped (in this recipe you cannot substitute dried herbs)
1 *Tablespoon parsley, chopped*

The fresh herbs above are given as a guide. You may use others as preferred or available. It is necessary to use this many fresh herbs to give the rice color.

Add the fresh herbs to the warm cooked rice, toss and serve.

Gruyère Risotto

Serves 4 to 6

Short-grained Italian rice is generally used for risotto and may be cooked in the same manner as in the basic rice recipe (see page 294).

4 *cups cooked Italian or long grain rice*

½ *cup Gruyère, cheddar, or other hard cheese, finely grated*

Place the cooked rice in a buttered ovenproof serving dish and stir in the Gruyère. Heat through in a medium oven (350 degrees).

Tomato Risotto

Serves 4 to 6

4 *cups cooked Italian or long grain rice*
½ *pound tomatoes, peeled, seeded, and chopped*
¼ *cup tomato juice*

In a buttered ovenproof serving dish combine the cooked rice, chopped tomatoes, and tomato juice and heat through in a moderate oven (350 degrees).

Risotto of *Fines Herbes*   *Serves 4 to 6*

4 *cups cooked Italian or long*
  grain rice
1 *teaspoon each of fresh parsley,*
  chives, chervil, finely chopped
  (if dried use ⅓ the amount)

Combine the cooked rice with the herbs in a buttered ovenproof dish and heat through in a moderate oven (350 degrees).

The Vegetables

Squash and Toasted Nuts

Serves 4 to 6

The squash family, which includes pumpkins and the Italian zucchini, affords a variety of eating pleasure all over the world. The summer squash has a soft rind and all you need to do is wash it. The winter squash has a hard rind and you need to cut it into pieces, remove seeds, rind, and stringy portions.

4 *yellow summer squash, cut either in ⅛-inch slices or in sticks*	1 *Tablespoon pistachios, chopped*
	1 *teaspoon salt*
	1 *teaspoon dill, chopped*
¼ *cup walnuts or pecans, chopped*	*Juice of ½ lemon*
2 *Tablespoons melted butter*	½ *teaspoon black pepper*

Bring the water to a boil and simmer the cut-up squash in 1½ quarts of lightly salted water until soft—about 10 minutes. Remove squash from saucepan, drain and keep warm. Sauté nuts in 2 Tablespoons butter until slightly browned. Add squash and all other ingredients and toss lightly until squash is coated with the nuts.

Zucchini Filled with Risotto

Serves 4 to 6

8 *zucchini squash, 6 inches long*	½ *clove garlic, minced*
	½ *onion, chopped*
½ *cup Italian or long grain rice (uncooked)*	½ *cup piñon nuts (pine nuts)*
	½ *cup fresh spinach, chopped*
1 *teaspoon curry powder*	½ *teaspoon salt*
½ *tart apple, diced*	2 *tomatoes, sliced thin*
1½ *cups water*	

Select firm zucchini and cut in half lengthwise. Boil in enough water to cover for 7 to 10 minutes until soft but firm. Drain. Using a pointed teaspoon, scoop out the seeds, leaving a firm shell. Place them side by side in a buttered shallow ovenproof serving dish.

Preheat oven to 400 degrees.

Put the rice in a medium saucepan, sprinkle with curry powder, add the diced apple, water, minced garlic, chopped onion, pine nuts, spinach, and salt, and simmer, covered, for 20 minutes, or until the rice is tender. Remove from the heat. Fill each zucchini shell with the flavored rice. Cover the top of each stuffed zucchini with thin slices of tomato and bake (400 degrees) for 10 to 12 minutes, or until heated through.

Serve with mixed grill, calf's liver, sautéed kidney.

Zucchini with Walnuts

Serves 4 to 6

1 *pound fresh zucchini, trimmed but unpeeled, cut into 1-inch pieces*
½ *cup olive oil*

½ *cup walnuts, coarsely chopped*
Juice of 1 lemon
½ *teaspoon salt*
¼ *teaspoon pepper*

Wash the zucchini, remove ends and cut into slices 1 inch thick. Heat the oil in a frying pan and sauté the zucchini until they begin to get soft. Drain off excess oil, add the chopped walnuts, lemon juice, salt, and pepper and sauté until soft, about 2 minutes.

PRESENTATION
Serve with luncheon cold cuts, fish or meat salads.

May be served hot or cold. If cold, chill after sautéing, and add a little more lemon juice.

Onions in Onion

Serves 4

2 *large onions*
1 *Tablespoon butter*
2 *Tablespoons flour*
¼ *cup milk*
½ *cup water in which onions were boiled*
½ *teaspoon salt*
¼ *teaspoon pepper*

Pinch dry English mustard
Dash Tabasco sauce
1 *can cooked pearl onions, thoroughly drained (or freshly cooked and peeled, 16–20)*
2 *Tablespoons Parmesan cheese, finely grated*

Cut the large onions in half horizontally. Simmer in enough lightly salted water to cover, until tender but firm—about 25 minutes. Drain, reserving ½ cup of the cooking water.

Make cups of the onion halves by scooping out centers and leaving only 3 outer layers. In a saucepan, melt the butter and stir in the flour to make a thick paste. Add the milk and the onion water, stirring constantly. Bring to a light boil until it thickens. Season with salt, pepper, mustard, and Tabasco. Add the drained pearl onions and heat them through.

Preheat oven to 400 degrees.

Fill each large onion cup with the pearl onions in sauce and sprinkle each with grated Parmesan cheese. Place the "onions in onion" in a baking dish and place under the broiler or in oven (400 degrees) until the tops are golden.

Serve with poultry, steak, roast beef, or leg of lamb.

Tomato Stuffed with Eggplant

Serves 4

4 *large ripe tomatoes*
Preheat oven to 400 degrees.

Eggplant salad (see page 31)

Skin the tomatoes by dipping them for 10 seconds in boiling water and then peeling. Cut out the stem of each tomato and scoop out the inside, leaving a firm shell.

Prepare the eggplant salad and while the salad is still warm fill each tomato with it. Place the tomatoes in an ovenproof dish and bake (400 degrees) for about 10 minutes or until the tomatoes are lightly cooked through.

Baked Tomato Stuffed with Mushrooms   *Serves 4*

Lightly baked large, firm tomatoes may be filled not only with sautéed mushrooms as indicated in this recipe, but with a variety of vegetables: cooked eggplant, chopped collard greens, spinach, or other fresh vegetables.

4 *large, firm tomatoes*
2 *Tablespoons butter*
½ *pound mushrooms (about 2 cups), sliced thin*
½ *teaspoon flour*
½ *teaspoon salt*
  Pinch each of dried rosemary, savory
3 *Tablespoons heavy cream*

Preheat oven to 400 degrees.

Skin the tomatoes by dipping them for 10 seconds in boiling water, then peeling. Cut out the stem and scoop out the pulp and seeds to form a cup.

Melt the butter in a frying pan, add the sliced mushrooms and sauté until they are soft—about 5 minutes. Dust them lightly with flour, add the salt, rosemary, savory, and cream, and stir until thoroughly mixed. Fill each tomato with the mushroom mixture and place them on a buttered ovenproof dish. Bake (400 degrees) for 8 to 10 minutes or until they are lightly cooked and thoroughly heated.

PRESENTATION
Serve the tomatoes *cut side down* on heated individual vegetable dishes garnished with a sprig of parsley or watercress. This offers a surprise when the tomato is cut open.

Tomato with Fried Oysters   *Serves 4*

The delicious combination of golden fried oysters, the bright red tomato shell, and delicate sauce make this a dish with a contrast in colors as well as an interesting variety of textures. In this section I am suggesting that it be served as an accompaniment to a meat, but it is ample for the main course of a luncheon or may be used as a dish in a buffet supper.

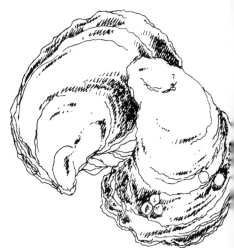

 4 *large tomatoes*
20–24 *small fresh oysters, shucked*
   Flour for dredging
   Beer batter (see page 373)
   Oil for deep frying
 2 *Tablespoons* sauce Béarnaise
   (see page 85)
1½ *Tablespoons* sauce rémoulade
   (see page 89)

Preheat oven to 275 degrees.

Select large, firm tomatoes. Skin them by dipping them for 10 seconds into boiling water, then peeling. Cut out the stems and scoop out the pulp and seeds to form a cup. Place them on a baking pan and keep them warm in oven.

Heat oil to 375 degrees.

Dry the oysters with paper towels and dredge them thoroughly in flour. Dip each oyster in beer batter and then fry them in the heated oil until they are golden brown.

Place them in the tomato shells.

Combine the *sauce Béarnaise* and the *sauce rémoulade* in a small bowl, then use this mixture to cover the top of each filled tomato. Reheat in oven (275 degrees) for 10 minutes. Serve warm.

Tomatoes and Glazed Avocado

Serves 4 to 6

Juice of ½ lemon
1 *large firm tomato*
1 *ripe avocado*

Salt and pepper to taste
Flour for dredging
½ *cup corn oil*

Mix lemon juice with enough water to make ¼ cup of liquid. Select a very firm tomato, not overripe, and cut into ¼-inch slices. Peel the avocado, remove the pit and cut into slices approximately the same size as the tomatoes. Sprinkle the avocado with the lemon juice and water, salt, and pepper, and dredge with flour. Heat the oil in a large frying pan and sauté the avocados and tomatoes until the avocado is a golden brown on both sides.

PRESENTATION
To serve, arrange the vegetables alternately on a hot plate.

Glazed Cranberries

Serves 4 to 6

2 *cups granulated sugar*
   (1 *cup for glaze,* 1 *cup to*
   sprinkle on afterwards)
   Juice of 1 *orange*
¼ *cup water*

Pinch each of ground cloves,
cinnamon
1 *pound fresh cranberries,*
   washed and drained

Preheat broiler

In a large saucepan combine 1 cup sugar, orange juice, water, cloves, and cinnamon, bring to a boil and cook for 3 minutes. Remove from the heat, add the cranberries, and stir until cranberries are completely coated with the syrup.

Using a slotted spoon lift the cranberries from the syrup and spread them out on a baking pan. Sprinkle with remaining cup of sugar.

Place under the broiler for 5 minutes. Allow the cranberries to cool and chill them before serving.

Glazed New Carrots

1 *pound tiny carrots*
  (1½–2 inches)
2 *Tablespoons butter*
½ *teaspoon sugar*

½ *teaspoon salt*
1 *Tablespoon chives, finely*
  chopped

Wash and scrub the carrots—there is no need to peel these very small ones. Drop into enough boiling water to cover and cook until they are tender but slightly undercooked—about 5 minutes. Drain.

Melt the butter in a frying pan, add the sugar and simmer until the mixture caramelizes but does not turn brown. Add the carrots and salt and sauté for 5 minutes, turning the carrots frequently.

PRESENTATION
Serve them immediately, sprinkled with chopped chives.

Carrots with Minted Dressing

1 *pound carrots*
1 *Tablespoon cider vinegar*
1 *Tablespoon honey*

1 *Tablespoon fresh mint, finely*
  chopped
½ *teaspoon salt*

Peel the carrots, slice, and drop into enough water to cover. Cook until tender—about 5 to 7 minutes. Drain. In a small bowl mix together the vinegar, honey, mint, and salt, and pour over the carrots. Heat quickly. Serve hot.

Minted Turnips

1½ *pounds (about 3 large) white*
   turnips, peeled and quartered
 3 *Tablespoons butter*
½ *teaspoon salt*

Pinch pepper
½ *Tablespoon fresh mint, finely*
  chopped

Peel and quarter turnips. Drop the turnips in enough boiling water to cover and cook until soft—about 25 minutes. Drain, then press the turnips through a sieve or purée in a blender. Place the puréed turnips in a saucepan over medium heat and stir until all moisture has evaporated. Stir in the butter, salt, pepper, and chopped mint. Serve hot.

VARIATION
For a different and subtle flavor substitute ⅛ teaspoon caraway seed for the fresh mint.

Casserole of Fresh Turnips and Greens   *Serves 4 to 6*

1 *pound small, fresh turnips*
  with green tops
2 *Tablespoons butter*
2 *Tablespoons shallots*
  (or onions), finely chopped

½ *teaspoon caraway seed*
⅛ *teaspoon cornstarch*
1 *ounce dry sherry*

Cut off turnip tops and set aside. Peel turnips, then place them in a saucepan, cover with water and bring to a boil. Cook for 25 to 30 minutes, until they are tender but not overcooked. Drain and keep them warm.

Wash and drain the turnip greens, removing the tough part of the stem. Chop the greens coarsely. Melt the butter in a large frying pan and sauté the chopped shallots until they are soft. Add the caraway seed and the chopped turnip greens and cook over medium heat for 5 minutes.

Cut the turnips into small (1 inch) cubes and add to the frying pan. Mix well and transfer to an ovenproof casserole.

Preheat oven to 400 degrees.

Dissolve the cornstarch in a small amount of the sherry and stir until smooth. Add the remaining sherry and pour over the turnips in the casserole, mixing lightly. Bake (400 degrees) for about 5 to 8 minutes, until heated through. Serve at once.

Braised Fennel

Serves 4 to 6

2 *pounds fennel, trimmed of*
  green tops and outside leaves
2 *large tomatoes, peeled,*
  seeded, and chopped
1 *teaspoon salt*

Pinch of pepper
Juice of ½ lemon
3 *Tablespoons Parmesan cheese,*
  grated

Preheat oven to 350 degrees.

Boil fennel in water to cover until tender—about 30 minutes. Drain, slice in half and cut away the hard core. Cut the fennel into ⅛-inch slices and arrange in a buttered baking dish. Add the chopped tomatoes, salt, pepper, lemon juice, and sprinkle with the grated cheese.

Bake (350 degrees) for 15 minutes or until the cheese is golden brown.

Braised Celery Root (Celeriac)

Serves 4 to 6

1 *pound (2 large) fresh or*
  canned celery root, peeled (or
  use canned and drained)
  Juice of 1 lemon
½ *cup brown stock, or tomato*
  juice (see page 45) (or use rich
  canned beef broth)

1 *teaspoon salt*
¼ *teaspoon pepper*
3 *Tablespoons Parmesan cheese,*
  finely grated

As soon as the celery roots are peeled, rub them thoroughly with half of the lemon juice to prevent them from turning dark. Boil in a covered saucepan until they are tender—about 40 minutes, depending upon size of roots.

Preheat oven to 400 degrees.

Drain and slice the celery roots ⅛ inch thick and arrange the slices on a buttered, shallow, ovenproof dish. Pour the stock over them and sprinkle with the remaining lemon juice, salt, pepper, and the Parmesan cheese. Bake (400 degrees) for 15 minutes. Serve at once.

Swiss Style Braised Red Cabbage

Serves 4 to 6

1 *head fresh red cabbage,*
   finely grated or shredded
1 *onion, finely chopped*
3 *tart apples, peeled and grated*
½ *pound bacon (or salt pork),*
   finely diced
½ *cup wine vinegar*

1½ *cups dry red wine*
1½ *Tablespoons raw rice*
1½ *Tablespoons red currant*
   jelly
1½ *teaspoons salt*
¼ *teaspoon pepper*

Preheat oven to 400 degrees.

Place shredded cabbage in an ovenproof casserole. Add the chopped onion, grated apples, diced bacon, vinegar, red wine, rice, currant jelly, salt, and pepper, and mix well. Cover the casserole and bake (400 degrees) for 2 to 2½ hours, stirring twice during the cooking period. Serve hot.

Beets and Ripe Olives

Serves 4 to 6

1 *pound small fresh beets, or*
   1 *No. 2 can of small beets*
½ *cup black olives, pitted and*
   coarsely chopped
½ *teaspoon sugar*

1 *teaspoon salt*
¼ *teaspoon pepper*
½ *teaspoon cornstarch*
½ *cup beet juice (from the*
   can or the cooking water)

Wash the beets and cook in boiling water until tender, about 25 minutes (unless using the canned variety). Reserve ½ cup of the liquid in which they were cooked and then drain the beets. Peel the beets, cut into small cubes, and place in a buttered ovenproof baking dish.

   Preheat oven to 350 degrees.

   Add the olives, sugar, salt, and pepper to beets. Dissolve the cornstarch in a little of the beet juice, add the remaining beet juice and pour over the beet and olive mixture in the baking dish. Heat in oven (350 degrees) for 5 minutes and serve hot.

Chestnut-Filled Cabbage Leaves

Serves 4 to 6

2 *cups chestnuts (canned may be used, drained)*
1 *head cabbage, trimmed of coarse, outer leaves*
6 *slices bacon, diced*
3 *Tablespoons onion, finely chopped*
¼ *pound pork sausage*
¼ *teaspoon powdered cocoa*
½ *teaspoon salt*
¼ *teaspoon pepper*
   Pinch each, marjoram and thyme

1 *Tablespoon capers, finely chopped*
2 *eggs, lightly beaten*
4 *Tablespoons butter, melted*
3 *ounces dry white wine*

If chestnuts are fresh cut a cross in the top of each, then boil for approximately 30 to 40 minutes, drain and shell them while they are still hot.

Chop chestnut meat coarsely.

Meanwhile poach the whole head of cabbage in boiling water for about 12 minutes. Drain well and carefully remove 4 or 6 outer leaves, blot them dry and lay them out flat to be filled. (Use remaining cooked cabbage as a cooked salad with vinaigrette sauce, for example, or use in one of my other recipes where cooked cabbage is called for.)

Sauté the bacon, chopped onion, and pork sausage in a large frying pan for about 6 minutes or until the onions begin to take on color. Add the chopped chestnuts, cocoa, salt, pepper, marjoram, thyme, and chopped capers, stirring occasionally, and cook for another 5 minutes.

Remove from the fire and stir in the beaten eggs.

Place a portion of the chestnut mixture in the center of each leaf and carefully roll the leaf around it, tucking in the sides to make a neat package.

Preheat oven to 400 degrees.

Pour the melted butter into a shallow, ovenproof serving dish; place the filled cabbage leaves in the dish with the flaps underneath and pour the white wine over them. Bake (400 degrees) for 25 minutes, basting frequently with the pan juices. Serve hot.

This may be served as a main course or as an accompaniment with pork or venison.

Mushroom Pepperoni   *Serves 4*

4 *small firm green peppers*
1 *Tablespoon butter*
3 *Tablespoons onion, minced*
2 *Tablespoons fresh bread*
  crumbs
1 *clove garlic, minced*
½ *pound mushrooms, sliced*
  very thin
1 *large tomato, peeled,*
  seeded, and diced

Juice of 1 *lemon*
1 *hard-boiled egg,*
  coarsely chopped
1 *teaspoon salt*
½ *teaspoon paprika*
¼ *cup milk*
2 *Tablespoons Parmesan cheese,*
  grated

Preheat oven to 450 *degrees.*

Slice off tops of peppers. Scrape out the seeds and white membrane leaving a cup. Blanch for about 15 minutes or until tender in simmering water, but do not overcook.

In a frying pan melt the butter, add the minced onions and sauté until they are soft. Stir in the bread crumbs and minced garlic. Add the sliced mushrooms, diced tomato, lemon juice, chopped egg, salt, and paprika and cook for 3 minutes. Pour in the milk and mix thoroughly.

Transfer the peppers to a buttered baking dish. Fill each pepper with the onion and mushroom mixture, piling it high. Sprinkle each with grated Parmesan cheese and bake (450 degrees) for 5 to 10 minutes or until the tops are golden brown.

Serve with veal, pork, beef.

Endive Filled with Mushroom and Avocado *Serves 4*

4 *large whole stalks of Belgian* *endive*	½ *avocado, coarsely chopped*
Juice of 1 lemon	1 *medium tomato, thinly sliced*
½ *teaspoon salt*	*Pinch sage*
4 *large mushrooms, finely* *chopped*	¼ *teaspoon pepper*
1 *Tablespoon butter*	2 *Tablespoons sour cream*
	3 *Tablespoons Parmesan or* *Gruyère cheese, finely grated*

Preheat oven to 350 degrees.

Select large firm endives and trim off outside leaves. Place the endives in boiling water to cover, add lemon juice and salt, and simmer for 15 minutes. Remove the endives and drain well.

In the meantime prepare the filling. Sauté the finely chopped mushrooms in butter until soft, remove from heat, chop avocado coarsely and add to mushrooms. Add tomato, sage, and pepper, and mix thoroughly.

Cut the endives in half lengthwise. Remove the center leaves, chop and add to the mushroom mixture. Fill each endive shell with the mushroom mixture and place in a shallow buttered baking dish. Spread the sour cream over the top of each filled endive, sprinkle with cheese and bake (350 degrees) until golden brown—about 10 minutes.

Orange Beets

Serves 4 to 6

1 *pound fresh beets*	2 *Tablespoons red wine vinegar*
2 *large eating oranges*	¼ *teaspoon cornstarch, dissolved* *in 1 teaspoon cold water*
1 *Tablespoon walnuts or pecans,* *finely chopped*	
½ *teaspoon sugar*	
½ *teaspoon salt*	
¼ *cup oil*	

Place the unpeeled beets in water to cover and boil until tender—about 25 minutes. Drain and skin them, then slice ¼ inch thick.

Using a very sharp knife peel the oranges, making sure to remove all the white pith. Slice the whole peeled oranges into ¼-inch thick circles and alternate with the beets in a shallow baking dish.

Mix together in a small saucepan the chopped nuts, sugar, salt, oil, vinegar, and dissolved cornstarch, and bring to a boil. Pour over the beets and oranges. This may be prepared in advance.

Preheat oven to 350 degrees.

Before serving, bake (350 degrees) until heated through—about 10 minutes.

Leeks au Gratin

Serves 4 to 6

1 *pound of leeks (both green and white parts), trimmed*
1 *Tablespoon butter*
1 *Tablespoon flour*
¼ *cup milk*
¼ *cup water in which leeks were cooked*

½ *teaspoon salt*
¼ *teaspoon pepper*
   Pinch cayenne pepper
2 *Tablespoons Parmesan cheese, grated*

Trim the leeks, using all the white and only the freshest part of the green stalk. Cut each leek lengthwise and then slice into 1-inch pieces. Wash thoroughly in a sieve under running water, and drain. Drop the leeks into a saucepan of boiling water to cover, and cook for about 20 minutes or until tender.

Preheat oven to 400 degrees.

Reserving ¼ cup of the water, drain leeks and transfer to baking dish. In the same saucepan (now completely emptied) melt the butter and stir in the flour to make a smooth paste. Add the milk and the ¼ cup of water in which the leeks were cooked. Simmer until the sauce has thickened. Season with salt, pepper, and cayenne.

Pour the sauce over the leeks, sprinkle them with Parmesan cheese and bake (400 degrees) about 10 minutes, or until golden brown.

Cauliflower *Amandine*

1 *pound fresh cauliflower buds*
2 *Tablespoons butter*
½ *cup sliced almonds*

½ *teaspoon salt*
¼ *teaspoon pepper*
2 *hard-boiled eggs, chopped*

Trim stalks off cauliflower, leaving only buds. Drop the cauliflower buds in enough lightly salted water to cover and cook for about 8 minutes, or until tender but not overcooked. Drain the cauliflower.

Melt the butter in a frying pan, add the cauliflower buds, sliced almonds, salt, and pepper, and sauté until the cauliflower buds begin to take on a bit of color. Sprinkle with the chopped eggs. Serve hot.

Brussels Sprouts with Chestnuts and Bacon

The seasonal tender young Brussels sprout is best served the instant it is cooked in order to retain a slightly crisp texture. Overcooking ruins it. Mixed with chestnuts, Brussels sprouts make a splendid accompaniment to a Thanksgiving dinner.

1 *pound fresh chestnuts, cooked*
   and drained (or canned and
   drained)
1 *pound Brussels sprouts, trimmed*
4 *slices lean bacon, diced*
1 *Tablespoon shallots (or onion),*
   finely chopped

Select and clean the tiny sprouts of any yellow leaves. Cook in lightly salted boiling water to cover, for no more than 8 minutes. While the sprouts are cooking, sauté the diced bacon in a frying pan until crisp; pour off the fat. Add the shallots and chestnuts to the bacon and sauté until shallots are lightly golden. When sprouts are cooked, drain them. Add the sautéed bacon, chestnuts and shallots and serve at once.

Sautéed Cucumber with Dill   *Serves 4 to 6*

1 *pound cucumbers*
1 *teaspoon salt*
2 *Tablespoons butter*

1 *Tablespoon fresh dill, finely*
chopped
Pepper

Peel the cucumbers and cut them across into 2-inch slices. Lay the pieces flat and cut them in half. Remove seeds. You should end up with slices of cucumber which look like wide rockers (curved at each end).

Place the cucumbers in a bowl, sprinkle with salt and allow to sweat for at least 30 minutes. Pour off the liquid, pat the cucumbers dry with paper towel. Sauté the cucumbers in butter over medium heat until they are lightly cooked—about 4 to 6 minutes. Sprinkle with finely chopped dill, season with pepper, and serve hot.

Spiced Lentils   *Serves 4 to 6*

½ *pound dried lentils*
1 *Tablespoon chutney,*
  finely chopped
1 *Tablespoon chow chow*
  (or piccalilli), finely chopped
2 *cloves garlic, minced*
1 *teaspoon cider vinegar*

1 *teaspoon salt*
2 *tomatoes, peeled, seeded,*
  and diced
1 *cup cooked ham, diced*
  (or cooked bacon, crisp and
  crumbled)

Soak lentils overnight. Drain, rinse, and boil in water to cover for 1 hour or until tender. Drain.

Preheat oven to 350 degrees.

In a shallow ovenproof serving dish combine the drained lentils with the chopped chutney and chow chow, the minced garlic, the vinegar, salt, diced tomatoes, and ham. All of this may be prepared in advance and heated in the oven (350 degrees) for about 15 minutes just before serving.

Purée of Peas
Serves 4 to 6

3 *pounds of peas,*   1 *teaspoon fresh mint, finely*
  fresh or frozen   *chopped*
1 *Tablespoon heavy cream*   ½ *teaspoon salt*
2 *Tablespoons butter*   *Pinch each of pepper and sugar*

Drop peas in enough boiling water to cover and cook for 5 to 6 minutes. Drain and allow to cool, then press the peas through a sieve or purée in a blender. Place the puréed peas in a saucepan. Add the cream and butter and stir, over medium heat, until the purée is smooth. Stir in the chopped mint, salt, pepper, and sugar.

Purée of Chestnuts
Serves 4 to 6

This particular purée of chestnuts is an elegant and very rich accompaniment to game, or perhaps a roast of pork or lamb. Most of the preparation may be done in advance, although I suggest adding the butter and cream just before serving.

1 *pound chestnuts, peeled*   3 *Tablespoons butter*
3 *ounces semi-sweet chocolate* ½ *cup heavy cream*
2 *Tablespoons honey*

NOTE: If you are using fresh chestnuts, to peel them easily, score each nut with a sharp knife and place on a baking sheet in a hot oven (375 degrees) for 15–20 minutes. Peel while still hot. If you are using dried chestnuts, cover with water and soak for 5 hours before cooking.
Place the peeled chestnuts in a saucepan with water to cover (or half milk, half water if you prefer), break the chocolate into small pieces, add to chestnuts and simmer, covered, for 45 to 50 minutes, or until the chestnuts begin to fall apart. During the final 5 minutes of cooking time reduce almost all the liquid in the pan by boiling. Drain the cooked chestnuts and put through the fine blade of the meat grinder into the saucepan. Stir in the honey, butter, cream, and serve hot.

Purée of Minted Red Beans   *Serves 4 to 6*

1 *pound dried red kidney beans*
   (or use canned and drained)
½ *onion, finely chopped*
¼ *cup ham ends, finely chopped*
   (or bits of bacon)
2 *Tablespoons butter*

1 *Tablespoon fresh mint, finely*
   chopped
1 *cup sour cream*
2 *Tablespoons chives, finely*
   chopped

Combine the beans and chopped onion and ham in 1½ quarts of water and cook, covered, for about 1½ hours or until the beans are very soft. Drain the beans, stir in the butter, and press them through a coarse sieve (or purée in blender).

Preheat oven to 350 degrees.

Place purée in an ovenproof serving dish, stir in the chopped mint and heat in oven (350 degrees) for 10 minutes before serving. Serve topped with sour cream and chopped chives.

Crisped Onions in Beer Batter   *Serves 4 to 6*

Onion rings, 4–6 per person
1 *cup flour sifted with* 1 *teaspoon*
   salt

Beer batter (see page 373)
Oil for deep frying

Heat oil to 375 degrees.

Peel large onions and slice very thin. Separate into rings. Select the best rings and dredge them in the sifted flour. With a slotted spoon or long-handled fork dip each ring into the beer batter and fry in oil (375 degrees) until golden. Serve hot.

Vegetables in Beer Batter

Serves 4 to 6

Crisply fried, the vegetables I suggest here retain all of their flavor to a degree which no other method of cooking can equal. They also retain their texture because they're slightly undercooked. Mixing them will give even more variety to your meal.

½ pound each, after trimming, raw: {
    cauliflower
    broccoli
    zucchini
    asparagus
    eggplant, peeled and sliced

Juice of 1 lemon
1 *teaspoon salt*
1 *cup flour*
   Beer batter (see page 373)
   Oil for deep frying

Preheat oil in deep-fryer to 375 degrees.

Trim away the cauliflower or broccoli stalks, leaving only the small buds. Slice the unpeeled zucchini into 1-inch pieces. Use only the tips of the asparagus. Wash the vegetables, then sprinkle them with lemon juice.

Mix salt with flour and dredge the pieces of vegetables well in the mixture. Dip the pieces in beer batter, making sure they are coated completely, then carefully drop into hot oil (375 degrees) and fry until golden brown and crisp. Drain on absorbent paper. Keep warm until all have been cooked. Serve immediately.

Blossoms in Beer Batter   *Serves 4 to 6*

Nasturtium, squash, or pumpkin blossoms, Hawaiian orchids, or, in fact, any kind of blossom in beer batter becomes a conversation piece and adds a touch of modest glamor to a dinner. You may serve them, crisp and golden, with drinks, or dusted with powdered sugar atop a pumpkin pie, or with any number of desserts.

1 *dozen large blossoms (any kind)*   *Beer batter (see page 373)*
1 *cup flour, sifted with* 1 *teaspoon*   *Oil for deep frying*
  salt

Heat oil to 375 degrees.

Wash the blossoms carefully, drain and pat dry. Dust them with sifted flour and salt, then dip into beer batter. Fry (375 degrees) until golden brown.

PRESENTATION
As an appetizer with drinks, serve them piled on a tray with a small bowl of dip in the center. As a dip, I suggest 1½ ounces puréed anchovies mixed with ½ cup sour cream and 1 teaspoon prepared mustard.

Salads

As Accompaniments
Primarily Main-Course Salads
Before or After Main-Course Salads

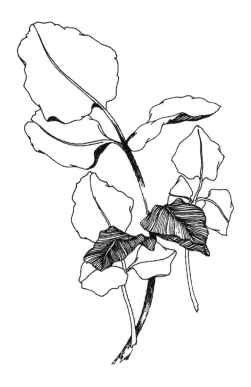

Considering the supreme wealth of materials available in America, salads are surprisingly limited—mainly "mixed greens," fruit salads, or those awful combinations that dieticians must have concocted. But delicious salads can be made using herbs, plants, vegetables, eggs, meat, poultry, and fish—in other words, every edible material in proper combination. And you can thus enjoy a much greater variety.

The average American also makes the mistake of dousing too many salads with mayonnaise—for example, on potatoes, to make "potato salad," or cabbage to make "cole slaw." More variety and originality can be achieved by limiting the use of mayonnaise and using instead such materials as sour cream, wine vinegar, broth, and unusual herbs and seasonings to vary the usual oil and vinegar base. A salad should be light and perfectly balanced—a contrast of flavors and textures.

Since cooked ingredients as well as raw are widely used in salads, leftovers can be utilized with imagination. Also, since the blend or combination is generally the important thing, you can take advantage of what the season affords and can readily substitute locally available materials.

As Accompaniments

Primarily Main-Course Salads

Before or After Main-Course Salads

As Accompaniments

Swiss Potato Salad

Serves 4 to 6

This warm potato salad is delicious with cold cuts, boiled beef, or spicy meat dishes.

3 *pounds potatoes (about 7 medium size), cooked and peeled*

½ *cup beef or chicken broth, hot (see pages 43 or 44) (or use rich canned beef or chicken broth)*

1 *teaspoon salt*

1 *teaspoon pepper*

1 *Tablespoon prepared mustard*

1 *Tablespoon white wine vinegar*

2 *Tablespoons peanut or corn oil*

1 *ounce sago cheese, finely grated*

1 *Tablespoon chives, finely chopped*

6 *slices bacon, cooked crisp, drained, and chopped*

Slice the potatoes while still warm. In a small bowl, mix together the hot broth, salt, pepper, mustard, vinegar, and oil. Pour this over the potatoes, toss lightly, and sprinkle the grated cheese on top. Serve warm, garnished with chives and crisp chopped bacon.

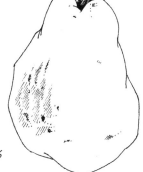

Pear and Potato Salad

Serves 4 to 6

This recipe is a simple variation of the preceding Swiss potato salad and makes a splendid accompaniment to either cold meats or a steaming platter of boiled beef and vegetables, or perhaps as one salad on a buffet table.

Using recipe for Swiss potato salad, substitute 4 cups (1½ pounds) ripe but firm pears, peeled, sliced, for 1½ pounds of potatoes. Combine 4 cups pears with 4 cups potatoes, then proceed according to recipe.

Watercress Salad with Mustard Dressing   *Serves 4 to 6*

2 *bunches watercress*
2 *Tablespoons peanut or corn oil*
1 *Tablespoon prepared mustard*
½ *teaspoon mustard seed*
1 *Tablespoon red or white wine vinegar*

½ *teaspoon salt*
½ *teaspoon pepper*
2 *hard-boiled eggs, chopped*

Remove and discard the larger stems from the watercress and wash, drain, and dry thoroughly. Refrigerate to chill for at least ½ hour before dressing.

In a salad bowl mix together the oil, mustard, mustard seed, vinegar, salt, pepper, and chopped egg. Add the drained watercress and toss until the cress is thoroughly coated.

Salad of Onions and Ripe Olives   *Serves 4 to 6*

This salad provides a spicy accompaniment to hearty casserole dishes, pork and beans, etc.

4 *medium Spanish onions, peeled and sliced paper thin*
½ *cup red or white wine vinegar*
1 *teaspoon salt*
2 *cups green ripe California olives, pitted and diced*

3 *pimientos, diced*
2 *cloves garlic, peeled and crushed, or minced*
1 *cup olive oil*
⅛ *teaspoon ground coriander*

Put the thinly sliced onions in a bowl, pour the vinegar over them, sprinkle with salt, and place in the refrigerator for at least 1 hour.

Remove from the refrigerator, add the olives and pimientos and crushed garlic, and then pour the olive oil over all. Add the coriander and mix well before serving.

PRESENTATION
Transfer to a salad bowl garnished with lettuce leaves or serve on lettuce leaves on individual plates.

NOTE: The term "green ripe" olives may not be familiar to you. Olives are usually either unripe and green, or ripe and black. But there is a variety grown in California which is still greenish when ripe. If you can't get them, use either the usual green or black or, better still, a combination.

Spicy Pepper Slaw   *Serves 4 to 6*

A fine complement to fish or any dish, even a sandwich.

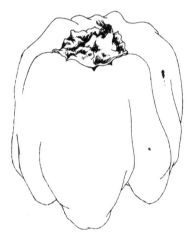

1 *2-pound head of green savoy*
cabbage, shredded
5 *green peppers, sliced*
½ *cup shallots (or scallions),*
finely chopped
1 *Tablespoon salt*
1 *teaspoon pepper*
½ *cup peanut or corn oil*
2 *Tablespoons red or white*
wine vinegar

Slice the cabbage into a large salad bowl by cutting as thin as possible, or by using a shredder or slicing machine. Remove the seeds from the green peppers, cut away the white part, and slice as thin as possible. Add the ½ cup of very finely chopped shallots and salt. Allow the mixture to rest for one hour.

Then remove the cabbage, green pepper, and shallots to a dry kitchen towel and twist the ends of the cloth tight to squeeze out moisture. Return to the salad bowl.

Prepare a dressing of the pepper, oil, and vinegar, and pour over the vegetables. Toss well and serve chilled.

Salad of Cooked Carrots with Dill Dressing

Serves 4 to 6

Serve as accompaniment to hot or cold poultry dishes. It is ideal on a buffet.

15 *medium carrots, cooked and thinly sliced*
½ *medium onion, peeled and finely chopped*
 1 *Tablespoon fresh tarragon or 1 teaspoon fresh dill, finely chopped (If using dried herbs cut amount in half.)*

¼ *teaspoon black pepper, freshly ground*
½ *teaspoon sugar*
¾ *teaspoon salt*
 2 *Tablespoons peanut or corn oil*
 1 *Tablespoon red or white wine vinegar*

Mix and serve chilled.

Raw Mushroom and Endive Salad, Lemon Dressing

Serves 4 to 6

Serve as a dinner accompaniment for game, especially in winter.

12 *large mushrooms*
  Juice of 2 lemons
 4 *Belgian endives, cut into thin strips*
 1 *teaspoon salt*
½ *teaspoon black peppercorns, crushed*

¼ *teaspoon savory*
 1 *Tablespoon chives, chopped*
½ *cup celery, finely chopped*
 3 *Tablespoons olive oil*

Wipe the mushrooms with a damp cloth, trim off hard root end, and slice the mushrooms very thin. Pour the lemon juice over them at once, coating them well. Toss in the endives then add the salt, pepper, savory, chives, celery, and the oil. Mix well and chill. Serve in a salad bowl.

Primarily Main-Course Salads

Salad of Raw Mushrooms with Ham and Artichoke

Serves 4 to 6

This salad makes
a lovely luncheon main-
course dish. It is also
good as a light supper.

½ *pound mushrooms,*
  sliced paper thin
1 *Tablespoon lemon juice*
2 *slices boiled ham, cut in*
  thin strips
2 *Tablespoons onion, finely*
  chopped
6 *hearts of artichoke (fresh,*
  frozen or canned), cooked,
  drained, and coarsely chopped
4 *Tablespoons olive oil*

2 *Tablespoons red or white*
  wine vinegar
½ *teaspoon salt*
  Pinch each of pepper, savory
  Lettuce leaves

NOTE: If you use frozen artichoke hearts they must first be cooked for 15 minutes; the kind that come in cans or jars are already cooked. Fresh artichokes should be boiled 30 to 40 minutes, or until leaves pull away easily; then remove all leaves, scrape away the thistle, trim root— 4 large fresh artichokes would do for this recipe.

Wipe mushrooms with damp cloth to remove any grit; trim off the hard end of stems, but do not peel. Cut lengthwise into paper-thin slices, and sprinkle with lemon juice. Combine the mushrooms, strips of ham, finely chopped onion and artichoke hearts.

In a small bowl, beat together the oil, vinegar, salt, pepper, and savory, and pour over the salad. Serve well chilled and garnished with leaves of lettuce.

Beet and Sausage Salad

Serves 4 to 6

This can make a good luncheon main course dish or can be served as an accompaniment to baked ham, boiled beef, smoked meats, etc.

2 *pounds fresh beets or*	*Pinch sugar*
1 *No. 2 can*	1 *teaspoon salt*
10 *ounces cooked pork sausage*	1 *Tablespoon red or white*
1 *medium onion, finely chopped*	*wine vinegar*
4 *hard-boiled eggs, sliced*	*Pinch of marjoram*
2 *Tablespoons peanut or corn oil*	

Cook the beets, if fresh, in boiling salted water until tender. Drain, peel, and cut into thin slices. Remove the skin from the cooked pork sausage. Cut into thin slices and mix with the beets. Add the chopped onion and sliced eggs.

In a small bowl mix together the oil, sugar, salt, vinegar, and marjoram. Pour the oil dressing over the salad and mix gently. Chill before serving.

Green Bean and Onion Salad

Serves 4 to 6

This may be served as a luncheon salad, for supper, in a buffet, or with a mixed grill main course.

2 *pounds small whole green*	½ *teaspoon salt*
beans	½ *teaspoon pepper*
1 *Tablespoon prepared mustard*	⅛ *teaspoon savory*
1 *Tablespoon olive oil*	1 *small onion, finely chopped*
½ *Tablespoon red or white*	6 *slices bacon, cooked crisp,*
wine vinegar	*drained, and chopped*

Trim off the ends of the beans and cook in barely enough boiling salted water to cover until they are slightly underdone—about 15 minutes. Drain and set aside to cool.

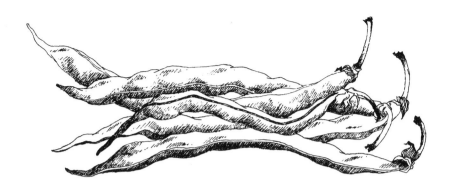

Prepare the dressing in a salad bowl, mixing together the mustard, oil, vinegar, salt, pepper, savory, onion, and bacon. Add the beans to the dressing, mix well and chill before serving.

Avocado with Sliced White Radish Salad   *Serves 4*

This salad makes a refreshing luncheon main course in the summer, and I often serve it outdoors.

2 *ripe avocados*
½ *lemon*
2 *cups medium-sized white radishes, grated or sliced paper thin (If not available use the small red radishes.)*
½ *medium onion, grated*

1 *teaspoon salt*
2 *Tablespoons olive oil*
1 *Tablespoon red or white wine vinegar*
Pepper to taste
Chives, finely chopped

Cut the unpeeled avocados in half lengthwise and remove the seed. Rub the exposed fruit with lemon. Cut the top and tail from the radishes, wash and drain. Slice them, unpeeled, paper thin, or grate them into a bowl. Then grate the onion into the bowl. Add the salt and allow the mixture to rest for 30 minutes.

Twist the radish and onion mixture between kitchen or paper towels to remove all moisture and return to a dry bowl. Add the oil, vinegar, and pepper, and mix well. Fill each avocado half with one fourth of the mixture, and garnish with finely chopped chives. Serve well chilled.

Bouillabaisse Salad

Serves 4 to 6

A chilled bouillabaisse salad, in the best tradition of the Mediterranean fishing ports, makes a glittering and unusual main course for a luncheon or an elegant beginning to a very special dinner party. Together, the lobster, shrimp, bass, mussels, and clams—the tender bits of "fruits of the sea," as they are called—produce a fragrant and delicious broth.

 1 *2-pound live lobster (about*
    ½ pound of lobster meat)
12 *raw shrimp (about 6 ounces),*
    peeled and de-veined
 1 *pound of striped bass (or halibut),*
    cut across backbone into 2-inch pieces
16 *mussels in shells*
12 *clams in shells*
 3 *cloves garlic, peeled and minced*
 ½ *cup olive oil*
 1 *cup dry white wine*
 ⅛ *teaspoon thyme*
 4 *Tablespoons shallots (or*
    scallions), finely chopped
 4 *medium tomatoes, peeled,*
    seeded, and coarsely chopped
 3 *Tablespoons brandy*
 ½ *cup tomato juice*
 1 *teaspoon salt*
    Pinch cayenne

Cut the live lobster in half lengthwise and then divide each half into three pieces (or have your fish man do it). Leave these pieces intact but remove the meat from the lobster claws. Place this meat together with the lobster pieces in a large saucepan. Add the shrimp, bass, well-scrubbed mussels and clams, garlic, oil, white wine, thyme, shallots, tomatoes, brandy, tomato juice, salt, and cayenne. Cover the saucepan; bring just to a boil, then reduce heat and simmer for 15 minutes. Cool the bouillabaisse, chill, and serve in large soup plates.

Julienne of Cold Turkey and Pineapple   *Serves 4 to 6*

This salad is ideal as a summer luncheon main course.

1 *pound cooked turkey breast,*
  cut in julienne strips (A
  julienne strip is about the
  width of a matchstick.)
1 *large pineapple, peeled*
  and cut in julienne strips

½ *pound fresh berries (blue-*
  berries, raspberries, straw-
  berries)

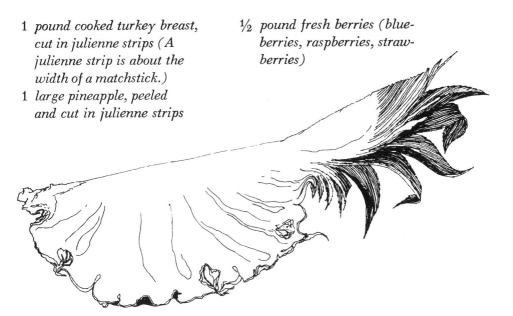

Slice the breast of turkey as thin as possible, then cut the slices into narrow strips. Remove the outer skin of the pineapple and then cut large slices, cutting from top to bottom around the hard core. Cut these slices into thin strips and mix gently with the strips of turkey in a salad bowl or large plate. Wash and prepare whichever berries are to be used (or a mixture of them) and sprinkle them over the turkey and pineapple.

DRESSING

1 *cup mayonnaise*
  Juice of ½ lemon
2 *ounces water*

½ *teaspoon honey*
2 *Tablespoons heavy cream*
  Salt and pepper

To prepare the dressing, put the mayonnaise in a small mixing bowl, add the lemon juice, water, honey, heavy cream, and season to taste with salt and pepper. Chill. Serve the dressing separately.

Salad of Pig's Knuckles and Spiced Autumn Squash

Serves 4 to 6

This unusual salad is, I think, a good example of the advantage of combining an old world favorite—pig's knuckles—with squash (hubbard, butternut, or acorn), a very popular American product. It should be served as a main course.

3 *pig's knuckles (or use cooked, bottled)*
1 *Tablespoon pickling spice*
1 *cup wine vinegar*
1 *Tablespoon salt*
1 *pound squash (hubbard, butternut, or acorn), unpeeled and seeded, cut into 2-inch cubes*
1 *medium onion, finely chopped*
2 *medium dill pickles, chopped*
1 *green pepper, finely chopped, after seeds and white ribs are removed*

1 *Tablespoon prepared mustard*
1 *Tablespoon red or white wine vinegar*
2 *Tablespoons olive oil*
  Leaves of lettuce for garnish

Cook the pig's knuckles in lightly salted boiling water uncovered until tender—about 1½ to 2 hours.

Meanwhile pour 2 quarts of boiling water into a large saucepan, add the pickling spice, vinegar, and salt, and the pieces of squash. Cook until tender but still firm—about 20 minutes. Drain. Remove the outer skin from the squash and place the flesh in the salad bowl.

Drain the pig's knuckles, remove the outer skin and discard; cut away the meat from the bones and cut into small cubes. If you use the cooked, bottled pig's knuckles, dice them in the same way. Combine the diced pig's knuckles with the squash, add the chopped onion, pickle, and green pepper, the mustard, vinegar, and oil. Mix thoroughly and chill before serving. Garnish with leaves of lettuce.

Dilled Cabbage and Ham

Serves 4

This hearty dish will serve as a main course for luncheon or supper.

1½ to 2 pound head cabbage,
   shredded
  4 ham steaks, 6 ounces each
  2 cups water
  1 cup dry white wine
  1 Tablespoon prepared mustard
  1 Tablespoon olive oil

1 Tablespoon red or white
  wine vinegar
½ Tablespoon brown sugar
½ teaspoon salt
¼ cup fresh dill,
  finely chopped

Shred the cabbage like sauerkraut by cutting as thin as possible or use shredder or cutting machine. Cook for 5 minutes in boiling salted water. Drain the cabbage and cool.

Simmer the ham steaks in 2 cups of water mixed with the cup of white wine for 25 minutes. Remove the steaks to cool and reduce the water/wine broth to half by boiling rapidly. Cool the broth and add the mustard, olive oil, vinegar, sugar, salt, and dill. Toss the cabbage in this dressing and serve well chilled alongside the ham steaks.

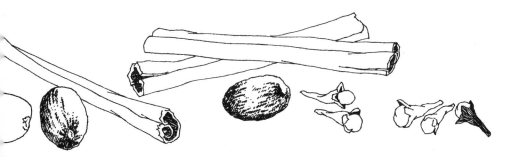

Luncheon Salad Bowl with Cold Meats   *Serves 4 to 6*

This nourishing and colorful luncheon salad bowl remains on my Stonehenge menu the year round. I serve it in a large wooden salad bowl, and we always bring it to the table, pour the dressing on and toss just before serving. I would suggest some crisp breads and a dessert to complete the luncheon menu.

1 *Boston or 2 bibb lettuce*
1 *head romaine lettuce*
3 *small breasts of chicken (about 6 ounces), cooked, sliced, and cut into julienne strips*
4 *slices (about 6 ounces) cooked ham, cut into narrow strips*
2 *slices (about 6 ounces) cold roast pork or beef, cut into thin strips*
3 *slices Swiss cheese (Gruyère or Emmenthaler), cut into thin slices*
4 *hard-boiled eggs, cut into quarters*
1 *cup tiny cherry tomatoes or 4 regular tomatoes, peeled and quartered*

4 *strips bacon, cooked crisp and drained*
6 *anchovy filets*
½ *cup country dressing (see page 89)*

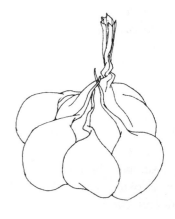

Wash and drain Boston or bibb lettuce, shake and dry thoroughly; then line the side of a salad bowl with the leaves. Cut the romaine across into 2-inch chunks, wash and drain until free of moisture, and place in the bottom of the bowl. Place the meat and cheese strips in separate mounds around the center of the pile of cut lettuce. Use the quartered eggs and tomatoes as garnish for the edge of the bowl and lay the crisp bacon and anchovy filets across the top. Just before serving at the table, pour the country dressing over the salad and toss lightly.

Greek Salad of Vegetables with Anchovies and Olives

Serves 4 to 6

This highly seasoned, colorful Greek salad is one way to bring to your luncheon table a touch of the Mediterranean. You can easily serve it as an appetizer or a main course for luncheon, choosing a substantial dessert to complete the menu. It is particularly good with barbecued meat. If fresh artichokes are not available, use the frozen hearts cooked according to directions. Do not overcook any of the vegetables, as a slightly crisp texture is important to this salad.

½ cup olive oil
12 medium mushrooms, wiped
    with a damp cloth and cut in
    quarters
1 teaspoon leaf oregano
2 medium onions, finely chopped
4 medium tomatoes, peeled,
    seeded, and chopped
1 medium eggplant, peeled
    and diced
2 cooked artichoke hearts, cut in
    quarters, or 1 package frozen
    artichoke hearts
    Juice of 3 lemons
½ teaspoon salt
12 anchovy filets
3 cloves garlic, peeled and finely chopped
12 black olives, pitted

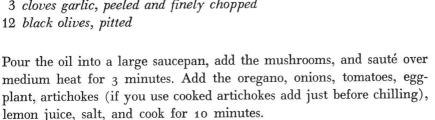

Pour the oil into a large saucepan, add the mushrooms, and sauté over medium heat for 3 minutes. Add the oregano, onions, tomatoes, eggplant, artichokes (if you use cooked artichokes add just before chilling), lemon juice, salt, and cook for 10 minutes.

Allow the salad mixture to cool, then transfer to a salad bowl. Add the anchovy filets, garlic, and olives and chill well before serving.

Before or After Main-Course Salads

Beef and Cheese Salad

Serves 4 to 6

This salad is most appropriate as an appetizer, especially when no meat is planned for the meal, or as a main course for a summer luncheon or supper.

1½ *pounds cold boiled beef*
  1 *medium onion, finely chopped*
  ½ *cup Swiss cheese,*
     cut into small cubes
  4 *small potatoes, cooked,*
     peeled, and sliced thin
  1 *Tablespoon prepared mustard*
  ½ *cup beef stock (see page 44)*
     (or use rich canned beef
     broth)
  2 *Tablespoons peanut or corn oil*
  1 *Tablespoon tarragon vinegar*
  1 *teaspoon salt*
     Pepper to taste
  1 *Tablespoon chives, chopped*

Cut away the fat from the beef, and slice about ¼ inch thick, then cut into 1-inch strips. In a salad bowl mix the beef strips, the finely chopped onion, cheese cubes, and slices of potatoes.

In a small bowl, mix together the mustard, beef stock, oil, vinegar, salt, and pepper. Pour over the beef and cheese mixture, sprinkle with chopped chives, and serve at room temperature.

Celeriac Salad with Ham and Olives   *Serves 4 to 6*

I prefer this salad served alone as a first course or combined with other hors d'oeuvres.

3 *medium celery roots (celeriac)*   ½ *teaspoon dry English mustard*
   Juice of 1 lemon   ½ *pound cooked ham*
1 *cup mayonnaise*   1 *cup black and green olives,*
1 *teaspoon salt*   *pitted and thinly sliced*

Peel the celery roots and grate very fine. Place in a salad bowl and sprinkle at once with lemon juice to prevent them from turning brown.

Mix the mayonnaise, salt, and mustard together, and pour over the grated celery root. Cut the ham in thin strips and add with the sliced olives. Mix and serve well chilled.

Salad of Zucchini and Hearts of Palm,   *Serves 4 to 6*
Lemon Dressing

This salad should be served primarily as an hors d'oeuvre or appetizer.

6 *small zucchini*   1 *clove garlic, finely chopped*
   Salt   ¼ *teaspoon pepper*
   Juice of 3 lemons   1 *teaspoon salt*
¼ *teaspoon marjoram*   1 *No. 2½ can hearts of palm*
¼ *teaspoon oregano*   3 *Tablespoons peanut or corn oil*

Trim the ends off the zucchini and scrub but leave them unpeeled. Cut into thin strips about the size of a pencil. Place them in a large salad bowl and sprinkle lightly with salt. Add the lemon juice, marjoram, oregano, garlic, pepper, and additional salt if necessary. Cut the hearts of palm into similar size thin strips and add them. Pour the oil over the salad, mix well, and chill before serving. (This salad is best made several hours before serving, allowing the vegetables to absorb the flavor of the herbs.)

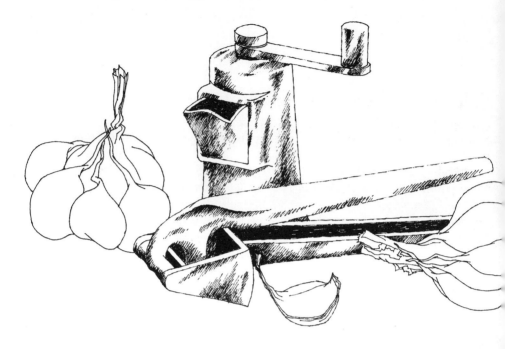

Wilted Spinach and Egg Salad

Serves 4 to 6

This tasty salad goes well after almost any main meat or poultry course.

 6 *slices bacon*
1½ *pounds fresh spinach*
 3 *hard-boiled eggs,*
   finely chopped
 2 *Tablespoons onion,*
   finely chopped
 1 *teaspoon salt*
 ½ *teaspoon pepper*

2 *Tablespoons olive oil*
1 *Tablespoon red or white*
  wine vinegar
1 *Tablespoon chicken stock (see*
  page 43) (or use rich canned
  chicken broth)
  Pinch curry powder

Fry the bacon and drain on absorbent paper. Meanwhile wash and drain the spinach (it will require several thorough washings to remove sand). Break off the stems and discard.

In a large salad bowl mix the drained spinach leaves and the finely chopped eggs and onion, the crisp bacon broken into pieces, the salt and pepper.

In a small saucepan heat the oil, vinegar, chicken stock, and curry powder. A few minutes before serving, pour the hot oil and vinegar sauce over the salad and mix well.

Salad of Endive, Grapefruit, and Orange, with Honey Lemon Dressing

Serves 4

I suggest this salad after hot roast poultry main courses, especially when there is no other fruit on the menu.

4 *Belgian endives*	12 *orange sections*
12 *grapefruit sections*	4 *strips of pimiento*

DRESSING

2 *Tablespoons honey*	½ *teaspoon ginger*
3 *Tablespoons lemon juice*	1 *teaspoon sesame seeds, lightly*
½ *teaspoon salt*	*toasted*

Wash and drain the endives, trim off and discard any outside browned leaves. Cut each endive lengthwise into quarters. Line 4 quarters, cut side up, on each plate and lay alternate grapefruit and orange sections across them, using 3 of each on each plate. Lay a strip of pimiento across tops of the sections.

In a small bowl, mix together the honey, lemon juice, salt, ginger, and sesame seeds (toasted lightly in the oven). Pour the dressing over the individual salads and serve cold.

Desserts

Dessert Basics   Pies
Frozen Desserts   Cake Desserts
Miscellaneous Desserts

The success of your meal depends on the selection of the right dessert; a dinner is not truly a great experience unless the finale provides exactly what your palate craves as a perfect ending. If you have served heavy opening courses that may have included a stuffed *crêpe* or a *quiche,* creamy sauces or rich accompaniments, then simplify the ending with something fruity that will be light and refreshing. But if your opening and main courses have been relatively simple, top the meal off with a rich, satisfying and unforgettable dessert.

The careful preparation of a batter and the baking of a cake are, of course, important, but remember that the good butter-cream filling is just as important to make the whole delectable.

In planning a dessert, let yourself be guided by what is in season. Fruits in their prime provide the best challenge for an inspired creation and they offer variety the year around.

Dessert Basics

Pies

Frozen Desserts

Cake Desserts

Miscellaneous Desserts

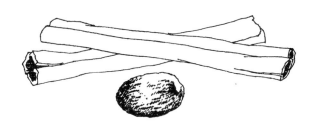

Dessert Basics

Basic Sponge Cake *Roulade*

Serves 8 to 12 (depending on fillings and additions)

(for one 12 × 18 inch baking pan)

This easily prepared basic *roulade,* a thin but surprisingly resilient, firm sponge cake, may be spread with a wide variety of fillings, flavored pastry creams, or ice cream and soft fresh fruits. Or it may be rolled and covered with your favorite icings, or decorated as a *Bûche de Noël* (Christmas Log).

5 *eggs*
½ *cup granulated sugar (¼ cup for yolks, ¼ cup for whites)*

½ *cup all purpose flour, sifted*
Grated rind of 1 lemon

Preheat oven to 400 degrees.

Cut piece of waxed paper 12 inches by 18 inches to fit the baking pan. Butter the paper, lay it butter side up on baking pan and set aside.

Separate the eggs: the yolks in one large mixing bowl and the whites in another. Add ¼ cup of the sugar to the yolks and beat until light yellow. Add the remaining ¼ cup sugar to the whites and beat until they form soft peaks. Fold half of the egg white mixture into the yolks and blend in the sifted flour and grated lemon rind. Fold in the remaining whites.

With a palette knife or spatula, spread the *roulade* mixture over the prepared paper on the baking sheet. Bake (400 degrees) for about 10 minutes, or until lightly browned but still moist.

Remove the *roulade* from the oven and cool on the baking pan for at least 10 to 15 minutes, then turn it upside down onto another piece of paper lightly sprinkled with sugar and carefully peel off the baked paper. Roll the *roulade* in the sugared paper and wrap in a dry kitchen towel until ready to fill.

Basic Pie Dough

For one 9 to 10 × 2 inch bottom pie shell

1½ *cup sifted flour*
 8 *Tablespoons cold butter, cut
     in pieces*

4 *Tablespoons shortening*
3½ *Tablespoons water*
¼ *teaspoon of salt*

Put the sifted flour in a pile on a pastry board. Make a well in the flour and put the butter and shortening in it. With your hands, mix the butter and shortening into the flour until it becomes a granulated texture. Make another well in this mixture. Add water and salt and mix in with your fingers only until the water is absorbed. Do not overmix. Form the dough into a ball, flatten out slightly with your hand, wrap in a damp towel and refrigerate for 1 hour, or until cool.

Preheat oven to 375 degrees.

Lightly butter a pie plate. Roll out the dough and line the pie plate. Trim edges and press rim with fingers to prevent shrinkage.

Lightly butter the bottom of another pie plate and place on top of the dough inside the original pie plate. Chill in refrigerator 15 minutes. Turn pans over and bake, bottom side up (375 degrees), for 25 minutes, until golden brown.

If this recipe is to be used for quiche, substitute the following baking time:

Bake (375 degrees), bottom side up, for 5 minutes. Turn pans over and bake for 10 minutes more, until crust is slightly browned.

Sweet Pie Dough

For two 10 × 2 inch piecrusts

If you require only one 9 to 10 inch piecrust, cut the ingredients in half and eliminate the heavy cream. Or if you make the following recipe and use only half the dough, the unused portion can be refrigerated for up to a week.

 4 *Tablespoons almond paste*
     Dash of vanilla
 1 *egg yolk*
12 *Tablespoons (1½ sticks) butter*

½ *cup granulated sugar*
 1 *Tablespoon heavy cream*
2¾ *cups all purpose flour, sifted*

Mix almond paste, vanilla, and egg yolk to make a smooth paste. In another bowl, cream the butter and sugar, then blend in the almond paste mixture. Mix in the heavy cream.

Put the sifted flour on a pastry board and make a well in the center. Put the egg mixture in the well. With your fingers, mix in a little at a time, only until the flour and egg mixture becomes absorbed. Do not overmix. Form dough into a ball and flatten out slightly with your hand. Wrap in a damp cloth and refrigerate for one hour or until cool.

Preheat oven to 375 degrees.

Lightly butter a pie plate. Roll out dough and line the pie plate. Trim edges and press rim with fingers to prevent shrinkage. Lightly butter the bottom of another pie plate and set inside lined plate, on top of dough.

Turn the plates over and bake, bottom side up, (375 degrees) for 5 minutes, then turn them over and bake for 10 to 12 minutes more or until lightly browned.

Pastry Cream

Yield 2 cups

2 *Tablespoons cornstarch*
1½ *cups milk (½ cup to dissolve cornstarch, 1 cup for cream)*

2 *whole eggs*
¼ *cup granulated sugar*
½ *teaspoon vanilla extract*

Dissolve cornstarch in ½ cup cold milk, rubbing through fingers to break up lumps.

In another bowl, with a wire whisk, mix eggs and sugar, then combine egg mixture with the dissolved cornstarch.

In a saucepan, bring remaining 1 cup milk to a boil, then add it in a thin stream to the egg mixture, stirring constantly with whisk.

Return this to the saucepan and cook over low heat, stirring it constantly until it thickens to a custardy consistency or has begun to bubble. Remove from fire and add vanilla extract.

Basic Butter Cream

1 *cup granulated sugar*   1 *cup confectioners sugar, sifted*
¾ *cup water*   ½ *pound butter, unsalted*
4 *egg yolks*

In a saucepan, bring the granulated sugar and water to a boil and cook until it reaches 234 degrees on a candy thermometer, or a medium soft-ball stage.

Place egg yolks in a large bowl and stir in confectioners sugar. Add the hot, boiled sugar mixture in a thin stream and beat at medium speed, until mixture is cooled.

In another bowl, whip the butter until creamy, then beat into the egg yolk mixture until well blended and light. (Keep in a cool place until ready to use. Do not refrigerate before using.)

Simplified Butter Cream

The following is a quick method for making butter cream and may be substituted for the classic butter cream recipe above.

¾ *cup unsalted butter*   ¾ *cup confectioners sugar, sifted*
2 *egg yolks*

Beat butter and egg yolks at medium speed until smooth—approximately 10 minutes. Adding a small amount at a time, mix in the sugar and beat until smooth. (Keep in a cool place until ready to use. Do not refrigerate before using.)

VARIATIONS
Any of these ingredients may be folded into finished butter cream:

1 *Tablespoon vanilla extract*
1 *Tablespoon liqueur (Grand Marnier, Cointreau, kirsch, etc.)*
1 *Tablespoon strong coffee*
2 *ounces chocolate, melted*

Pies

Swiss Apple Custard Tart

Serves 6 to 8

1 *9 to 10 × 2 inch prebaked*
  sweet dough piecrust (see
  page 347)
6 *medium green apples, peeled,*
  cored, and grated
  Juice of ½ lemon
2 *Tablespoons flour*
⅛ *teaspoon cinnamon*
⅛ *teaspoon ginger*
  Grated rind ½ lemon
¼ *cup sugar, depending upon*
  tartness of apples
½ *cup milk*
4 *eggs*
1½ *cup light cream*

Preheat oven to 375 degrees.

Peel and core the apples, grate coarsely, and sprinkle immediately with lemon juice. Spread the grated apples over the prebaked sweet dough piecrust.

In a bowl, combine and thoroughly mix the flour, cinnamon, ginger, grated lemon rind, and sugar. Stir milk into the flour mixture.

In another bowl, beat eggs and cream together. Pour the beaten eggs and cream into the flour mixture and stir with a whisk to a smooth batter. Pour this custard mixture over the apples.

Bake (375 degrees) for 30 minutes or until the custard is completely set and golden in color.

Swiss Plum Tart

Serves 8

  1 *9 to 10 × 2 inch unbaked sweet*
     dough piecrust (see page 347)
 ½ *cup cake crumbs*
  2 *Tablespoons blanched al-*
     monds, slivered
2½ *cups fresh plums (dark*
     Italian if possible), quartered
     and pitted
 ¼ *cup apricot glaze*
     (If not available, see below.)
  1 *Tablespoon confectioners*
     sugar

Preheat oven to 400 degrees.

Line the pie dish with the unbaked sweet dough piecrust. Spread the cake crumbs and slivered almonds over the dough. Arrange the plums attractively over almonds, with skin on the bottom.

Bake (400 degrees) for 30 minutes or until the plums are soft and the crust is baked through and brown around the edges.

Remove the tart from the oven. Brush the apricot glaze over the top of the plums with a pastry brush. Cool.

PRESENTATION

Just before serving, sprinkle confectioners sugar over top of the tart.

To make an apricot glaze, heat ¼ cup apricot jam or preserves with 1 teaspoon water until it melts, then put through a sieve to remove any lumps.

Deep Dish Rhubarb Rosa

Serves 8

6 *medium stalks rhubarb, peeled,*
  and cut into small pieces
1 *cup sugar*
¼ *cup water*
1 *Tablespoon cornstarch, dis-*
  solved in 3 Tablespoons water
1 *cup soft bread crumbs*
5 *eggs, separated*
1 *cup sour cream*
¼ *teaspoon cinnamon*
1 *ounce brandy or kirsch*
8–10 *zwieback*
½ *cup melted butter*
½ *cup bottled sauce Melba,*
  optional

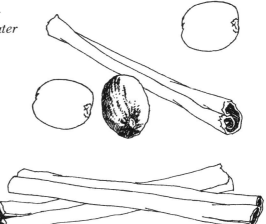

Preheat oven to 425 degrees.

In a saucepan, bring rhubarb, sugar, and ¼ cup water to a boil. Reduce heat and simmer for 10 minutes. Add dissolved cornstarch and stir into cooked rhubarb. Pour into a large bowl and cool.

Mix bread crumbs with egg yolks and stir into cooled rhubarb. Mix sour cream, cinnamon, and brandy, and fold into the rhubarb. Beat egg whites until stiff and fold into rhubarb.

Line the bottom of a 2 inch high, 1½ quart earthenware casserole or baking dish with zwieback, and pour ½ cup melted butter all over. Pour rhubarb mixture over zwieback. Bake for 20 minutes (425 degrees), or until top is lightly browned and center is no longer soft.

Serve warm. If a sweet sauce is desired, serve with sauce Melba on the side.

Chilled and Frozen Desserts

Daiquiri Pie

Serves 8

1 *9 to 10 × 2 inch prebaked,*
  sweet dough piecrust
  (see page 347)
3 *Tablespoons freshly squeezed*
  lime juice, strained
  (about 2 limes)
1 *Tablespoon unflavored gelatin*
4 *eggs, separated*
  Pinch salt
1¼ *cups granulated sugar (¾*
  cup for filling mixture, ½ cup
  for egg whites)

3 *Tablespoons white rum*
1 *cup heavy cream (for decorat-*
  ing)

In a small saucepan combine lime juice and gelatin and heat until dissolved. Set aside to cool.

In the top of a double boiler over simmering water, mix the egg yolks, salt, and ¾ cup sugar, stirring with a wooden spoon until thick and smooth. Stir in the gelatin mixture and cook for an additional 3 minutes, stirring constantly. Remove from the heat and stir in the rum. Set aside to cool slightly.

Beat the egg whites, adding the remaining ½ cup sugar gradually until firm peaks are formed. Fold beaten whites into the warm custard. Pour the mixture into the piecrust and chill for an hour. (This pie freezes very well. If frozen, remove from freezer and place in refrigerator for 2 hours before serving.)

PRESENTATION
Just before serving, whip the heavy cream, and with a pastry tube or spatula, decorate the entire top of pie with the whipped cream.

Strawberry or Raspberry Parfait

Serves 6

1 *Tablespoon unflavored gelatin*
1 *Tablespoon flour*
¾ *cup sugar*
1 *quart heavy cream (3 cups*
  for gelatin mix, 1 *cup whipped*
  for folding into berries)
5 *egg yolks*
1 *teaspoon vanilla*
  Grated peel of one orange
1½ *ounces brandy or kirsch*
½ *pint fresh strawberries*
  (or raspberries), puréed in a
  blender
1 *pint fresh, whole strawberries*
  (or raspberries)

In a large saucepan, mix gelatin, flour, and sugar. Beat 3 cups heavy cream and egg yolks together and stir into the gelatin mixture. Stirring constantly with a wire whisk, cook mixture over medium heat for 10 minutes. Remove from heat and add vanilla. Pour into a large bowl and stir in grated orange rind and brandy or kirsch. Chill briefly until mixture is thickened slightly.

Mix together the puréed and the whole strawberries, reserving 6 for garnish. Whip 1 cup heavy cream and fold into strawberries. Fold strawberries and whipped cream into lightly thickened, chilled cream mixture. Spoon into champagne glasses. Chill until firm. Before serving, garnish with a whole strawberry in the center.

NOTE: If raspberries are substituted, blend with 1 Tablespoon sugar to sweeten them slightly.

Baked Alaska *Flambée*   *Serves 6 to 8*

I suggest you prepare this filled cake at least one day in advance of serving and store in the freezer. The final preparation can be done just before serving to produce a gala and delicious dessert for a special occasion.

1 *4 by 8 inch cake
   [basic* roulade *(see page 345)]*
1½ *pints vanilla ice cream,
   softened to spreading consistency*
1 *cup orange sections (If
   canned, drain well.)*
1 *cup grapefruit sections (If
   canned, drain well.)*

4 *ounces Grand Marnier or
   Cointreau*
3 *eggs*
2 *Tablespoons confectioners
   sugar*

FOR FLAMBÉE

4 *tablespoons (½ stick) sweet
   butter*

1 *Tablespoon granulated sugar*

Place cake on platter. Spread half of the softened ice cream on the cake. Alternate the orange and grapefruit sections on the ice cream. Sprinkle with half of the Grand Marnier or Cointreau. Cover the fruit with other half of ice cream. Place in freezer.

MERINGUE
Preheat oven to 400 degrees or heat broiler.
Separate the eggs and beat the yolks and confectioners sugar together until the mixture is light yellow. Beat the whites until they begin to form soft peaks; then fold in the egg yolks and continue beating until they hold peaks. Don't be alarmed if the egg yolks soften the whites at first; they will firm up as you continue beating.

With a spatula, completely cover the sides and top of ice cream with meringue. Place in oven (400 degrees) for about 2 minutes or under the broiler for about ½ minute or until the meringue is lightly browned.

In a chafing dish at the table or in a small saucepan, melt the butter and stir until it takes on a golden color, add the sugar and remaining half of the Grand Marnier or Cointreau. While very hot, set alight and pour it flaming over the meringue. Cut in thick slices and serve immediately.

Frozen Orange Soufflé Grand Marnier   *Serves 8*

6 *egg yolks*
¾ *cups sugar*
2¾ *cups heavy cream, whipped*
   (2 cups for soufflé, ¾ cup for
   topping)

3 *ounces Grand Marnier*
8 *cleaned orange shells*
   or soufflé cups
   Powdered cocoa (optional)

Combine egg yolks and sugar. Beat until stiff. Fold 2 cups of the whipped cream into the egg yolk mixture, then fold in the Grand Marnier. Fill the orange shells or soufflé cups with the mixture and place in the freezer for at least 2 hours.

At serving time, top the soufflés with the additional ¾ cup of whipped cream, using a pastry tube or spatula. Sprinkle with powdered cocoa if desired.

Cake Desserts

Chilled Cream Cheese Cake
Serves 8

1 9 to 10 × 2 *inch prebaked sweet*
dough piecrust (see page 347)
8 *ounces cream cheese*
   (at room temperature)
1 *cup confectioners sugar*

Grated rind of 1 lemon
1 *Tablespoon unflavored gelatin*
2 *Tablespoons water, boiling hot*
1 *cup heavy cream*

Beat the cream cheese, sugar, and grated lemon rind until smooth. Dissolve the gelatin in the boiling water and stir until smooth. Whip the cream.

Add one fourth of the cheese mixture to the gelatin, stirring until thoroughly mixed. Fold this into the rest of the cheese mixture, then fold in the whipped cream and pour into the cooled piecrust. Score the top with a knife to decorate. Chill for 1½ to 2 hours before serving.

New England Walnut Torte
Serves 8

12 *egg yolks*
 1 *cup granulated sugar*
   (¾ cup for egg yolk mixture,
   ¼ cup for egg whites)
 6 *egg whites*
¾ *cup sifted flour*

¼ *cup sifted cornstarch*
¾ *cup walnuts, ground*
½ *lemon rind, grated*
   Basic butter cream
   (see page 348)
½ *cup walnuts, chopped*

Preheat oven to 400 degrees.

Butter and lightly flour a 10 inch cake pan and line with a circle of waxed paper.

Combine the egg yolks with ¾ cup sugar and beat until thick and light colored. In a separate bowl, beat the egg whites until they stand in soft peaks. Sprinkle with ¼ cup sugar and beat only until the sugar is thoroughly mixed—do not let the whites become stiff. By hand, fold one-third of the egg whites into egg yolk mixture. Fold in the flour, cornstarch, ground walnuts, grated lemon rind, and the remaining egg whites. Pour into the cake pan.

Bake (400 degrees) 25 to 30 minutes or until the cake springs back to light touch. Allow cake to cool.

Remove from the cake pan and cut the cake into two layers. Cover the bottom layer with one-quarter of the butter cream; sprinkle with half the chopped walnuts. Place the second layer on top, spread the remaining butter cream on top and sides of cake. Sprinkle the rest of the chopped walnuts over the top and side.

Wine Cream Roll

Serves 6

1 *sponge cake roulade (see page 345)*
1½ *cups dry white wine*
½ *cup granulated sugar (¼ cup for wine mixture, ¼ cup for eggs)*

4 *Tablespoons (½ stick) butter*
3 *eggs*
2 *Tablespoons cornstarch*
Powdered sugar
Seedless grapes (optional)

Prepare *roulade* according to directions.

Combine the white wine, ¼ cup of the sugar, and the butter in a saucepan and bring to a boil. Remove from the heat.

In a bowl combine the eggs, remaining ¼ cup sugar, and the cornstarch. Mix well and add to the wine mixture. Return to low heat and stir rapidly until the custard is thick and smooth. Set aside to cool.

Remove the towel from the *roulade*, spread out flat and cover the surface with the wine cream filling. Carefully roll like a jelly roll and refrigerate for at least 1 hour before serving. At serving time sprinkle top with powdered sugar.

NOTE: If you have some seedless grapes available, spread them on the cream filling before rolling.

Zuger Kirschtorte   *Serves 8*

There are cakes and there is the *Zuger Kirschtorte*. Whether you're on a diet or not, I doubt if you will be able to resist the rare flavor of this cake, which is not overly sweet, and a perfect climax to a festive dinner.

The torte—a crumbly combination of textures—is a light sponge cake, soaked when cool with a heavily kirsch-flavored syrup and covered with butter cream and crisp, golden meringue; then coated on the top and the sides with flaky toasted almonds. With this recipe, you may discover, or perhaps rediscover, the satisfaction of creating a truly splendid old world torte.

THE SPONGE CAKE

4 whole eggs
2 egg yolks
¾ cup granulated sugar
½ cup sifted all-purpose flour

6 Tablespoons sifted cornstarch
5 Tablespoons butter, melted and
  cooled to lukewarm

Preheat oven to 350 degrees.

Butter a 9 inch cake pan and dust lightly with flour. The cake pan must have at least a 2 inch rim. If it does not, tie on a collar of waxed paper or aluminum foil, buttered.

In a large bowl, combine the eggs, egg yolks, and sugar and beat at high speed until thick and light yellow. The mixture will triple in volume.

Sift together the flour and cornstarch and with a spatula fold into the egg mixture. Add the melted and cooled butter and mix only until the butter is completely absorbed.

Pour the batter into the cake pan and bake (350 degrees) for 25 to 30 minutes or until golden brown on top and springy to the touch. Cool the cake in the pan for 5 to 10 minutes and unmold onto a sugared square of waxed paper.

THE ALMOND MERINGUE

½ cup egg whites (4 egg whites)
1 cup granulated sugar
⅓ cup blanched almonds, finely ground

½ Tablespoon flour

Reduce oven to 275 degrees.

Beat egg whites with ⅓ cup of sugar, until they form soft peaks. Gradually add another ⅓ cup sugar until it is absorbed and the egg whites form stiff peaks.

Mix together ⅓ cup sugar, ground almonds, and flour, and fold into the beaten egg white mixture until thoroughly blended.

Using waxed freezer wrap (or baking paper), cut off two square pieces and with a pencil, trace a 9 inch circle on each square. Dust lightly with flour and place each square on a baking sheet. Using a pastry bag with a small tube, cover the circles with meringue. Start with a small dot in the center and continue circling until the drawn circle is completely covered (like a coiled rope). Or, use a spatula and spread the meringue to the size of the circle about ½ inch thick.

Bake (275 degrees) for about 30 minutes or until a light gold color and crisp. Turn off the oven and let the meringues cool in the oven.

KIRSCH SYRUP

¼ cup sugar   2 Tablespoons kirsch
½ cup water

Bring the sugar and water to a boil and then let cool. Add kirsch.

ADDITIONAL INGREDIENTS

Basic butter cream recipe (see page 348) flavored with 1 Tablespoon kirsch
½ cup blanched toasted almonds (for decoration)
Powdered sugar (for decoration)

To assemble the cake, cut off a paper-thin layer of the brown crust from the top and bottom of the sponge cake. (This permits the syrup to soak into the sponge cake easily.) Brush top, bottom, and side of the cake with the kirsch syrup.

Cover one meringue with about ¼ inch of butter cream. Place the kirsch-soaked sponge cake on top of the meringue. Spread the top of the sponge cake with about another ¼ inch of butter cream. Place the second meringue on top of the butter cream. Trim the meringue all around to fit exactly the size of the sponge cake. Spread the rest of the butter cream all around the sides of the cake. Holding the bottom of the cake in one hand, press the toasted almonds around the side of the cake. Lightly sift powdered sugar on top of the cake.

Swiss Chocolate Cake

THE CAKE

1½ *pounds semi-sweet chocolate*
4½ *cups all purpose flour, sifted*
  1 *pound unsalted butter, cold*

Pinch salt
⅔ *cup cold water*

NOTE: It is important to roll out the dough in a cool part of the kitchen. An overheated room will melt the butter and the dough will become too sticky to roll. If the dough should become sticky, place a sheet of waxed paper on top of the dough and roll the dough out. Peel off the waxed paper after you have finished rolling the dough out.

Cut ½ pound of the chocolate into little pieces and melt in a small bowl over simmering water.

Pour the flour into a large bowl. Cut the butter up, one stick at a time, into small pieces, add the salt, then with two knives or a pastry blender, work the butter into the flour until the dough has formed large, coarse crumbs. Add the cold water and mix with a fork until the water is completely absorbed. Pour in the melted chocolate and mix thoroughly with a fork. Scrape the dough out of the bowl. Form into a ball and place in the refrigerator for 30 minutes.

Preheat oven to 375 degrees.

Flour a flat surface and sprinkle the dough with flour. Roll into a rectangle. The dough will be heavily marbleized with butter. Fold one third of the dough to the center. Fold again, and roll out a second time. Cut the dough into two equal pieces. Lay one 12 by 15 inch piece of waxed freezer wrap or baking paper on a flat surface and cover generously with flour. Place one piece of dough in the center. Roll dough to fit the paper rectangle and press the edges to fit. Slide the paper and the dough onto a baking sheet, sprinkle with flour, and bake (375 degrees) in the middle rack of the oven for 25 minutes while preparing the second sheet of dough. Repeat the same procedure. When cooked, remove the dough from the baking sheets and slide onto grease-proof paper to cool.

THE CREAM FILLING

½ *pound semi-sweet chocolate*   ⅓ *cup granulated sugar*
1½ *cups heavy cream*

Cut ½ pound of chocolate into small pieces and melt in a small bowl over simmering water.

Combine the cream and sugar and whip until the cream forms soft peaks. Gradually pour in the melted, cooled chocolate and continue to whip until the mixture is smooth, the chocolate is completely absorbed, and the color is uniform.

FORMING THE CAKE

Cut the cooled pieces of cake in half and peel off the paper. Place one layer of cake on a plate and cover with a quarter of the chocolate cream. Add the remaining layers of cake, covering each one equally with the chocolate cream. Reserve enough of the chocolate cream to frost the sides.

Decorate with chocolate curls.

THE CHOCOLATE CURLS

½ *pound semi-sweet chocolate*

Cut the chocolate into small pieces and melt in a small bowl over simmering water.

Pour the melted chocolate onto a smooth, cool surface and spread as thin as possible. Allow the chocolate to harden, but not to dry, for several minutes. Then, holding a large kitchen knife so that only the last half inch will scrape the chocolate, start in an upper corner, an inch from the top, and scrape the hardened chocolate away from you. If the chocolate is the right temperature—not completely dried—it will form a curl. Repeat until all the chocolate has been made into curls. If your kitchen is too hot, the curls will melt, but you can, as you make them, put them on a plate and refrigerate.

Sprinkle the chocolate curls over the top of the cake.

The cake should be kept in the refrigerator until you are ready to cut into squares and serve.

Lemon Cream Roll

Serves 6

1 *sponge cake* roulade
   (see page 345)
2 *cups water*
½ *cup sugar (¼ cup for lemon
   juice mixture, ¼ cup
   for eggs)*
4 *Tablespoons (½ stick butter)*
   Juice of 2 lemons, strained
3 *eggs*
   Grated rind of 1 lemon
2 *Tablespoons cornstarch*
   Powdered sugar

Prepare *roulade* according to directions.

Place the water, ¼ cup sugar, butter, and lemon juice in a saucepan, and bring to a boil. Remove from heat.

Combine the eggs, remaining ¼ cup of sugar, grated lemon rind, and cornstarch, stir until smooth and add to the heated lemon juice mixture. Return to low heat and stir rapidly until custard is thick and smooth. Set aside to cool.

Remove towel from *roulade*, roll out flat, and spread the lemon cream evenly over the entire surface. Roll like a jelly roll and place in the refrigerator for at least 1 hour before serving. At serving time sprinkle top with powdered sugar.

Miscellaneous Desserts

Apple Charlotte with Brandy Sauce

Serves 6

8 to 10 *slices firm-textured*
white bread, trimmed of crusts,
buttered on one side
8 *green cooking apples*
4 *Tablespoons (½ stick) butter*
¼ *cup sugar*

Grated rind of 1 *lemon*
1 *teaspoon cinnamon*
1 *teaspoon ginger*
½ *teaspoon ground cloves*
3 *ounces applejack or Calvados*

Preheat oven to 400 degrees.

Line the bottom and sides of a 1½ quart Charlotte mold or casserole with the bread slices, buttered side to the mold.

Peel, core, and slice apples. Melt butter in a large skillet. Add the sliced apples, sugar, grated lemon rind, cinnamon, ginger, cloves, and applejack. Sauté until apples are slightly softened. Pour into the mold, allowing excess to form a dome above the rim.

Bake (400 degrees) for 20 minutes, then cover with aluminum foil and bake another 20 minutes or until the apples are completely cooked and the edges of the bread have browned slightly. Cool for at least 1 hour before unmolding and serve with brandy sauce.

BRANDY SAUCE

½ *cup apricot glaze (if not*
available, see below)
1 *ounce brandy*
1 *cup apple juice*

Juice of 1 *lemon*
⅛ *teaspoon ginger*
1 *teaspoon cornstarch, dissolved*
with a little of the apple juice

Combine all the ingredients except the dissolved cornstarch in a saucepan and bring to boil. Add cornstarch mixture. Bring back to boil. Remove from heat and serve warm.

NOTE: To make an apricot glaze, heat ½ cup apricot jam or preserve with 1 teaspoon water until it melts, then put through a sieve to remove any lumps.

Bread and Butter Pudding with Raspberry Sauce

Serves 6 to 8

3 or 4 *day-old crusty rolls*
1 *stick butter (¼ pound)*
4 *eggs*

½ *cup granulated sugar*
2 *cups light cream*
½ *teaspoon cinnamon*

RASPBERRY SAUCE
1 *cup Melba sauce, bottled*
½ *cup puréed or whole ripe*
   raspberries

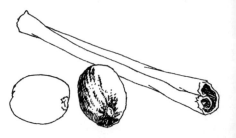

Preheat oven to 375 degrees.

Cut the rolls in slices ½ inch thick and cover the bottom of a shallow
9-inch diameter ovenproof dish with one layer of these slices. Melt the
butter and pour over the bread, turning the slices over to soak up all the
butter. Beat the eggs, mix in the sugar, cream, and cinnamon, and pour
this over the buttery bread.

Bake (375 degrees) for about 30 minutes, or until top is golden
brown and custard is set. Serve at room temperature.

Combine the Melba sauce with raspberries and serve separately.

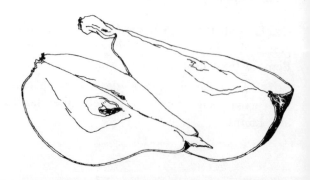

Poached Fresh Pears with *Crème au Kirsch* *Serves 4*

4 *large pears*
1 *quart water*
⅔ *cup sugar*
1 *ounce kirsch (if not available, you may substitute any other liqueur or brandy)*

2 *cups pastry cream (see page 347) (1 cup for filling, 1 cup for sauce)*
1 *cup heavy cream, whipped*
3 *Tablespoons pistachio nuts, finely chopped*

Select large firm pears, peel, leaving stem. Core from bottom leaving a ¾ inch hole.

Bring the water and sugar to a boil in a saucepan. Place the pears in the syrup leaving stem and approximately 1 inch of the top of the pear out of the syrup. Lower heat to simmer, cover, and cook until the pears are tender but still firm—about 8 to 10 minutes. Be careful not to overcook them. Drain and cool.

Whip ½ ounce of the liqueur into 1 cup of pastry cream and use this to fill the holes in the bottoms of the pears.

SAUCE
Strain the remaining 1 cup pastry cream through a fine sieve, add the remaining ½ ounce liqueur and fold in the whipped cream. Chill.

PRESENTATION
If you are serving these at the table a pedestal type bowl is appropriate. Place the chilled pears in the bowl, pour the sauce over them. Sprinkle with chopped pistachio nuts.

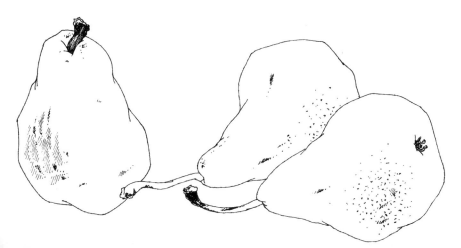

Chocolate Mousse

4 *egg whites*
1 *cup sugar*
¼ *teaspoon cream of tartar,*
   dissolved in 1 *teaspoon water*

½ *cup water*
12 *ounces semi-sweet chocolate,*
    melted and cooled
1 *pint heavy cream, whipped*

Beat egg whites until stiff.

In a small saucepan, combine sugar, dissolved cream of tartar, and ½ cup of water. Cook mixture until it reaches the soft ball stage (232 to 234 degrees on a candy thermometer). Add cooked sugar mixture in a thin stream to egg whites, blending at medium speed until cooled.

Fold in cooled, melted chocolate and whipped cream.

Pour into a mold and refrigerate for 3 to 4 hours before serving.

Zabaglione Creole

I find that hot, foamy zabaglione poured over fresh strawberries or any soft fruits of the season, appeals to almost everyone—especially those who pass up rich cakes or tarts. Zabaglione is always prepared a few minutes before serving. A metal or heatproof glass bowl resting in a saucepan above simmering water makes a perfect double boiler for easy whisking of the zabaglione.

3 *egg yolks*
1 *cup dry white wine*
   Juice of 1 *lemon*
2 *Tablespoons sugar*
   Pinch powdered ginger

Beat the egg yolks and add all of the above ingredients in the top of a double boiler over simmering but not boiling water. Beat with a wire whisk until the mixture becomes light and frothy. Serve at once in high stem glasses either poured over fruit or, of course, zabaglione can be served by itself in individual glasses.

FRUITS
¾ *cup fresh strawberries, sliced*
¾ *cup fresh or stewed cherries,*
   sliced peaches, or sliced apricots

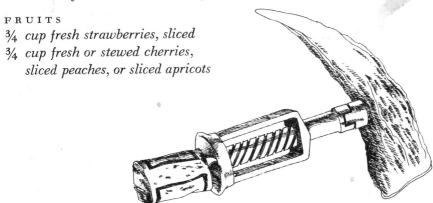

White Wine Sapphire

Serves 6

½ *bottle dry white wine*
¾ *cup sugar*
   Juice of 3 oranges
   Juice of ½ lemon
2 *Tablespoons unflavored gelatin*

1 *cup water*
2 *cups heavy cream, whipped*
1 *cup heavy cream, whipped,*
   for garnish

Pour wine into a saucepan, add sugar and boil over medium heat for 10 minutes. Remove from heat. Add orange juice and lemon juice and set aside.

In another saucepan sprinkle gelatin in cup of water to soften. Place over low heat and stir until gelatin is dissolved. Remove from heat and stir the wine mixture into the dissolved gelatin.

Pour into a large bowl and chill until the mixture slightly mounds on a spoon. Fold in 2 cups heavy whipped cream, and pour into a glass bowl. Chill until firm.

Unmold onto a chilled serving platter and garnish with a border of whipped cream.

Acorn Squash Country Style

Serves 4

2 *acorn squash, cut in half*
    and cleaned of seeds
4 *ounces butter (one stick)*
    Pinch salt for each half
    of squash
½ *ounce white rum*

1½ *cups (approximately)*
    honey or maple syrup
 1 *pint vanilla ice cream (or less,*
    depending on appetites)
¼ *pound walnuts, chopped*
½ *teaspoon powdered ginger*

Preheat oven to 450 degrees.

Cut each squash in half and remove the seeds. Put 1 ounce butter in each half cavity. Sprinkle each with a pinch of salt. Fill the cavity of each to ¾ full with the white rum and honey or maple syrup. Bake for 40 to 45 minutes (450 degrees) until the vegetable marrow is soft. Cool.

Serve with a scoop of vanilla ice cream in each half. Combine walnuts and ginger and sprinkle on top.

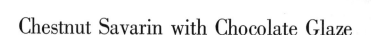

Chestnut Savarin with Chocolate Glaze

Serves 6 to 8

3 *cups heavy cream (1 cup to*
    melt chocolate; 1 cup whipped,
    to fold into purée; 1 cup,
    whipped, for serving platter)
4 *ounces semi-sweet chocolate,*
    broken into pieces

2 *pounds canned chestnuts, after*
    draining off water (If dried
    chestnuts are used, see note.)
¾ *cup sugar*
2 *ounces maraschino liqueur*
¼ *cup honey*

CHOCOLATE GLAZE
½ *cup light corn syrup*
½ *cup (2½ ounces) semi-sweet*
    chocolate, shaved

¼ *cup heavy cream*

Heat 1 cup heavy cream in a saucepan and stir in chocolate until melted. Set aside to cool.

Place drained chestnuts in a bowl and mix in the sugar, liqueur, honey, and cooled chocolate-cream mixture. Blend in a blender until smooth and thick. (You may have to do it in two loads.) Pour into a large bowl.

In a separate bowl, whip 1 cup heavy cream and fold into the puréed chestnuts. Rinse a savarin mold with cold water and shake out excess water. Pour mixture into the mold and *refrigerate* until firm.

Prepare chocolate glaze. Place a bowl over a saucepan of very slowly simmering water. Pour syrup into the bowl and mix in chocolate until melted. Remove from heat and stir in ¼ cup heavy cream. Set aside to cool.

Unmold savarin onto a chilled serving platter. Whip the remaining 1 cup heavy cream and use it to fill the center of mold. Pour chocolate glaze over all.

NOTE: If using dried chestnuts, reduce quantity of cream to 2 cups, using as follows: 1 cup to fold into whipped purée and 1 cup, whipped, for serving platter.

Put 2 pounds peeled dried chestnuts in a saucepan with enough milk to cover and add 1 cup sugar. Bring to a boil, reduce heat, and cook over medium heat for 20 minutes. Remove from heat, add shaved chocolate, and stir until blended. Set aside and cool. Stir in liqueur and honey, and blend in a blender until smooth and thick. Pour into a large bowl. Proceed with balance of recipe.

Beer Batter

and pâte à choux

Through the years I have found that the greatest reward of cooking creatively is often found in simplicity. My beer batter is a good example of what I mean. Beer batter is far from new—it has been used extensively in Europe for a long time, but ingredients do change from continent to continent and this is particularly true with flour and beer. Here in America I have tried countless versions of this batter—I have used eggs, then no eggs but substituting oil or butter instead. None of these combinations brought the result I wanted until I tried it with nothing but American all-purpose flour and light domestic beer, with salt and some paprika for color.

And here it is—made in minutes—the simplest batter imaginable, to give that special light, crisp touch. Notice especially how grease-free your shrimp or other deep-fried foods emerge from the oil. Now that you have the batter, use your own imagination in utilizing it. One of my own particular favorites is a sort of bouquet of vegetables with bits of meat or fish—all deep fried in beer batter: tiny croquettes or dumplings, buds of cauliflower or other vegetables in season. Have you ever eaten a nasturtium flower deep fried? Try it—it is really very good. Chicken, fish, game, and seafood as well are delicious fried with this batter.

I also use beer in my *pâte à choux*. It makes a superbly light dough and is particularly effective in the various recipes throughout my book that call for it.

Beer Batter

1 *can light domestic beer*   1 *Tablespoon salt*
   (12 ounces)   1 *Tablespoon paprika*
1 *cup all-purpose flour, sifted*

Pour the beer into a mixing bowl. Sift the flour, salt, and paprika into
the beer, stirring with a wire whisk until the batter is light and frothy.
Beer batter may be used at once or after standing several hours. When
using the batter, whisk it from time to time to keep it thoroughly mixed.

   You can keep the batter a week or more in the refrigerator but it is apt
to retain the flavor of the ingredient that has been dipped in it. So if
you are using it again do so with a similar-tasting material.

Pâte à Choux   *Yield 1 quart*

1¼ *cups light domestic beer*   *Dash salt*
    (or water)   1¼ *cups all-purpose flour*
 1 *stick butter (8 Tablespoons)*   6 *eggs, medium size*

In a heavy-bottomed saucepan over medium heat, combine the beer,
butter, and salt, and bring to a boil. Pour in the flour all at once and stir
vigorously until the dough rolls away from the sides of the pan and
forms a mass. Remove from the fire and allow the dough to cool to lukewarm, about 15 minutes. Beat in eggs, one at a time. Beat dough by
hand or more quickly in a mixer. Once the eggs are thoroughly blended
into the dough, it is ready for use.

   Put in a bowl, cover with damp cloth, and refrigerate if not using
immediately.

Index

A Note About the Author

Albert J. Stockli, Commandeur *of the* Commanderie des Cordons Bleus, Maître de Cuisine & Chevalier *of the* Confréries des Chevaliers du Tastevin, *and* Confrère *of the* Compagnons de Bordeaux, *was born in Switzerland in 1919. There, after his formal schooling, which included several semesters learning Restaurant and Hotel Administration, he began his real, practical training as an apprentice to some of the great chefs of Europe. He has continued to practice and learn—as a chef on the Holland-America and Dutch East India Lines, Chef Steward for the War Shipping Administration from 1941 to 1946, and as chef in various hotels and restaurants in the United States, including those of the famous Restaurant Associates chain. In 1965 Mr. Stockli, then a vice-president, left Restaurant Associates and he and his wife, Helen, moved to Connecticut; there they now operate their own restaurant, the Stonehenge Inn.*

A Note on the Type

The text of this book was set in Waverly, the Intertype version of the type face called Walbaum. The original cutting of this face was made by Justus Erich Walbaum in Leipzig in the early 1800's. Young Walbaum began his artistic career as an apprentice to a maker of cookie molds. How he managed to leave this field and become a successful punchcutter remains a mystery.

Waverly is a wholly modern type face, if not by definition, certainly by association with the designs of our best contemporary typographers.